The United States through Arab Eyes
An Anthology of Writings (1876–1914)

Introduced, selected, and translated by Nabil Matar

EDINBURGH
University Press

Edinburgh University Press is one of the leading university presses in the UK. We publish academic books and journals in our selected subject areas across the humanities and social sciences, combining cutting-edge scholarship with high editorial and production values to produce academic works of lasting importance. For more information visit our website: www.edinburghuniversitypress.com

© editorial matter and organisation Nabil Matar, 2018

Edinburgh University Press Ltd
The Tun – Holyrood Road
12 (2f) Jackson's Entry
Edinburgh EH8 8PJ

Typeset in 10/12 Goudy Old Style by
IDSUK (DataConnection) Ltd

A CIP record for this book is available from the British Library

ISBN 978 1 4744 3435 5 (hardback)
ISBN 978 1 4744 3436 2 (paperback)
ISBN 978 1 4744 3437 9 (webready PDF)
ISBN 978 1 4744 3438 6 (epub)

The right of Nabil Matar to be identified as Editor of this work has been asserted in accordance with the Copyright, Designs and Patent Act 1988, and the Copyright and Related Rights Regulations 2003 (SI No. 2498).

The illustration on the front cover is from Mikhaᵓil Rustum, *Diwan* (1909), 183.

Contents

Section 2. Women and Gender

Section 3. Identity and Americanization

Acknowledgements

I wish to thank many colleagues and friends who helped me during the last three years while I worked on this text.

I start with Professor Hani Bawardi, University of Michigan, Dearborn, whose book on *The Making of Arab Americans* and his friendship first motivated me to this new area of research. I also wish to thank Professor Muhammad Shaheen of the University of Jordan for his suggestion of texts and for discussing with me his translation strategies. And of course, Professor Wadad Kadi, who has been my mentor since our AUB days: she was ever ready with her philological insights and assistance. I benefited from the various panels at MLA and MESA that dealt with Arabic literature and history in the United States, and from conversations with Professors Nouri Gana, Tahia Abdul Nasser, Waïl Hassan, Suha Kudsieh, Nizar Hermes and others.

I am grateful to Ms Samira Kawar for introducing me to her ninety-two-year-old Jerusalemite mother and sending me the newspaper article and comments by Mr Hazem Nusseibeh ("Lest we forget – Christian Palestinians of Jerusalem", *Jordan Times*, 15 July 2017). I wish to thank Ms Nawal A. Kawar of the Library of Congress for her help in locating a lost document. I am very grateful to Ms Amy Frankfurt for her support and inspiration; Ms Meghan Philips for her research on Native Americans in early-twentieth-century newspapers; and Mr David Faust of the Wilson Library at the University of Minnesota who sent me links to digitized copies of early Arabic newspapers in the United States. Many students in my classes on "Arabic Writings" at the University of Minnesota read and commented, sometimes quite insightfully, on sections of the introduction. Thanks are also due Professor Katharine Gerbner who convened (and continues to convene) the Atlantic Workshop at the University of Minnesota, and to Professor Kirsten Fischer, who offered me insightful comments. I am grateful to the (then) Chair of the English Department, Professor Ellen

Messer-Davidow, for extending to me funds which I used to conduct research at the NYPL in Spring 2016. I am also grateful to Professor Erika Lee for giving me the opportunity to share with her and her seminar an early version of my introduction, and for her inspiring role in the Immigration Center at the University of Minnesota – where I spent many an hour going through the extensive collection of material on early Arab America. On 26 April 2018, I gave the Farhat J. Ziyadeh Distinguished Lecture in Arab and Islamic Studies at the University of Washington, based on the research in this book. I am grateful to Professor Selim S. Kuru for the invitation and to the family of the late Professor Ziyadeh for sponsoring the lecture.

I wish to thank my former student Ian Larson, who has been my friend for years, and who is preparing to launch on a new phase in his life. His comments on the typescript of this book were invaluable. And last but not least, I wish to thank my life-long friend Professor Mohammad Asfour, winner of the State Award for Excellence in Translation (Cairo, 2017), for agreeing to go over the translation; I could not have hoped for sharper and more experienced eyes than his.

As always, I think of Abraham and Hady, in Atlanta and Ramallah respectively, forging ahead in life. Sons of immigrants, may they ever celebrate their multiple identities as Americans and Arabs, adopting the best from those tumultuous worlds.

I was awarded the Samuel Russell Chair for the Humanities during my work on this book which enabled me to complete my research in a timely manner. I am grateful to Dean John Coleman and to Associate Dean Ana Paula Ferreira for their support, and to Mr and Mrs Gesell of St Paul, Minnesota, who generously endowed the Chair.

This book is dedicated to G.H. for whom immigration to the United States offered the opportunity to realize dreams, to achieve goals, and to excel. Since we met four decades ago, she has been a friend and a confidante. But on that day in July 2006, she was pure heroism – "always, always" to be remembered, cherished, and thanked.

Some Notes on the Translation

With the exception of Khalil al-Sakakini's letters, the texts below were written and published during the period commonly known as the *Nahda* – the Renaissance of Arabic thought and literature which started in the second half of the nineteenth century. After centuries of decline under Ottoman rule, writers from Greater Syria and Egypt revived their mastery of classical Arabic at the same time that they started studying Western literature and publishing novels and articles to entertain and edify their compatriots from the Mediterranean to North America.

The authors below wrote in the same formal Arabic that is used in mass media today. It is simple, clear, and pragmatic, without the rhetorical flourish that had marked it during the previous centuries. In their writings about the United States, they aimed at a truly transnational readership, extending between New York and Beirut, Buenos Aires and Cairo, and so they used language and diction that were to be accessible and uncomplicated to the widely different reading communities. Only Mikha'il Rustum and Prince Muhammad ʿAli aspired to some sophistication in style;[1] even so, the former firmly indicated that he wrote in a simple style, so much so that his verse came to be known as the "Rustumite Verse" for its lucidity and near-colloquial strain.[2] The prince used an elegant and educated language, avoiding (as did others) the internal rhymes in prose, the cumbersome adjectives, and the long winding sentences of earlier centuries.

Excepting him, all the writers of the selections translated below were Christian, but all shared in promoting an inclusive perspective that would appeal to the intellectual circles in the home countries as well as to emigrants who were adjusting to their new American environment. Religion rarely intruded into their writings, and although the prince sometimes quoted Qur'anic verses, he expressed an exuberant tolerance and engagement with other religions (he had earlier traveled to and written about Japan).

In translating the texts, I have remained close to the original in both style and content. On some occasions, I omitted or added words because authors used turns of phrases which, literally translated into English, would make awkward sense. I have not had reason to "interpret" – much as translation is always an act of interpretation. The authors were presenting arguments, descriptions, accounts, and polemics, and therefore, they avoided ambiguity and uncertainty. They were also eager to promote the Arabic language, and if there was a strong undercurrent to their writings, it was the narrative of Arabic as language and culture that defined them in the *mahjar*/land of emigration and that also tied them to their homelands – which they were unsure they wanted to leave forever.

The translations below present the first Arab/Arabic writings about the United States, reflecting the views and confusions of the first emigrants who were still unsure about their future plans. In trying to articulate a master narrative of departure, settlement, and in some cases, return, the writers were addressing their communities inside the United States at the same time that they engaged in transnational discussions.

NOTES

1. Rustum was born in 1849 in Shwayr, Lebanon, emigrated in 1891, and died in 1922: see Linda K. Jacobs, *Strangers in the West: The Syrian Colony of New York City* (New York: Kalimah Press, 2015), 436. Prince Muhammad ᶜAli Tawfiq (1875–1955) was the younger brother of Khedive Abbas II and heir presumptive of Egypt and Sudan.

2. *Al-Hilal* 16 (1908), 48.

For G.H.
and that heroic day in July 2006.

PART I

Emigration, the Arab *Nahda*, and the United States of America – An Introduction

We must leave the ship right now. We don't want them to send us back to our country.

No one will be sent back from here. If they force me on another ship, I will jump and swim to the city [New York]. Rabiʿ Jaber, *Amayrka* (2012)

The above words are from a novel about early Lebanese emigrants to America. They were desperate to enter the United States and not to be sent back to the poverty and repression of their Ottoman-ruled homeland. So desperate were some emigrants that in 1902, a Syrian woman, Alexandra Youssef, jumped from a train and committed suicide as she was being deported by the Immigration Inspectors (*New York Times*, 24 October). Such a view of America as a land of refuge and opportunity continues today, but it has been marred by the image of America as an imperial power with military might and global ambition. In *What They Saw in America* (2016), James L. Nolan included in his study of four foreign writers about America the views of Sayyid Qutb (1906–66), a leading ideologue of the Muslim Brotherhood in Egypt, who visited the United States between 1948 and 1950.[1] Qutb traveled from Boston and New York to California and Colorado, and after returning to Egypt, he wrote with anxiety and anger about a country that he saw had become a leader of Western imperial hegemony in the Middle East.

But unlike Alexis de Tocqueville, Max Weber, and G. K. Chesterton, whom Nolan discusses, Qutb did not have the educational exposure, the social status, or the intellectual background that the three Europeans had. Qutb came from a small and impoverished region of Egypt, which helps to explain why he was bewildered by the cultural differences he saw in big cities in the United States. There is no denying his sometimes petty tirades (against American barbers, for instance), but then, unlike the other writers, he had not grown up in de Tocqueville's aristocratic surroundings with the privileges of tutors and mentors, did not have the encyclopedic knowledge of Chesterton or his access to libraries, and he never underwent the rigorous philosophical, economic, and political training of Weber. While he did leave his mark on modern Islamic thought, it was at a level by far more limited in its analytic and conceptual framework than the work of the other three Europeans. In Nolan's discussion, Qutb appears as an Arab/Muslim who simply criticized America because it was different and "immoral." But besides ignoring the vast cultural and social differences that separate Qutb from the other writers, Nolan also ignored the political context against which the Egyptian visitor was writing – a context that did not exist for the other three writers. Qutb's vituperative tone was in reaction to America's support of the establishment of a Jewish state in Palestine and the expulsion of the native Muslim and Christian population – as an article published as early as 1946 in al-Risala shows, and as in Qutb's scathing essay on American foreign policy in which the Egyptian denounced the hegemony of the Western White Man over the peoples of the East.[2]

Had Nolan looked back half a century earlier at other Arab visitors and emigrants, he would have found Arabic writings about America that were vastly different in tone and content from Qutb's. For in the late 1880s, as "Turkish" emigrants began to arrive in America, they did not see the country as a hegemonic world power intent on dominating their homeland, nor had the seeds of conflict in the Middle East in the form of the Sykes-Picot agreement (1916) and the Balfour Declaration (1917) been cast – of which Qutb was deeply aware. Nor had the Ottoman Empire to which all the Syrian (that is Lebanese, Syrian, and Palestinian) emigrants belonged yet collapsed. Before 1914, America was not yet seen as an empire and the emigrants saw a land offering economic opportunity and intellectual freedom. Excitedly, and, without fear of censorship,[3] they wrote about their experiences and disseminated their views in newspapers and books throughout the United States, and in letters sent to Arabic journals in cities stretching from Damascus to Beirut and from Cairo to Jerusalem – the centers of the Arab Nahda. Not unlike other arrivals in the United States, they wrote to their compatriots about the new land, becoming the first men and women, authors and clergy, peddlers and princes who made the much-admired social, political, and cultural uniqueness of America known to Arab readers overseas. Contrary to what has been maintained, these Arabs wrote a lot about America before WWI:[4] in 1898, an Egyptian cleric visited America and returned to write about "The Wonders [ʿajaʾib] of America" in the first issue of al-Manar, a periodical edited by the Islamic reformer Rashid Rida. The wonders consisted of industrial innovations, high-rise buildings (over twenty storeys), trains, and ships; the author hoped that his readers would learn to emulate the inventive spirit of Americans. The travelogue by Prince Muhammad ʿAli in 1913 shows a breadth of perspective that makes the author fit better in the social and intellectual milieu of de Tocqueville, Weber, and Chesterton than Qutb: the prince had read de Tocquville, and in 1912, he did not have any political anxiety about America.

The Arabic corpus of the early emigrants reveals the tensions, confusions, and challenges which they faced in the United States. That the writings were in Arabic is important: they were intended for members of the Arabic-speaking community and revealed how members of that widely spread community thought about, remembered, and analyzed

their experiences. The corpus described, with honesty (although not necessarily without exaggeration or misunderstanding), the United States
as Arabs truly saw and negotiated it.[6] The memoirs and poems, essays
and travelogues, stories and discussions present a model with which
to write today's challenges of migration. As the Moroccan critic Saʿid
Yaqtin wrote: recent immigrants/refugees to Europe should emulate the
early emigrants/immigrants to the United States and establish literary
and cultural ties both with their host communities and their homelands.[5]
New arrivals should learn from their new societies, enrich their linguistic
and cultural identity, and then contribute to their host countries. His
words recall the motto of *Kawkab America* in 1892 (in English), the first
Arabic newspaper in the United States: "Helpful relations and good
understanding between the East and the West."

*

At first, emigration officers used "Turk" to define all arrivals from the
Ottoman regions, although the *New York Times* had used the phrase
"Maronite Arabs" as early as 25 May 1890 ("Sanctified Arab Tramps").
But after 1899 the emigrants were classified as "Syrians," and except for
the Egyptian writers, all emigrants discussed below viewed themselves
as "Syrians"; in the case of the Lebanese writers, they were Syrians
from "the Lebanon" which had enjoyed some administrative autonomy
since 1860. Khalil Sakakini, who was from Palestine, did not, however,
refer to himself during his American sojourn except as a Jerusalemite.
But in his dealings and exchanges with fellow emigrants, as in the case
of many others, there was little indication that he or they saw differences among themselves because of their different countries of origin:
they all felt united by their Arabic language. Rustum often praised
the Arabic language and glorified Arab civilization; in 1905, Ameen
Rihani used the phrase "Syrian Americans,"[7] but it did not catch on
as a designation and both "the Syrian *umma*"/nation[8] and "Syrians"
remained the dominant terms in use.[9] At the same time, writers concurred that they were from "Arab countries", thereby folding Syrian
with Arab: as Rihani wrote in 1908, his soul remained "both Arab and
eastern,"[10] and many business advertisements in the first almanac published by 1907 emphasized the owners' use of the Arabic language in
their transactions. In the introduction to his 1907 almanac, Dr. Naguib
Abdou repeatedly used phrases such as "*al-ʿalam al ʿArabi*"/the Arab
World, "*al-bilad al-ʿArabiyya*"/the Arab Countries, and "*abnaʾ al-lugha
al-ʿArabiyya*"/Sons of the Arabic Language, at the same time that he
continued to address himself to our "Syrian brethren." The Syrians' and
other Arabs' pride in their language consolidated a communal sense of

identity which was celebrated as far away as Egypt where a letter was sent to the *Hilal* magazine in 1907 asking for a report on the role of "our brethren the Syrian Christians in spreading the Arabic language in the New World." The reply emphasized how much the Syrians have "retained their Arabic language and have labored to revive its literature by founding newspapers, writing books, composing verse, and establishing societies."[11] The Syrians/Arabs imagined themselves as a community united across continents and seas by their language; as Abdou indicated in his advertisement to his almanac, he wanted to reach all the "sons of the Arabic language around the world."[12]

In clinging to Arabic/Arabicity, the emigrants anticipated the ideological role the language would play in the 1916 revolt against the Ottomans: it was the Sharif of Mecca, by means of his newspaper, *al-Qibla*, who helped define for Arabic-speakers a political and civilizational role that separated them from the Turks in a hoped-for United Arab Kingdom. It was from Mecca that Arab/Arabicity became revolutionary and politicized. Meanwhile, racially maligned in the American press, often demeaned and intimidated, the Syrians/Arabs in America turned to Arabic to show that they were a people with a legacy of greatness in science and geography, imagination, and achievement. Their language and their history were their defenses against racial slurs and social denigration.

The early emigrants traveled widely around the country, whether as correspondents for journals in the Middle East or as entrepreneurs, as laborers or as peddlers/*ba⁽at al-jizdan* (as they were known among their compatriots): "No region was too remote or forbidding to them."[13] As Mikhaʾil Rustum joked: "Two men succeeded in discovering the North Pole. If there is to be a third, he will be a Syrian peddler."[14] While some sought homesteads in states as sparsely inhabited as the Dakotas, others settled in the main cities where they encountered for the first time in their lives new and different religious and ethnic communities. The views they developed and articulated about those communities reflected their different levels of exposure, from an educated man like Khalil Sakakini who assisted Columbia University professor Richard Gottheil (1862–1936) in his research and editorial work, to men and women who had to learn a few words of English in order to eke out a living on the streets; and from Egyptian government officials sent on state missions, to women who had to confront Arab male chauvinism and cultural restrictions. Like Qutb, many wrote in periodicals and in local Arabic newspapers about "the America that I had seen"/*Amayrka al-lati raʾayt* (his title).[15]

With the America they had seen, the emigrants had no quarrel, so much so that in 1898, Syrian Jibraʾil Ward/Rose patriotically volunteered to fight in the war against Spain in Cuba, eager to defeat the "tyranny" that he had read about in the newspapers. And so too did many others from Lebanon, Syria, and Palestine fight in WWI – many of whose pictures he included in his 1919 book, along with the "Compliments of the Ramallah Young Men's Society, 145 of whose members were with the colors."[16] Interestingly, a large number of emigrants had gone to America to avoid Ottoman military service, and when America went to war in 1898 and 1914 and needed volunteers, some argued that their Christian faith prevented them from going to battle – which prompted the priest of the Syrian Orthodox Church in Brooklyn to write an article showing how Christianity did not oppose war.[17] Whatever criticisms the Syrians leveled at the new country, they were not of America's destabilizing role in the Middle East:[18] rather, in the pre-WWI period, their criticisms focused on America's harsh industrialization and its brutal labor conditions – criticisms that many European travelers, from the English writers Frances Trollope (1779–1863) and G. K. Chesterton (1874–1936) to the French thinker Alexis de Tocqueville (1805–59), also expressed and that were scathingly described in the 1906 American classic, Upton Sinclair's *The Jungle*.

One of the many reasons why Syrians went to the United States was because they had learned about it from the European and American missionaries who had been establishing schools in the Ottoman Empire since the first quarter of the nineteenth century. The missionaries later included native Arabs who went to America, converted to Protestantism, and subsequently returned to proselytize in Lebanon and Syria.[19] In this educational respect, the United States contributed to the development of the Arab *Nahda*,[20] a contribution that was recognized by a thinker such as Farah Antoun in 1902 but that has not been adequately studied in the history of Arab cultural transformation. Albert Hourani, in his magisterial work on the Arab *Nahda*, examined the influence of British and French thought and civilization on the changes that occurred in the nineteenth- and twentieth-century Arab World (1798–1939), but he said nothing about the influence of the United States which was inspiring the Arabs' modernization and their rising sense of self-confidence.[21] After all, the Arabs learned about the United States without having to endure invasion and colonization (as in the French invasion of Egypt in 1798 and the colonization of Algeria in 1830, and the British occupation of Egypt in 1882).[22] In fact, before WWI, the United States had very little political presence in the Arab World: in his memoir, the Egyptian khedive ʿAbbas Hilmi II (reg. 1892–1914) showed how much France, Britain, and Italy were active in Egyptian and North African domestic and foreign affairs (Italy occupied Libya in 1912) – making no reference at all to the United States.[23]

The Arabic-speaking peoples of Egypt and the eastern Mediterranean were heavily exposed to British and French influences that had started with Muhammad ʿAli at the beginning of the nineteenth century (reg. 1805–49). The Egyptian ruler had sent students and scholars to France to study new fields of knowledge and administration. These students were followed by travelers and diplomats who visited Paris, London, and other parts of Europe.[24] After their return, and inspired by their exposure to European civilization and languages, men such as Rifaʿa al-Tahtawi (1801 –73), ʿAli Mubarak (1823–93), Ruhi al-Khalidi (1864–1913), Ahmad Faris al-Shidyaq (1805–87), Francis Marrash (1836–74), Jurji Zaydan (1861–1914), Muhammad al-Muwaylihi (1858–1930),[25] Muhammad Kurd ʿAli (1876–1953), Khalil Sakakini (1878–1953), and others became some of the greatest Arab writers and intellectuals of the nineteenth and early twentieth centuries. However, they had not been intent on emigration: they visited the West and returned to their homelands in Lebanon, Palestine, Syria, and Egypt with memories of what they had liked or disliked. The few who emigrated and settled permanently in England and France were mentioned by Zaydan, who listed their family names in his travelogue of 1912.[26]

These immigrants to Western Europe did not leave behind them writings comparable to the output of their counterparts in the United States. The latter, after clearing Barge Office (and after 1892, Ellis Island), wandered into "Little Syria" in lower Manhattan,[27] and then moved out into the rest of the country. Large numbers had arrived in the hope of making money in America and then returning home, and it is not clear how many of them saw themselves as immigrants intent on settling permanently, or as emigrants who would stay for a set period of time and then go back with what they imagined would be wealth and fortune. In these cases, including the traveling visitors and the writers in the home countries, all expressed admiration for how much America had freed itself of imperial British rule and had risen to "supersede the European countries in output."[28] They were delighted to learn about former American presidents visiting the Arab East, Egypt in particular, not as imperial lords like the British, the French, or the Prussians, but as citizens eager to see, and sometimes to praise, local achievements. In 1878, former president Ulysses S. Grant toured Egypt and the region, having earlier invited to dinner at the White House a member of the Egyptian delegation to the 1876 Philadelphia Fair, Idwar Ilyas, who later published a charming account of his dinner at the "White Palace" and the visit of the wife of President Grant to the Egyptian section at the Fair. Having suffered under the aristocratic French and British models of governments, the new arrivals transposed the values of European history onto the American soil: in 1907, one advertisement for silk products on 35 Broadway, New York City, used the rallying cry of the French Revolution (plus one further term), "Liberty, *Justice*, Fraternity, Equality", to praise the American spirit of industry.[29] In 1910, the Cairo- and later Damascus-based *al-Muqtabas*, edited by the notable Syrian scholar Muhammad Kurd ᶜAli, summarized the speech of Theodore Roosevelt during his March visit to Egypt and Sudan in which he praised the schooling system in those countries that integrated Muslim, Christian, and Jewish children.[30] President Roosevelt, who was greatly admired in the Arabic press for having crushed monopolists and overpowered "the kings of steel and oil," visited Egypt and Sudan after ending his term in office, where he gave a number of motivational speeches urging his Arab audience to rely on themselves in building up their society: *al-Muqtabas* summarized his speeches and prominently featured them.[31] Such admiration had inspired a poem based on the "meaning of an American poem" in praise of America.[32] If, as Rasheed El-Enany observed, Britain and France were "at once the malady and the remedy" for Arab writers and travelers,[33] the United States was the remedy without the malady – which is why when "Syrian Americans" returned to their homelands, they "idealized the social and political life of the United States," as Philip Hitti reported in 1924.[34]

In the 1850s, the United States sent an archeological expedition to Palestine,[35] and in 1866, it established the nucleus of the first modern university in the Middle East. The Syrian Protestant College introduced Western knowledge to the students who enrolled in its Ras Beirut buildings. But it was a knowledge that was guided by religious and conversionary goals[36] – which is why it was the founders of the College who published the first "authorized" translation of the (Protestant) Bible into Arabic. The translation was overseen by a team led by New York-born Cornelius Van Dyck who revolutionized Arab culture by insisting (as had been the Protestant tradition since Luther) on the use of the vernacular/Arabic in Christian worship which was either conducted in Latin and Syriac by the Catholics and Maronites, or in Coptic and Greek by the Orthodox.[37] From the campus of the College (renamed in 1920 the American University of Beirut), new ideas were disseminated and discussed, ranging from Charles Darwin's *Origin of Species* and the debate about whether Shakespeare was really Francis Bacon or not, to descriptions of elections in America; there were also publications of medical books such as al-Razi's treatise on smallpox (1873). "Who is the traveler," asked Najib ᶜAzury, author of the 1905 classic *The Awakening of the Arab Nation in Turkish Asia* and who lived for a few years in New York before returning to the Middle East, "who has not been impressed by the admirable organization of the American University in Beirut?"[38]

The majority of the emigrants were Christian, both Orthodox and Catholic, but one of the first recorded immigrants to the United States was a Syrian Muslim: "Hi Jolly." He arrived in the early 1850s with camels for the United States Army, after which he got married and settled in Arizona. Although there is a memorial for him in the Quartzsite Cemetery, Arizona,[39] Hadji ᶜAli (his original name) was not known to later emigrant writers. In 1898, the newly founded Beirut periodical *Al-Machriq* reported how the first emigrants to the New World (Brazil) had been Christian Palestinians from Bethlehem and Jerusalem, who were later followed by Syrians/Lebanese, who sold holy trinkets from "the Holy Land."[40] But in 1911, Ray Harroun won the inaugural Indianapolis 500; he had been born in 1879 in Spartansburg to parents who had emigrated from Lebanon earlier in the century.[41]

In 1909, Jamil Butrus Hilwa stated that after the Christians wrote back to their relatives about their successes in America, others belonging to "Muslim denominations, Druzes, and Matawilah [Shiᶜite]" started emigrating so that the number reached 300,000.[42] It has been estimated that 10 per cent of the emigrants were educated,[43] and so, soon after arriving, they started publishing books on topics ranging from Christian hagiography to the Qurᵓan, from an Arabized *Romeo and Juliet* to the *Muqadimmah* of Ibn Khaldoun, and from the *Diwan of ᶜAntar* to a translation of Victor Hugo's *Les Misérables* to a biography of Mar Maroun. The various religious communities established their own newspapers,[44] and they distributed them from North and South America to the Middle East and as far away as Australia and the Philippines. From all parts of the United States, emigrants contributed to the newspapers by sending letters, news accounts, essays, poems, and opinions: they saw themselves as establishing a vast reading but not, unfortunately, buying public in America – as authors and newspaper editors complained.[45]

In the 1898–9 volume of *al-Diyaᵓ*, a journal edited in Beirut/Cairo by the Lebanese reformist Ibrahim al-Yaziji (1847–1906), an article celebrated the literary revival of "this [Arab] nation both in the homeland and thousands of miles away."[46] Various emigrants published essays in the Cairo-based *Hilal*, which, as the list of its sales agents shows, was read in the United States, Canada, Mexico, Cuba, San Salvador, Honduras, Brazil, Argentina, Chile, Basra, Iraq, Baghdad, Goa, the East Indies, Beirut, and Damascus.[47] Even in Mecca, soon after the beginning of the Arab Revolt (10 June 1916), the local newspaper, *al-Qibla*, started reporting on responses to the revolt from Arabs living in the United States, and praising "the nationalist spirit of the emigrant Syrians" (11 Shawwal 1335/30 July 1917). A few days earlier, the newspaper had reported what *Mirᵓat al-Gharb*, "one of the biggest Arabic newspapers in the world", wrote in praise "of the king of Hijaz, he who rules over the hearts of all Arabic-speakers [*lughat al-dad*]," adding that "none of the emigrants would have left the homeland had authority been held there by the Arabs and for the Arab homeland" (7 Shawwal 1335/26 July 1917).[48]

Struggling to find a place in a new society and caught in the tension between integration and memory, emigration and immigration, the pre-1914 writers of the texts below did not think of themselves as building a national narrative or history in the United States; they still had not envisioned where their future would be and whether they were destined to return to their homelands or to settle in America. But from their confusion and adventure, success and failure, they produced the first portrait of America through Arab eyes – a portrait that should not be ignored in the study of writings by pre-1914 immigrants to the United States.[49] Further, in recent scholarship, there has been much emphasis on Arab American immigrant narratives in novels, autobiographies, films, essays, and poems. But before this (chiefly) English output, there was an Arabic *Ur*-output by Arab emigrants and visitors who showed their compatriots the changes in their understanding of America: from a "land of gold," as Ameen Rihani had been told, and "the mother of wonders"/*um al-ʿajaʾib* as one 1898 article described it,[50] to a land of hard work and competition, of brutal capitalism and soul-killing greed. As Jamil Butrus Hilwa, who worked as a translator in the immigration bureau in New York, stated, America was a land of struggle in which only the fittest survived, deliberately echoing the language of Darwin.[51]

By sheer coincidence, the texts below are bookended by two travel accounts, the first belonging to 1876, the year in which the first Arab visited and later published about the United States, and the second to 1913, when the first ever Arab travelogue about North America was published in Cairo. Just after the sinking of the *Titanic* in the summer of 1912, Prince Muhammad ʿAli traveled from Egypt to the United States and Canada, after which he published his travelogue. The two authors, Idwar Ilyas and Prince Muhammad ʿAli, were Egyptian dignitaries and therefore saw the United States from "above": in fact, the latter wrote in the aristocratic manner of Alexis de Tocqueville – with additional insights from Ibn Khaldoun. Another visitor, the Lebanese Bulus Effendi al-Khawli, a university professor, wrote a short account about the "greatness of America" in 1906, but he also added criticisms of America based on his reading of Darwin and Marx.[52] These writers were not poor, were not intent on immigration, and were not culturally insecure; they could observe, comment, and be amused at American peculiarities. During the Philadelphia Fair, Ilyas wrote:

> People looked and wondered especially when they came to our Egyptian exhibit and saw its marvels. But then they asked me and others in the delegation odd questions that do not cross anyone's mind. For instance: one wanted to know how the silkworms were raised after seeing natural silk; another asked whether eggs were hatched into chicks by industrial methods; some asked for an Arabic newspaper to keep as a memento. A woman asked us to write her name in Arabic on a visiting card, while another asked about marriage customs and polygamy, and many other questions that only a foreigner would ask.

He and a few other writers described their experience in America from a position of distance and safety. But the larger number of Arab arrivals were the "small" emigrants who wrote from "below," forced by circumstance to become what anthropologists might call "participant observers." They described the full range of their experience of America: arrival and search for work, success and fear, hunger and despair, and, in one case, near cannibalism. As they met with races and ethnicities they had not known in the Middle East, many of them adopted the Americans' racist discourse against Native Indians, Chinese, and other minorities. However, there were some among them who challenged that discourse and showed commiseration and compassion. And while compatriots in the homelands debated and discussed the "West"/*al-gharb* – how good or bad it was, what to adopt or not adopt – the emigrants were in 'the trenches' and wrote about their encounter with: (a) new racial and ethnic **minorities** in America, and (b) their uncertainty about the role of **women** in a society that permitted women the "indecency" of swimming with men while at the same time offering them opportunities to become financially independent. Also in America, the writers discovered the need to negotiate (c) their Syrian-Arab **identity** in the face of a powerful culture that threatened them with Americanization/*ta'amruk*. Many of the emigrants assimilated into American life and identity, but there were many others who (d) came, saw, and then **returned**.

(A) THE MINORITIES

Arriving in the United States, the Arabs came face to face with peoples they had not seen in their home countries. Inevitably, and as they started learning English, adapting to their surroundings, and interacting with the general public, they picked up the prevalent discourse of American racism. It may well be that those who were literate among them had also read some of the racist articles and reports that had been translated from English and French and published in Arabic periodicals in the Middle East. Historically, racial differentiation had not marked Arabic thinking in the period under study. More divisive were the religious and the social stratifications: Christian, Muslim, Jewish, Nusayri, Druze, etc., or urban vs peasant, and prince vs commoner. But in the United States the dominant divide was racial,[53] and so emigrants, eager to be integrated, accepted it; even the two Egyptian visitors fell victim to some expressions of bigotry. To varying degrees, they all learned "to curse."

The Chinese

From 1882 on, the Chinese confronted wide discrimination that sought to stop their immigration into the United States.[54] When the new arrivals mixed with the Chinese immigrants, living not too far from them in Lower Manhattan, they repeated the general conviction about the racial superiority of the white race over all other races. But, in 1892, *Kawkab America* reported sympathetically about Chinese attempts to challenge Congress's denial of citizenship to them (13 May and 30 September 1892), and the editor described a wonderful Chinese wedding in New York – although he ridiculed the religious rituals which he could not understand. He and other writers were appalled at the Chinese addiction to opium – ignorant of the British policy to inundate China with Indian opium in order to subdue the population. Prince Muhammad ᶜAli described the shoddy conditions of the Chinese in San Francisco but he was not unsympathetic to their plight, and he merged the Chinese with the Japanese in his desire to undermine the alleged racial categories that underpinned advanced civilizations. Although he was familiar with the phrenological explanations for the inferiority of the "Yellow Race," he praised the victory of the Japanese over the Russians in the 1904–5 war, eager to refute those who "believe that only the White Race is capable of advancement."[55] Like many poets and writers in his native Egypt, there was pride in the "Eastern" victory over the "Western" Russians.[56]

Other Arabic writings however, both in the United States and overseas, did not express sympathy. In the first issue of *al-Muqtabas* in 1906, an article praised the American Renaissance that was built on the shoulders of "a flood of immigrants from Europe," but it denounced the Chinese who sucked the good out of the country, just like "the bird of prey carrying its prey in its talons."[57] A year later in New York, Abdou repeated those exact words.[58] After the Boxer Rebellion and the massacre of Christians became known in the United States, the "heathen" attack provoked the ire of the majority-Christian emigrants; even nine years later, in 1909, Rustum wrote a scathing and racist poem about "the Massacres in China and the killing of foreigners and all Christians."[59] In that same year, 1909, Hilwa warned about the "yellow danger," followed in 1910 by mention of the "yellow menace" in al-Muqtabas (5 [1910], 424).

The Native Americans

As there were differing views of the Chinese, so there were of the Native Americans/Indians. In the second half of the nineteenth century, White Americans were still celebrating their victory over the Indians and their near total seizure of the land: Indians had been corralled in arid reservations, driven out of the main cities, and cleared off the territories which emigrants were claiming as homesteads. Travelers and emigrants wanted to identify with the American whiteness that controlled economic and political power, and one way to confirm (to themselves) and to assert (to outsiders) that whiteness was to do what white Americans did: denigrate the non-white, turning the Indians into the bête noire of their writings.

In 1876, Idwar Ilyas adopted the American discourse of triumphalism over Indians, although he did not mention in his travelogue any meeting with them. He vilified them after listening to his American hosts from whom he picked up words such as "lynching."[60] As the English traveler Frances Trollope had noted less than half a century earlier, it was from her conversations with Americans that she "heard the statements which represent them [Indians] as treacherous and false almost beyond belief in their intercourse with the unhappy Indians."[61] Like her, Arabs had had no idea about Indians but still they adopted the derogatory views and repeated them both in the United States and overseas. An article in the Beirut-based periodical al-Jinan in 1883 and translated from the New York Tribune mentioned how the Indians "waged war on us," killing and pillaging the "whites."[62] A year later, another article in the same periodical spoke of "savages . . .who still lived like Bedouins in the stone age";[63] a writer in al-Muqtataf explained that "the law of evolution/irtiqaʾ demonstrates how the whites will fight and overcome the blacks who might just become extinct in the same manner that the original inhabitants [of the United States] have become extinct."[64] In the United States, Kawkab America reported how Indians slaughtered their chiefs when they became senile (19 July 1895), and over a decade later, Abdou listed many of the Indian names that were used in America, adding that the Indians were the original inhabitants of the land: thus Connecticut is "Long River (Indian)" and Arizona is "Sandy Hills (Indian)." But then, he added that the "Indian Tribes" lived in the "Indian Territory" after they had been "expelled from the United States" – a callous reference to their Trail of Tears;[65] while over 3,000 of those "Indian Americans" were sent to schools in Arizona – another callous reference to the American government's attempt at forcible integration.[66]

A correspondent (muktatib) in the United States, Yusuf Jirjis Zakham, wrote for al-Muqtabas in Cairo how the Indians lived "like wild animals," and although he mentioned that out of the 276 million acres the Indians had possessed of fertile lands they were left with only 7 million, he still added that they were "hard-necked, spending their time and life wandering from place to place." He was not surprised therefore that those Indian "savage peoples" were going extinct, and in looking at paintings and photographs and circus shows, he thought them similar in features to "Chaldeans and Bedouins."[67] In 1910, he again denounced the Indians for still living a "savage/hamajiyya life";[68] and halfway across the world in Palestine, Haifa-based ᶜAbdallah Mukhlis, who had been reading about Alaska and its "Eskimos", appealed to Ibn Khaldoun's terminology that the native populations in America were similar to bedouins/badawa: they lacked industry and were therefore savage/hamaj.[69] Three years later, Orthodox Priest Basil Kherbawi wrote in New York how those "savage tribes that were used to a life of wandering for hundreds of years developed characteristics more savage than human – which can never be changed."[70] Additionally, emigrants fell victim to the captivity genre of narratives that had been popular in the United States since the beginning of the nineteenth century (and further back to Mary Rowlandson in the 1680s) and that had contributed to the negative and violent image of the Indians in the White American imagination. In 1895, Kawkab America reported about a white boy who was captured by the Indians and made to live among them – until he escaped.

But, when an American newspaper described how Indian children were told to celebrate Columbus Day, because "had not Columbus reached here, they would not have had the good education they were having," the Kawkab editor commented sarcastically that the newspaper forgot how Columbus had slaughtered the ancestors of those children, stolen their lands, and enslaved them (14 October 1892). As knowledge grew of the history of the destruction of the North American Indians, some Arab voices rose in sympathy: before returning to Egypt from the United States in 1908, the secularist reformer Farah Antoun (1874–1922) stood one day before Niagara Falls and called: "Do you remember, O waterfall, the day when your river bank was the home of those pitiful Indians before others reached you and usurped their land, unjustly and brutally?"[71] But the most sympathetic depiction of the Indians, and the first in Arabic print, was written by a gold prospector who actually visited Indians in Alaska: Jibraʾil ʿAssaf Mirʿi. Although he retained the view of their "savagery" which could only be eradicated by their Christianization, he praised their dedication and hard work, the beautiful schools and churches they had built in Metlakahtla, their endurance at times of hardship, and most importantly, the kindness they expressed to the poor even among the "white" race.

Another description of the Indians appears in the travelogue of Prince Muhammad ʿAli. Although he, too, used terms like "savages"/*mutawahhishin* about the Indians ("the savage Shoshone tribes," 159), he offered detailed descriptions of their lives, habitations, conditions, and crafts. He discussed their origin, wondered about similarities between them and the blacks of Africa, and reflected on the cruelty of white discrimination against them. It is significant that by the end of his journey, and after seeing so much suffering among the Indians, he lambasted humanity (and not just the Whites) for failing to come to their help. Like de Tocqueville, he was appalled at the poverty and destitution that he saw,[72] but while Mirʿi had stayed with Indians, eating and conversing (in signs) with them, Prince Muhammad ʿAli observed them from a distance, and it is to the credit of these two writers, coming as they did from different social and religious backgrounds, that they took pains to write compassionately. A year later, the Catholic periodical *Al-Machriq* reported from Beirut how Pope Pius X (reg. 1903–14) had denounced to the American bishops the horrible treatment of Native Indians.[73]

Other groups

Ilyas wrote the first Arabic description of the Quakers, praising them for their honesty and moral conduct. In 1875, *al-Jinan* published a long article by Salim al-Bustani about the origins and beliefs of the Mormons; a few years later, another article in the same periodical stated that in Utah, and because of the prevalent custom of polygamy, the number of males had increased by 5,000.[74] Abdou mentioned the sect/*shīʿa* of Mormons who had practiced polygamy,[75] and in 1911, an article in *al-Muqtabas* alluded to them and to their beautiful temple in Utah (finished in the 1890s), adding that some of them had married more than ten wives, and so, "the government of the United States denies entry to every immigrant who upholds or practices multiplicity of wives."[76] The priest Kherbawi gave a short account of the Mormons, and mentioned the killing of "their prophet and his brother."[77]

Although there was a large Irish presence just north of Little Syria on Washington Street, there was not much reference to them in Arabic writings – notwithstanding frequent violent encounters.[78] Jibraʾil Ward, however, included a picture of the "bold and zealous Ibrahim al-Kha-wand, known as Abu Raffoul, one of the daring and courageous Syrians who served the Syrian community in many ways, most important of which was to break the back of the Irish thugs who used to attack, insult, and demean our [Syrian] countrymen."[79] Still, all Ward's friends who enlisted with him to fight in Cuba in 1898 were Irish, and much as he was buddies with them, he could not but make fun of one of them who did not know left from right. Other Syrians repeated the stereotypes about the Irish in American discourse: *Kawkab America* reported a teacher asking his student what poverty meant. The student answered, "My father tells me poverty is New York on Sunday when you cannot find a single beer to drink" (2 August 1895); and New York-based Mikhaʾil Rustum, in the first Arabic book to be printed in the United States,[80] included a joke about the Irish (*ayrishi*). But on 5 March 1895, the Irish held a nationalist rally in New York in which they raised green flags and called for revolution to save the home country/*watan* from the English (*Kawkab America*, 8 March), inspiring the Syrians to similar patriotism, without, however, the revolutionary fervor. In the 1911 *Book of Khalid*, the first novel written by an Arab in America (in English), Rihani praised the kindly Irishman with whom his Lebanese hero, Khalid, lodged.

Meanwhile, writers differed in their designations of the *zunuj*, *ʿabid*, and *sud*,[81] although few of the emigrants seem to have "seen" and therefore commented on them. (After the failure of Reconstruction, there was a large migration of African Americans to the North.) *Kawkab America* reported on the riots in Harris County, Georgia by the "Sons of Ham" (22 February 1895) stemming from their dire poverty, and how they were beaten down by the U.S. Army; a week later, on the occasion of the funeral of Frederick Douglass, it praised "the great orator among those of his race/ *abnaʾ jildatihi*," adding that he was married to a white woman (1 March 1895). But when Mexico refused to admit black/*ʿabid* emigrants from the United States because of the "violence and unrest they caused," Syrians were pleased that they, along with the Irish and the French, were welcomed (*Kawkab America*, 19 July 1895). However, and influenced by some Protestant hymns that he had picked up before his emigration from one of the many American schools in Lebanon,[82] Rustum expressed shock at continued racial segregation in America:

> In Syria, we used to sing a hymn which began as follows: "Whites and blacks are equal – because our redeeming Lord came to all." But here, we should reverse the prayer: "Blacks and whites are far apart – the two races do not even ride the same [street]-car." Notwithstanding the laws of the land, the religious teachings of

Christ, and the toleration shown by the American race to the negroes/zunuj, the situation in the South remains contrary to what we would have expected. The whites separate themselves from the blacks who have specially designated places to ride; they also have separate restaurants and separate clubs. In everything, they are apart from the white race. Furthermore, the Samaritans do not mix with the Jews. What happened to all the men and funds that were expended in the cause of liberating the slaves and for establishing equality among mankind?[83]

A summary of a "European" article about America published in a Beirut periodical in 1906 mentioned "crucifying and whipping" of blacks, a reference to Ku Klux Klan practices, while another article discussed the various shades of black among the zunuj/Africans – summarizing a much-repeated discussion in American racism – to the point where one correspondent in Beirut, who had been reading a scientific magazine, inquired whether the blacks could be whitened by "electricity."[84] But a resident of Province Island, Shihadeh Shihadeh, wrote an article in which he praised President Roosevelt for adding Booker T. Washington, the black man, to his staff, because the latter "was a noble man who served his community and would thereby help in resolving one of America's biggest problems: the problem of the blacks."[85] Prince Muhammad ᶜAli noticed the hierarchy of white over black in employment: all the cooks and waiters on the train were sudaniyyin,[86] he wrote, but their supervisor was white, as were the drivers and inspectors.[87] He did not, however, write about them in the detailed manner of the Indians or the Chinese because, for him, they were not unlike the black Sudanese/Nubians who were also employed in Egypt in menial labor. Generally, emigrants were totally unaware of or did not comment on racism against blacks: even when Jibraᵓil Ward was suspected of being a Spanish spy because he was not white and had a dark complexion, he did not elaborate. Over half a century later, Sayyid Qutb denounced the racist practices of Americans after he experienced them first hand.

The racist attitudes of Arab emigrants reflected their anxiety about the racist attacks on them which described them as ᶜarab, turko, dako, and dinko, as priest Kherbawi bitterly observed.[88] As early as 1890, the emigrants had been denounced as "Arab Tramps: Wretched Maronite Beggars Infesting the Country" who made their living begging in front of churches on Sundays (New York Times, 28 May); in 1894, Kawkab America, wishing to reform the community, denounced the Syrians for constantly fighting and suing each other, becoming an udhuka/laughing stock for Americans, from Denver, Colorado to Shenendoah, Pennsylvania

(7 December); on 24 October 1905, the *New York Times* reported that the Syrians in Lower Manhattan used knives against each other – Maronites against Orthodox Christians (not much different, however, from the 1860s violence depicted in Martin Scorsese's *Gangs of New York*).[89] The Syrians were riotous, always ready to blow the "trumpet for a battle of the Armageddon type" (*New York Times*, 29 October 1905). In 1907, Congressman John L. Burnett listed the Syrians as the "most undesirable of the undesirable peoples of Asia Minor,"[90] and an article in the *New York Times* on 30 September 1909 described them as "Turks of the Mongolian race" – which was a good reason to bar them from citizenship, as had happened with "the Chinese, Japanese, Burmese, and their half-breeds."[91]

By the beginning of the twentieth century, some Syrian emigrants began to seek naturalization and were afraid of not being categorized as White and of being associated with the "Turks" and the "Mongolians."[92] Rustum jokingly wrote that:

> What had saved the Syrians in particular, and the Turks in general, after that Mongolian attempt to deny them citizenship, was the advent of the celebration of the birth of Jesus the Nazarene and of Thanksgiving. On both occasions, Americans need the Ethiopian rooster, which they call turkey. It had been better for them to name it Mongol and slaughter as many as they wanted to satisfy themselves."[93]

It was in this charged climate that Hilwa was asked by the "great Syrian reformer and editor Naʿum Effendi Mukarzil" (editor of *al-Hoda*) to write his book: there had been a recent racist attack on the "sons of Syria by an American" writer who described them as "descendants of the Mongols." Hilwa explained that such vicious attacks should motivate the Syrians to "examine their social conditions in order to establish a set of historical and economic texts" that refute such allegations.[94] In the 1915 case of Dow v. The United States, the Syrians won in court and became officially "Caucasian,"[95] but still, in 1917, Rihani wrote (perhaps tongue-in-cheek) of how much he wished that his father had married one of the "native daughters" of America so that he would have been born like the officer he met on board an American destroyer: a "ruddy-cheeked, blue-eyed, raw-boned, chin-in-the-air lad."[96] "Caucasian"/white as he was, Rihani wanted to become American.

Emigrants and travelers, Christians and Muslims, were deeply impressed by what they saw of American religious toleration. On 9 February 1900, Rihani gave a resounding speech in New York praising *al-tasahul al-dini*/religious tolerance in Europe and the United States and calling on his fellow countrymen to promote it.[97] From its first issue in 1892, *Kawkab America* used both the Hijri and the Christian calendars on its front pages, signifying its recognition of both religious traditions; Rustum was ever proud that the emigrants had overcome their religious differences and he always mentioned Muslims and Druze in his anecdotes about the Syrians in America. But the emigrants did not seem to recognize one of the distinctive marks of America which had been praised as far back as de Tocqueville: the institutional separation between church and state. The writers admired toleration but they did not understand that it was part of the American political system because they did not feel they could ever be part of the political life in the Ottoman Empire, which to many remained their home country.[98] Some Christian writers recalled the persecution they had experienced at the hands of Ottoman officials, on whom they poured their wrath, but they credited persecution to Turkish ethnocentrism and not to Islam. After 1908, the Ottoman administration discriminated heavily against its Arab Muslim and Christian subjects alike, but the latter were the more vulnerable. Still, priest Kherbawi went out of his way to laud the toleration of the Qurʾanic tradition – as against Turkish bigotry. He described the suffering Christians endured at the hands of Ottoman administrators and corrupt rulers – and then added:

> Far be it that the Muslim bad treatment of Christians stems from the religion of Islam . . . On the contrary, the religion commands moral and upright treatment of Christians and others. But the ignorance of some and the designs of others have disguised the bad treatment as part of religion. Islam, however, has nothing to do with them and their deeds. We cannot but admit that there are among the Muslims a noble community whose members are not deceived by selfish schemes and who know what the truth is. They are honorable and have treated and continue to treat their Christian neighbors with respect and courtesy, knowing that if God had wanted, He would have created us all as one *umma*.[99]

Sakakini was angry when he learned of Christian bigotry against Muslims in Jerusalem, and in turn, Prince Muhammad ʿAli praised the piety of Christian Americans who did not eat Sunday lunch until after church prayer was over; he also enjoyed organ music in what he thought was a church, and admired a marble cross that an old woman had erected outside Los Angeles for Father Serra: "This is the way in which religious memorials should be preserved – which we do not see in our country," he noted.[100] It is significant that in all his meetings with emigrants and immigrants during his travels, the prince did not mention the Christian or Muslim religion of individuals – although he noted Jews.

Jews

As anti-Semitism was on the rise in Europe, the Arabic press both in the Middle East and in the United States took up the defense of the Jews. The first issue of *al-Jinan* attacked a book that had recently been published and that maligned the Jews/*al-Isra'iliyyin*;[101] and two years later, in 1872, it published another article in defense of the Jews; in 1881, *al-Muqtataf* translated the reply of British Rabbi Adler against anti-Semitic writings, crediting hostility to Jews to "Germanic fanatics."[102] On 13 January 1892, *Kawkab America* decried the treatment of Jews in Russia and their expulsion from their homes; a few months later, on 13 May, it denounced the "Polish Anti-Semitic Riot" (in the English page of the newspaper). Anti-Semitism increased in the wake of the Dreyfus Affair in France (1894) and in 1898, the conservatively Islamic *al-Manar* condemned the bigotry against Jews in that country, blaming it not just on religious fanaticism, but also on the envy of French newspaper editors who were greedy for the wealth of the Jews. "We hope," concluded the author, "that the European disease will not reach our East."[103] But Western myths about Jews were already traveling to the Middle East, thus the query which one reader sent to the editors of *al-Bayan* in that same year, Ibrahim al-Yaziji and Bishara Zalzal, inquiring about the Wandering Jew. The editors warned that it was a silly myth of the ancients.[104]

Both in the *mahjar* as in the East, authors viewed the Jews as part of their home society because there were Jewish communities in the main cities of the Levant, from Beirut to Damascus to Jerusalem to Cairo – a *millet* protected by Ottoman (and Islamic) law.[105] As early as 1870, Butrus al-Bustani had called in his *al-Jinan* for "brotherhood" among Turks, Arabs, Druze, Jews, Maronites, Orthodox and others,[106] while Rida in *al-Manar* praised the Ottoman *dewlet* for so welcoming Jews fleeing from persecution that the Jews started thinking of establishing an independent homeland for themselves in Palestine![107] This religious inclusiveness crossed the Atlantic with the emigrants and in 1893, a Jewish merchant by the name of Ezra al-Sitt was described as one of the "sons of the homeland"/*awlad biladina* who joined his Syrian brethren at the New York Exhibit to sell his wares (*Kawkab America*, 6 December).[108] In fact, during the 1884 journey of the four Lebanese to the United States as recorded by Priest Kherbawi, Arabic-speaking Jews played a most helpful role. In 1900, there was a New York report about the "*jihad*" of the Maronites against their corrupt clergy in which they joined together with the Catholics, the Orthodox, the Jews, and all other concerned Syrians.[109] In 1908–9, Jurji Zaydan, editor of the Cairo-based *al-Hilal*, treated the Christians, Muslims, and Jews of the Arab world as one community, rejecting thereby the European anti-Jewish images that he had used in one of his earlier novels.[110] In his travelogue, Prince Muhammad ʿAli periodically mentioned meeting with Jews: having been familiar with Jews in the homeland, he as well as the Arab emigrants did not see any difference with them because they all belonged to the same linguistic and cultural world. In 1919, Jibraʾil Ward gave brief biographies of the young Syrian men who had fought in WWI on the side of the Allies, along with other Syrians who were respected writers and businessmen whom he had known. One of the entries was the following:

From Yusuf Hakim, 71 Wall Street, New York

(The author): Yusuf Hakim is a noble and generous man from one of the old Jewish/*Israʾiliyyin* families in Damascus. Like others, he came to this land and with energy, dedication and the other qualities for which he was known, sought the path of success. He started working with dedication and achieved what he wanted. His prosperous business in olive oil is the greatest proof of his brilliant abilities and he is ever willing to express his nationalist feelings and his deep love to everything that is Syrian. Not a project is started but he supports it: more than once, he has contributed to charities.[111]

That is why some emigrants turned to Arabic-speaking Jews for help, and Rustum reported how two of the first Lebanese emigrants met with a Jew in Gibraltar who accompanied them on their journey to the United States. His name was Solomon Yona Ṭawil.[112] This association might help to explain why the Syrian emigrants were often compared by American writers to Jews.[113]

Significantly, the religious tolerance of the emigrants and visitors ran counter to the exclusivity of American society where the White Protestant establishment discriminated against Catholics and Jews (and others). While Jews were often depicted in a negative light (Michael Dobkowski, *The Tarnished Dream: The Basis of American Anti-Semitism*, 1979), the emigrants called for unity among the Arabic speakers in the *mahjar*, regardless of religion. For them, the Jews were part of the mosaic of Arab emigrants in the United States as they had been part of the mosaic in the homelands. Intellectuals writing in both verse and prose advocated for diversity in unity among the various denominations and groups.[114] And although religious tensions and squabbles continued among the emigrants, men like Rihani, Khalil Gibran, Sakakini and others tried to consolidate a unity that was not possible back home where the religious and educational institutions were powerful and crippling;[115] in fact, Gibran and Sakakini rebelled against their respective churches and were excommunicated. The America in which the emigrants lived was not secular (thus the Scopes Trial of 1925), and it is unlikely that any of the emigrants would have conceived of himself as "secular," but many advocated for religious inclusion of Christians, Muslims, and Jews in a manner that mainstream America did not, and they did so not only in their writings and social programs, but also in their vision of the homeland. It is this spirit of openness that contributed to the making of one of the earliest secularist thinkers in Arabic: Farah Antoun.[116]

(B) WOMEN

One of the major challenges that faced emigrants was the changing role of women. Abdou included an advertisement about a kimono store owned by a Miss Saʿdi al-Hajj which she had placed in his almanac. She stated that in the United States, women were equal to men in word and deed: and so "Syrian and American" patrons should visit her store which she had established eleven years earlier (1896) on 44 Broadway, Suite 414, New York City.[117] Women were pursuing their own economic initiatives in America, and from Egypt, Warda Yaziji contrasted the eastern woman with her "European and American" counterpart, and praised the latter for writing newspaper articles and studying astronomy and chemistry. There was such interest among the readership of periodicals and newspapers to promote the role of women that (Philadelphia- and later New York-based) al-Hoda newspaper designated space for women writers from its very establishment in 1898. A year later, ʿAfifa Azan wrote about the need for decency in Syrian women's attire (29 March 1899),[118] and a decade later, ʿAfifa Karam, a frequent contributor to the newspaper, wrote: "The Syrian woman is being discussed by two groups of men. One group seeks to educate, enlighten, and edify her, and the other seeks to keep her in ignorance. They represent two camps: the camp of reform and the camp of defeat . . . To which camp, O reader, do you belong?"[119]

In some respect, this tension reflected the social class of the observers: writers such as Ilyas and Prince Muhammad ʿAli, coming from wealth and status, wanted women to be conservative and modest – at a time when other women had been sent by their husbands to peddle and face danger and humiliation on the streets. The tension, which was also being discussed in Egypt by such writers as Qasim Amin (1865–1908) and his supporters (and detractors), explains the conflicted attitude towards women among Arab writers in the United States. A certain Haykal Effendi al-Khoury set down the basic rules for women: "1. Working. Loving. Praying. Weeping with the weepers. Staying awake when others are asleep, that is, when the children are asleep. 2. Wiping tears off the cheeks of the sorrowful. Endurance. Patience. Cheering the demoralized and helping the weak," and other duties.[120] Similar advice had been offered to women by Miss Maryam Yusuf al-Zammar, who stated: "It is not important to be educated, to read and write, learn music or be able to parse or peruse newspapers. Rather, women should heed my advice and they will surely find it true: they should practice gentility, avoid flippant humor with people they do not know, avoid unnecessary conversation, shun gossip, shun envy; and they should receive their guests with a smile."[121]

Such views did not go unchallenged both in the *mahjar* and in the East. The editor of *al-Hoda* came to the support of women: the doctor/Haykal Effendi, he responded, writes that love should be the strongest emotion in women. Why not in men, too, the editor asked, as did a certain Mrs Asma Sabir.[122] A book was sent to *al-Muqtabas* by Rafiq Bayk al-ʿAzm describing women in America as more virtuous than women in Egypt or Istanbul/*Istana*, debunking thereby the general fantasy about the dissolute West (which had been contested by Qasim Amin, but later constituted a main argument in Qutb's criticism). The women were also beautiful and well dressed, with a charm that was augmented by elegance, poise, and moderation. "A few days ago," the editor of *al-Muqtabas* wrote, "I read an advertisement by one whom I think is rich stating that he would pay 37,000 riyals to every *hurma*/woman who manages to escape from one of the palaces of the mighty in the East and agrees to marry an American."[123] In that same year, *al-Muqtataf* published an article praising American women for their attentiveness to their homes: they nurse their children, cook, wash clothes with their hands, and play the piano, unlike women in the east who imitate Parisian women living in carefree indolence. If Arab women, continued the article, imitated their American counterparts, there would be no unmarried men left in the Arab world.[124]

While educated women wrote in defense of their roles, large numbers of Syrian women faced a very different challenge because many came to the United States without husbands or supporters (the novel *Amayrka* describes one such woman).[125] Some came in pursuit of work and income, others of husbands, and others still to escape abusive and indolent husbands, as in the case of the mother of Khalil Gibran. These women showed courage in undertaking dangerous crossings at sea and on arrival, they joined the "army of peddlers" after which some fell victim to violence and dishonor.[126] From the start, there was concern about women leaving their husbands, but at the same time, the women could make money by adding an extra peddler to the household. A correspondent from St Paul, Minnesota, complained in *Kawkab America* about men sending their women to work on the roads, while they stayed at home and got drunk (10 January 1895). As women were being forced to work and exposed to abuse, there was need to protect the Syrian "noble reputation," urged the editor (*Kawkab America*, 7 June 1895).

As the influx of women continued, they became the subject of frequent newspaper exchanges. "A woman whose blood and mind are corrupted [by the desire for money] will forget her honor." The editor of *al-Hoda* denounced the stay-at-home men in the East: "twiddling their mustaches," men sent their women to "a land rife with immoralities and infidelities . . . Do not blame these miserable women; blame their idle husbands."[127] In January 1908, a debate was conducted in *al-Hoda* about "the need to end or to pass laws that prevent the emigration of the Syrian woman to America." The number of such women was rising, explained Yusuf Wakim, and there was no way of stopping them because the "greedy" agents in the port cities of the Ottoman Mediterranean and in Marseille (the usual European stop on the way to New York) profited from them. And so, he urged, every woman who emigrated without a supporter should be promptly sent back home. When the argument was made that women needed to emigrate because there was not enough work in the homeland, Yuwakim retorted that women were not made for labor and toil. But a counter-argument was presented: women freely chose to leave in order to make a living. Yuwakim wrote back: "Is money better than your honor," and did women not realize that their children would pick up bad habits in their mothers' absence?

The article published by Louise Seymour Houghton in 1911 about "Syrians in the United States" glamorized women peddlers. The peddler was a "free woman," she wrote, who enjoyed the autonomy of working "at her own pleasure," rather than immuring "herself within four noisy walls and being subject to the strict regime of the clock" at a factory.[128] Such a view was belied by the many articles in American newspapers that maligned these "single" Syrian women: as editor Arbeely noted, American writers were surprised that while in the East women were protected at home, in the United States they were being pushed to go into towns, even at night, knocking on doors, to sell their wares (*Kawkab America*, 5 June 1895). One report described a pregnant "Syrian" peddler who gave birth on the street – leading to denunciations by the "Americans" (*Kawkab America*, 19 July 1895); other women deserted their husbands and children and fell into prostitution. Syrians from all around the United States sent letters to newspapers describing the dangers and dire situations that peddling women – and men – faced, hoping to warn their compatriots about the shame and dishonor that Syrians met from Americans.

With their *kushé*/basket of marketable wares, women were easy prey:[129]

A Syrian woman by the name of Saghira, wife of Ilyas Yusuf Suleyman from Hadath al-Jubbeh [Lebanon] was peddling in South Royalton, Vermont. A coach driver asked her if she needed a lift, showing her sympathy for the heavy weight she was carrying. She agreed and he stretched out his hand and helped her into his coach and asked her where she wanted to go. She answered: "The train station." He told her that he was going in that direction, too, and would take her there. But, as he got close to the train station, he veered into a forest, pulled the woman down, and tried to rape her. She defended herself heroically and when he realized he could not satisfy his animalistic lust, he pulled out a knife to scare her. But she became stronger and fought back. Her clothes were torn and she was losing strength when some American women passed by who heard her screaming. The barbaric man fled, and the women helped that poor Syrian and went with her to the police station. The culprit was caught and a date was set for his trial, and he was condemned to eight years in prison. When the trial was over, one of the judges stood up and praised in public the heroism and chastity of that woman, adding that the Syrians are the most protective of their honor.[130]

But not all women were as lucky: "The wife of Jiryis Shahin from [the Lebanese village] Hardin and residing in Wilkes-Barre, Pennsylvania, about twenty years old, brownish in skin, stocky, with blue eyes: forty days ago, she left her house to peddle in order to make a living and nothing has been heard of her since."[131]

Wives who were unable to peddle were sometimes exposed to violence at the hands of their husbands – to the point of murder. In the light of such changes in the role of women, even Rihani urged women to stay at home, adding that the "striving woman" was the one who looked after her husband and family.[132] The priest Kherbawi denounced the Syrian women because they were transgressing traditional codes precisely because, as they argued, they were living in freedom. He blamed their looseness on their work as peddlers, changing from women behind the veil to women on the streets.[133]

Rustum did not bother with the peddling women and praised the Syrian women who emigrated for honorable reasons, arriving in New York, according to him, with money in their pockets.[134] They were civil and well-mannered: "An American woman bumped into a Syrian woman and so said, 'Excuse me,' which means 'My apologies.' The Syrian woman replied: 'And good evening to you, too'."[135] Not a single anecdote in his book was about the looseness of Syrian women; rather, in a poem that his daughter 'Afifa recited in Philadelphia in 1896, there was praise for the New York "Daughters of Syria" who prided themselves on knowledge and eloquence rather than on jewelry and ornaments, as was done in the past.[136] Prince Muhammad ʿAli did not bother with the peddlers and never mentioned them; addressing women in a higher social class, he urged them to remain faithful to "our customs and traditions" and learn everything that would help a woman "in fulfilling her duties to her husband and in properly raising her children."[137] At the same time, he admired the independence of American women and although he was unhappy at seeing them on *motocycles* (transliteration from French for "bicycles that run on petrol"), or dressed in *jupe courte*, he realized that such women were mothers of the American youth who were forging the new nation: "Most of a child's character is acquired from the mother and a nation will not improve unless the status of the mother is raised"[138] – a view that had been expressed by the Egyptian social reformer Qasim Amin, too. When he reached Colorado Springs, the prince was delighted to meet a Syrian woman (recognized by her accent), a merchant/*tajira* who owned a store in the hotel where he was staying.[139] Later in New York, he was impressed by "Madam" Sabbagh, the wife of Qaysar Sabbagh of the Syrian Unity Club, who represented to him the model of the Arab woman:

> Proof of her competence lay in her managing a large store for women's attire. Because of her dedication, perseverance, and graciousness, her store had become the best in that line of business. That a woman from the East, a foreigner in these parts, could rival and surpass American and European women is worthy of high regard. What added to my admiration of her was her sincere and genuine care for her compatriots: she was quite knowledgeable about the economic conditions in her country and on every occasion sought to help: she employed her compatriots in Syria to manufacture *dentelle* [lace] and export it for her to sell in America; this shows how deeply she upheld her duty to her compatriots. She gave them the opportunity to earn an honest living, encouraged them to work, and mitigated the burdens of life which are so overwhelming.[140]

After she gave a speech to welcome him, he described her as a spokeswoman for her "eastern sisters." He assured her that eastern men have come to realize the importance of education for women: "We shall, with God's help, imitate the Western ways in educating women and making them equal to their Western counterparts. But they will exceed them if they retain their Eastern moral values."[141]

(C) IDENTITY AND TA'AMRUK/AMERICANIZATION

Kherbawi recorded the first account about the experience of emigration from Lebanon to Philadelphia.[142] It is not known if the four men he described, who had arrived in 1882, ever returned or stayed on; but the narrator of the account, Tanyus Tadros, was still in New York and seemed to have prospered financially as advertisements in Abdou's almanac showed. With the passage of time, the exposure to American culture began to precipitate a crisis of identity so much so that in 1898, an article in one of the first issues of *al-Hoda* coined the term *musta'mrik* and in 1909, Rustum repeated *"muhajir muta'amrik"*/Americanized emigrant.[143] This crisis was not dissimilar to the anxiety faced in the home countries in regard to Westernization/*tafarruj* and Europeanization/*tamaddun Awrubbi*.[144] But in the United States, the danger of *ta'amruk* was stronger since the emigrants were cut off from their history and separated from their native villages and mother tongue.

In 1913, Kherbawi warned that within three or four generations, the Syrians in America would lose their *jinsiyya*/identity, become integrated (*indimaj*) and "americanized," and so refuse to return home.[145] *Mustamrik* was understood to imply "distinctiveness and superiority" and could be expressed by accepting the writings of someone such as Darwin, to which the non-*mustamrik* answered: "I leave Darwin to you and I remain an Easterner."[146] Evidently, emigrants wanted to remain "Arab" or "Syrian" – definitely keeping their foods and music – but they wanted to work and live in the new country: they did not see the need for changing their cultural and social habits. As Carol Fadda-Conrey has observed, the emigrants did not think that assimilation should be their goal.[147]

For Rustum, the most humorous commentator on the Syrian community in this period, *ta'amruk* was expressed in daily behavior. In his *Diwan*, he gave advice about social etiquette and the qualities of the "American" whom the Syrian was to emulate. *Ta'amruk* meant for the Syrian to learn not to eat garlic, unless he could seclude himself for a week; to remove his hat at meeting a lady; to polish his shoes; to not burp in front of others; to give up his seat on the train to a lady; to wash and comb his hair twice a day; to not scratch his head in public; to not leave a train while it is moving; and never to walk with a lady to his right.[148] Rustum was clearly concerned about social integration and wanted the new arrivals to be able to mix smoothly in their various environments. Unfortunately, however, there were American traits that the fresh emigrants adopted which were odious: whistling; lighting a match by scraping it on one's trousers; and pulling one's cap down the forehead.[149] Also objectionable to Rustum was the Americanized Syrian man who started wearing tight shoes and chewing tobacco, or the woman who wore a corset, or those who started using English instead of Arabic, and thinking in American terms – like the Egyptian man who gave his children the names of the cities in which they were born: Chicago; Philadelphia; Washington; McKinley (MN); and New York.[150]

Rustum was the first writer to focus at some length on the challenges to identity in America: for him, "American" should not replace Arab/Syrian, but be an added and enriching development. Importantly for him and others was the retention of the language of the homeland. One of the evils of emigration was "the loss of Arabic in the long run"[151] because the Arabic language and the recollection of the homeland were the essential constituents of identity. That is why he wrote poems about the cities of Syria and Lebanon so that readers would not forget the homeland, just as the Israelites, he added, composed songs in their Babylonian captivity.[152] In an anonymous dialogue written in 1898 and published in al-Hoda, the watani/nationalist denounced the mustamrik: "I remain an Easterner and my first father was Adam, whose language may well have been Arabic. May the East rise, and may its detractors fall."[153] But there were others who completely integrated into the ideology of Americanism: in 1919, Jibraʾil Ward wrote an account of his participation in the Spanish–American War in Cuba in 1898 in which he expressed love and fealty for the flag, great admiration for Colonel Roosevelt and the Rough Riders, and his support for the American ideals in the war against Spanish rebels in Cuba.

A common but disturbing form of Americanization was conversion to Protestantism – the same as had happened to the Native Indians in the Mirʿi account. In the context of Protestant–Catholic rivalry in the United States and in the Middle East, such conversion was repeatedly denounced by Catholic writers in Lebanon, who subsequently took a firm stand against emigration in al-Machriq. Given that the largest number of early emigrants were Lebanese and Catholic, church authorities warned about the dangers and difficulties of emigration. In 1902, al-Machriq published a report by Lebanese physicians after their annual meeting which stated that four-fifths of all returnees from the pollution and hardship of America suffered from tuberculosis and venereal diseases. As for "the corruption of religion and civility," the commentator added, "there is no end to that."[154] Two years earlier, the periodical began installments of a novel, adapted from French into Arabic, which went on for two years, and told the story of Fadil, a Lebanese who emigrates in order to make money. Al-Safar al-ᶜajib ila bilad al-dhahab/The Wondrous Journey to the Land of Gold had been written by a Jesuit priest and described America as a land of immoral books, bad newspapers, and evil companions. In America, the novel's hero encounters disease and tribulation, and so he returns to his home village only to find that his mother had died pining for him. But the sad ending has a silver lining: Fadil returns with his Catholic faith intact, having converted two of his Protestant American friends to Catholicism. Back in his Lebanese village, Fadil warns "people from going there."[155] In 1902, a short story told a desiring emigrant, one Abdallah Quzma, that leaving his home and family to make money in a foreign land was un-Christian.[156]

As there was fear of apostasy among Catholics to Protestantism and Americanization, so there was among Muslims who encountered fellow emigrants intent on converting them.[157] Abdou reported that one Hanna Awwad preached so convincingly that 100 Muslim families turned Christian.[158] This conversionary factor may have been instrumental in discouraging Muslims from emigrating since there were numerous known cases of Muslims who converted after their arrival in the United States.[159] Sakakini wrote in 1907 how a fellow Jerusalemite he met in New York by the name of Muhammad ᶜIssa al-Turi had converted to Christianity and took the name of Ibrahim Yusuf (22 February 1908) – and much as he missed his homeland, Yusuf told Sakakini that he would never go back because of his new religious affiliation (25 February 1908). On 28 December of that year, al-Hoda reported the conversion of Dawud Asᶜad al-Rishani, a Druze man, to Catholicism in St Louis, Missouri.

Of course, there were many good things to learn in the United States without necessarily becoming Americanized. At the turn of the twentieth century, a blind girl from Nazareth, Mateel Kaᶜwar (1892–1989), became the first Arab to be sponsored by American missionaries to a school for the blind in the United States, after which she returned to run a similar school in Jerusalem.[160] In 1907, the editor of al-Muqtabas, Muhammad Kurd ᶜAli, praised in an op-ed the Unitarian philosophy of Ralph Waldo Emerson, which encouraged Rihani, the year after, to visit Emerson's house.[161] The editor lauded the American Transcendentalist for his attack on greed and his call to combine "the love of gold with the love of literature."[162] A year before, in 1907, and under the influence of Walt Whitman, Rihani had become the first Arab poet to use free verse: "Walt Whitman is the inventor and trail blazer in this" kind of poetry, he wrote:

This new verse is called in French *vers libre* and in English free verse – that is free and unrestrained verse. It is the highest form of achievement in poetry among the Franks [sic], especially the English and the Americans. Shakespeare freed English verse from rhyme, and the American Walt Whitman freed it from meter.[163]

Two years later, Mark Twain made his way onto the pages of Rustum's garrulous text,[164] and in 1912, the Palestinian writer Khalil Baydas (1874–1949) wrote the first Arabic book on the history of flight, in which he celebrated the American Wright Brothers. In the next two decades, the United States offered Rihani and other emerging writers, such as Gibran, Naimy, Farah Antoun, and others, the space in which to experiment with new literary and intellectual themes.

In general, there were two formidable challenges that emigrants had to confront in their identity adjustment: America's work ethic, which put a premium on money-making and ceaseless labor; and political freedom. Both emigrants and travelers criticized the "greed" in American life – a theme that had also informed the writings of European travelers as far back as de Tocqueville. Rihani did not like the "bible" of endless work that was preached in the United States, and reminisced about the mountains and valleys of Lebanon: like Khalil Gibran, he always thought of returning to his village, and it is rather striking that Rihani, Naimy, Antoun, and Sakakini returned to their homelands, while Gibran died in New York but stated in his will that he wanted his body to be buried in his native village (and it was). Coming from Maronite and Orthodox villages in Lebanon with a long tradition of monastic asceticism and worldly renunciation, Naimy, Rihani, and others could not tolerate the brutal conditions to which Capitalism gave rise. Having to take on a menial job and finding himself cleaning floors in a paper mill, Sakakini constantly thought back on Jerusalem and its pleasant hills.[165] These writers were the first Arab critics of industrial pollution and the disastrous impact it had on ecology. Drawing on their own experiences in the smoggy cities of the United States, combined with their readings of the Romantic English poets, they yearned for pristine nature, clean air, tree-covered mountains and valleys: after all, they had come from the majestic mountains of Lebanon, near the holy valley of Qannoubin, or from the sacred hills and promontories of Jerusalem. Of course, only the literary writers among the early emigrants wrote against the dire impact of American materialism and nature-destroying industrialization: the peddlers and traders and entrepreneurs had no problem with the pursuit of wealth, even at the price of ravaging the environment. Much later, Qutb noted "the effects of materialism" not only on nature, but also on the "American psyche."[166]

The other challenge: coming from regions where the rulers were glorified and where subjects were at their mercy, the traveler Ilyas and numerous emigrant writers expressed admiration of the structure of government in the United States, the freedoms it granted, and the modesty of the American presidents – and their wives. Ilyas was impressed with Julia Grant when she came to the Egyptian section in the Fair and walked around with him, without putting on airs, asking questions and listening to his answers, without making him feel that he was an inferior – as, doubtlessly, he would have felt with the wife of the khedive, or with a European royal. *Kawkab America* reported how editor Arbeely had visited President Cleveland who praised the newspaper for serving "the Easterners, residents of America"; later in the year, the Syrian Miss Farida Fluti went to the White House and presented the president with a gift from Lebanon (17 March, 12 November 1893). The American president was a modest man willing to meet people of all walks of life. From New York, Rustum told another story (exaggerated?) about a lowly Syrian peddler:

> A peddler with his *kushé* was audacious enough to go to the White House and ask to see the president, the late McKinley [assassinated September 1901]. The answer came back that the president was busy. He said to the messenger: "Tell the president I am a Syrian man and would love to see him." So, the president came out and stood in front of him saying: "Do you want to see me?" He answered: "Yes, sir, I am honored to see you." The president then turned around and around saying: "Look at me carefully, from every side. Now you have seen me." The Syrian man laughed and offered the president a little artifact with the carving of Jerusalem on it. The president gave him 100 riyals.[167]

In 1899, Yusuf Nuᶜman Maᶜluf (Joseph N. Maloof, as he spelled it) published in New York a book in Arabic about the great figures of world history and dedicated it to his "Excellency William McKinley, President of the United States, Representative of 85 million free citizens, Champion of human rights, and exponent of the gosple [sic] of Liberty and Equality throughout the world." Maᶜluf included an Arabic translation of the American constitution, to inform his fellow Syrians, as he explained, of the rights they would enjoy in the land.[168] He clearly wanted to counter Tahtawi's translation of the French constitution and other documentary history over half a century earlier. The priest Kherbawi, too, included an Arabic translation of the Constitution in 1913. There was respect for the American institution of government which encouraged the emigrants to Americanize: and so, Jibraᵓil Ward translated his name into English: Gabriel Rose.

(D) RETURN

Emigrants expressed both admiration and uncertainty about emigration/immigration. As a result, an active dialogue on the pages of newspapers and periodicals in the United States and in the home countries ensued between those who had emigrated and those who had not. On 7 December 1894, editor Arbeely described in *Kawkab America* the "members of our Syrian people . . . [as] aliens in this foreign land," which, legally, they were. In 1896, Saj⁽an Effendi Sa⁽adeh described all Syrians as "temporary" residents,[169] and in 1898, Yusuf Effendi Dahir was certain that all the emigrants would return to Lebanon with the wealth they had accumulated.[170] In 1910, the American-based correspondent for *al-Muqtabas* rejected the use of the term immigrants/*muhajirin* because, he insisted, the Syrians had traveled to "America to trade, not to stay . . . they definitely had no intention of making America a new homeland."[171] Even those Syrians who had bought property, he insisted, had done so only to make money in order to send it back to their villages. They viewed the United States as the "land of gold" where they wanted to become rich – and then return to their homelands.[172] Whenever people drank coffee together, wrote the priest Kherbawi, they wished each other the following: "In expectation of your return to the homeland, God willing."[173] After the Young Turks deposed Sultan ⁽Abdul Hamid II and brought back the constitution in 1908, there was much elation among the emigrants: "Shall we return?" wondered one writer in that year,[174] and whenever Prince Muhammad ⁽Ali met emigrants, he called on them to return. But Hilwa, who worked for the immigration office and wanted his compatriots to become naturalized, explained that the constant desire of the emigrants to return was the main reason for their failure/*taqsir*.[175]

It is significant that while there was emigration, there was also return. After getting rich, some were eager to improve conditions in their homelands; others returned after failure and despair. The cause of their failure was the same as for many other emigrant communities: in her reference to the Irish in America, Trollope bewailed the dire and miserable condition of "the labouring poor of our country" who thought of "mend[ing] their condition by emigrating to the United States." Not only were racial distinctions marked between the "white labourers" and the Irish, but also, the newspapers were full of invective against them.[176] For similar racist reasons, many Syrian emigrants found themselves destitute and unsuccessful, unable to find proper employment. Some, like Khalil Sakakini, had no idea what they would do in the United States: he had thought he would make money and return to Palestine, but his diary shows how little prepared he had been for the American experience. Mikhail Naimy stated that he had never thought of settling in the United States,[177] and later in his life, he wrote in his memoir of how he had been drafted into the U.S. Army in 1918. But when the war was over, he was confused as to what his future would be like: "Should I return to Lebanon? What would I do in Lebanon? Should I go to New York? What would I do in New York?" Naimy remained in the United States until April 1932, the period of the Great Depression. Although the economic crisis was a factor in his decision to return, he explained that he had gone to the United States to study and not to make money, and after twenty years, he was tired of New York, and longing for "peace, purity, and simplicity." And so, with only $500 in his pocket, he sailed back to an ascetical life, ever remembering the energy and inventions of America, a country which "conquered the world with its merchandise, gadgets, and dollars" – and with chewing gum, too, which he found stuck on the slopes of his beloved mountain Sannin, near his village of Baskinta.[178]

Although Houghton stated that between 1894 and 1899, four to five hundred Syrians returned, the number could not but have been higher – as shown by the repeated *Kawkab America* advertisements of shipping companies, chiefly Fabre Line, to all those who "desired to return home," or Lloyd Steamship Co. to "transport emigrants."[179] Already in the mid-1890s, there had been debates among the Syrian Young Men's Association in New York about the pros and cons of emigration (*Kawkab America*, 10 January 1895); similar discussions and a "disputation"/*munazara*, in verse, appeared in Rustum's *Diwan*.[180] In 1909, after returning to Egypt, Farah Antoun published an article of warning against emigration and addressed it, "To those who seek to emigrate: Look and reflect before you leave."[181] Two years later, the protagonist in Rihani's *Book of Khalid* returned home from New York; by 1913, Kherbawi believed that 10 per cent of all emigrants would return.[182] In 1920, the father of Edward Said, Wadi' Said, returned to Palestine after having served in the U.S. Army.

Of course, many were those who returned but then found themselves disappointed in conditions at home, and so sailed back to the United States for good. Meanwhile, numberless and often nameless were those who died on the peddling roads, fell victim to crime/murder,[183] or committed suicide. After killing his wife, a Syrian lawyer in New York, Nasib Shibly, committed suicide, leaving the following note: "O my people/ *qawmi*, I am the first among you who is a murderer and a suicide. How horrible are these words. Forgive me."[184] Those who returned, or never lived to return, did not leave their stories – which is why the diary of Khalil Sakakani is so valuable. For in what could well be the first daily diary in Arabic, as Salim Tamari noted, he recorded events and emotions and dreams every day during his stay in the United States, from 1907 to 1908. It is striking that none of these dreams reflected immediate conditions or related to New York or Rumford Falls; all were about life in Jerusalem, and the friends and family there. Sakakini described the daily tribulations, hopes and despairs, joy and tears of the unsuccessful emigrant: he was unique in being a highly educated and cultured man and he recorded in brutal honesty his emotions in the face of hunger and loneliness, poverty and humiliation – doubtless, the plight of thousands upon thousands of working emigrants in the United States in the period under study. His diary shows the life of a man ill-prepared for emigration, without any business acumen, who hoped to teach and to assist scholars in their research but ended up working in a factory, hauling paper bundles and sweeping floors. His dreams always took him back to the genteel surroundings of Jerusalem, away from the industrial tumult which he did not know how to handle – and which he despised for its cruelty and drudgery. Sakakini reflected on emigration in a manner that others did not: he had the talent and the honesty to write down not just his experiences, but also his reactions, thoughts, and criticisms. His description of life in the paper mill presents a first-person insight into the social, financial and moral (or lack thereof) conditions of early-twentieth-century capitalism – anticipating the critique of mechanized and soulless labor in Charlie Chaplin's 1936 "Modern Times." Sensitive but confused and not without self-righteousness, he often distanced himself from his surroundings and looked from above not only on himself, but also on a whole class of people who were trapped in factories – denuded of the spiritual and the deeply meaningful. Day after day, Sakakini wrote about himself, perhaps the iconic emigrant, desperate for a livelihood but longing for a home that was thousands of miles away – and always, at the forefront of his thoughts and dreams, the woman he loved and had left behind and to whom he would eventually return.

*

Through Arab eyes, the United States between 1876 and 1914 was complex, challenging, alluring, and new: a place to make money, but also a place of frightening alienation; a country where there was freedom of expression, but also where there was racial discrimination at its most vulgar; and a country where potentials could be realized but where mechanization and labor-abuse killed the soul. It was a multiplicity of countries where some emigrants *ta'amraku* and were fulfilled by becoming immigrants, while others returned, eager to live again in the gentle mountains of Lebanon or the sacred hills of Jerusalem, without riches but with conflicted memories. The texts below show how the wealthy visitors saw what the peddlers did not, how women experienced what men did not, and how the educated reacted to what the illiterate never noticed. There was excitement as well as confusion, aspiration as well as delusion, admiration as well as criticism – reactions very different from Sayyid Qutb's half a century later.

In 1921, the Quota Limit Act was passed, restricting Syrian immigrants to the United States to 882 per year; ironically a year later, Philip Hitti, who had lived in the United States since 1914, published a series of articles in the widely circulating *Hilal* in Cairo about the laudable qualities of the American character. Two years later, the Immigration Act of 1924 belied his praise as it completely banned Arabs (and others) from entry into the United States – while continuing to allow in other White ethnicities. Still, twenty years later, an Egyptian author wrote to celebrate *sihr Amrika*/the magic of America,[185] known to the general Arab public through its movie industry (notwithstanding Orientalist depictions) and the educational institutions which presented to the Arab peoples from Iraq to Egypt the best in the ideals and the illusions of what is now a by-gone United States.

NOTES

1. James L. Nolan, Jr., *What They Saw in America* (New York: Cambridge University Press, 2016).

2. See the reproduction in '*Amayrka min al-dakhil bi-minzar Sayyid Qutb*, ed. Salah ᶜAbd al-Fattah al-Khalidi (Jidda, SA, 1986), 124–9. I am grateful to Dr. Samira al-Khawaldeh from the University of Jordan for drawing my attention to this book.

3. See Donald J. Cioeta, "Ottoman Censorship in Lebanon and Syria, 1876–1908," *International Journal of Middle East Studies* 10 (1979): 167–86.

4. Yusuf Shwayri maintained that the Arabs did not learn about the United States until after the end of WWI: *The New Arabic Travelogue: From Europe to the United States* (Beirut: al-Muʾassasa al-ʿArabiyya, 1998), 6 [in Arabic]. Kamal Abdel-Malek included only one entry from before 1914, *America in an Arab Mirror: Images of America in Arabic Travel Literature: An Anthology, 1895–1995* (New York: St. Martin's Press, 2005), 3–5. See also ᶜAbd al-Hayy Yahya Zallum, *Amayrka bi-ᶜuyun Arabiyya!* (Amman: Dar Ward, 2007); and ᶜAbd al-Karim Gharayibah, *Al-ᶜArab wa-l-Wilalayat al-Muttahidah min al-qidam ila al-khamis min Tishrin al-thani 2008* (Amman: Dar Ward, 2009).

5. *Alquds al-ᶜArabi* newspaper, 12 January 2016, accessed 13 January 2016.

6. One of the first descriptions of the American experience in English was written by Abraham Mitrie Rihbany, *A Far Journey* (Boston,

1914). See the study by Geoffrey Nash, *The Arab Writer in English: Arab Themes in a Metropolitan Language, 1908–1958* (Portland, OR: Sussex Academic Press, 1998).

7. *Rasaʾil Ameen Rihani*, ed. Albert Rihani (Beirut: Dar Rihani, 1959), 69 in a letter from Lebanon on 24 November 1905.

8. Ibid., 22 and 26 in a letter to Naʿoum Labaki, the editor of the periodical *al-Munazir*, in 1901. See the discussion of this term in Hani Bawardi, *The Making of Arab Americans* (Austin: University of Texas Press, 2014), 29–30 and the extensive survey in ch. 2, "Syrian Nationalism and the *Mahjar* Press."

9. Was that a withdrawal from the Arab *umma/al-umma al-ʿArabiyya* used as early as 1880? *Al-Jinan*, 1 May 1880: 264. See the studies on the "Syrianism" of Gibran, Rihani, and Naimy in the 8th, 9th, and 10th essays in *The Origins of Syrian Nationhood: Histories, Pioneers and Identity*, ed. Adel Beshara (London and New York: Routledge, 2011); and Akram Fouad Khater, *Inventing Home: Emigration, Gender, and the Middle Class in Lebanon 1870–1920* (Berkeley: University of California Press, 2001), 85–92. See also Thomas Philipp, "Participation and Critique: Arab Intellectuals Respond to the 'Ottoman Revolution'," in *Arabic Thought Beyond the Liberal Age*, eds Jens Hanssen and Max Weiss (Cambridge: Cambridge Univerity Press, 2016), 243–65.

10. *Rasaʾil Ameen Rihani*, ed. Rihani, 132.

11. *Al-Hilal* 16 (1907–8), 46–9.

12. Abdou, *al-Safar*, 417. See the discussion of the "imagined community" in the Arab-American critical tradition in Rebecca C. Johnson, "Importing the Novel: The Arabic Novel In and As Translation," *Novel: A Forum on Fiction* 48 (2015): 256 in 243–60.

13. Alixa Naff, "Lebanese Immigration into the United States: 1880 to the Present," in *The Lebanese in the World*, eds Albert Hourani and Nadim Shehadi (London: I. B. Tauris, 1992), 146.

14. Rustum, *Diwan Al-Gareeb fi-El-Garb, The "Stranger in the West"* (poem) [sic], vol. 2 (New York, 1909), 47. All references are to this edition.

15. *Amayrka min al-dakhil bi-minzar Sayyid Qutb*, ed. al-Khalidi, 103: from an essay published in November 1951, followed by other essays with the same title.

16. Jibraʾil Ward, *Kitab al-jundi al-Suri* (New York, 1919), 158.

17. The article was reproduced after the end of WWI by Ward, ibid., 116–18.

18. Such criticisms would emerge decades later, as Gregory Orfalea has shown: *Before the Flames: A Quest for the History of Arab Americans* (Austin: University of Texas Press, 1988).

19. As Jamil Butrus Hilwa stated as early as 1909, *al-Muhajir al-Suri*, 8. See also Rustum who praised the missionaries, *Diwan* (1909), 30.

20. See Abdallah Laroui's succinct definition of the *nahda* in *The Crisis of the Arab Intellectual*, vii: "A vast political and cultural move-ment that dominated the period of 1850 to 1914. Originating in Greater Lebanon/Palestine/Syria and flowering in Egypt, the *nahda* sought, through translation and vulgarization, to assimilate the great achievements of modern European civilization, while reviving the classical Arab culture that antedates the centuries of decadence and foreign domination," quoted in Abdulrazzak Patel, *The Arab Nahḍah: The Making of the Intellectual and Humanist Movement* (Edinburgh: Edinburgh University Press, 2013), 13. The American contribution was noted by Farah Antoun: "Syria's mod-ern *nahda* [dates] to the time of the arrival of the American and the Jesuit missionaries," *al-Munadhara al-diniyya bayna al-Shaykh Muhammad Abduh wa Farah Antoun*, introd. Michel Jiha (Beirut: Bisan, 2014), 168.

21. Albert Hourani, *Al-Fikr al-ᶜArabi fi ᶜAsr al-Nahda, 1798–1939* (Beirut: Dar al-Nahar li-l-Nashr, 1977), 3rd edn; the English origi-nal had appeared in 1962. Another study that ignores the American role is Hisham Sharabi, *al-Muthaqqafun al-ᶜArab wa-l-Gharb, ᶜAsr al-Nahda 1875–1914* (Beirut: Dar al-Nahar li-l-Nashr, 1978), 2nd edn, and so does ᶜAli Mahafza, *al-Itijahat al-fikriyya ᶜind al-ᶜArab fi ᶜAsr al-Nahda, 1798–1914* (Beirut: al-Ahliyya li-l Nashr, 1978) and Patel, *The Arab Nahḍah*. See also Nazek Saba Yarid, *al-Rahhalun al-Arab wa hadarat al-gharb fi-l Nahda al-ᶜArabiyya al-haditha* (Beirut: Muʾassasat Nawfal, 1979) whose focus is chiefly on the encoun-ter with Europe. For Arabs in America and Arab knowledge of America, Gregory Orfalea's *Before the Flames* remains the ground-breaking study in this field. See also Bawardi, *The Making of Arab Americans*, especially ch. 3. For brief discussions, see Carol Hakim, *The Origins of the Lebanese National Idea, 1840–1920* (Berkeley: University of California Press, 2013), 170–2; and Ami Ayalon, "The Arab Discovery of America in the Nineteenth Century," *Middle Eastern Studies* 20 (1984): 5–17, although the article ignores a large number of sources.

22. As Rashid Khalidi noted, "the American schools were seen as the most politically neutral," *Palestinian Identity: The Construction of Modern National Consciousness* (New York: Columbia University Press, 1997), 52. See also "The Option of 'America'" in Christine Beth Lindner, *Negotiating the Field: American Protestant Missionaries in*

Ottoman Syria, 1823 to 1860 (PhD dissertation, University of Edinburgh, 2009), 100–5.

23. *ʿAhdi: Mudhakirat ʿAbbas Hilmi al-Thani, khedewi Misr al-alakhir 1892–1914*, trans. Jalal Yahya (Beirut: Dar al-Shuruq, 1993). As Mounir A. Farah has shown, until diplomatic relations were established between the United States and the Ottoman Empire, the Americans in the Middle East had not presented themselves as Americans, but as *"Ingliz"*/English: *The United States Identity from its Origin to 1876 in Syria* (PhD dissertation, New York University, 1986), ch. 2.

24. The vast majority were sent to the first capital. But there was an attempt to establish educational contact with Russia, too: thus the journey of Muhammad ʿAyyad al-Tantawi to teach Arabic in St Petersburg. He wrote an account about his experience between 1840 and 1850. He died in 1861 and was buried in the Tatar Cemetery in St Petersburg. I am grateful to Professor Suha Kudsieh for sharing with me her work-in-progress on Tantawi. Later, after the Russians started schools in Palestine, Mikhail Naimy went to the Nazareth school, the *maskobiyya*, after which he spent five years in a Poltavian seminary (1906–11).

25. See Yves Gonzalez-Quijano, "Reading Muhammad al-Muwaylihi's Description of Paris: A Modern Egyptian Glimpse of the West at the Beginning of the 20th Century," *Middle Eastern Literatures* 13 (2010): 183–9.

26. *Rihla ila Awrubba 1912*, ed. Qasim Wahab (Abu Dhabi, 2002), 123 on England; and 83 on France. In 1876 and 1877, the first Arabic newspapers were published in London: *Mirʾat al-ahwal* and *al-Nahla*. But unlike the ones to be published in America later, those two were partly subsidized by the British government.

27. A "Little Syria Exhibit" was held at the University of Minnesota, 10 October 2013 to 15 January 2014. See also Louis Werner, "Little Syria, NY," in *Saudi Aramco World* (November/December 2012): 2–9; and *An-Nahar*, www.annahar.com/article /479376 (3 October 2016, accessed 14 October 2016). Other "Little Syria" exhibits have been held, all to some extent glamorizing Washington Street in Lower Manhattan; but when Mikhail Naimy recalled his arrival there in 1909, he described the "Syrian neighborhood in Lower Manhattan as one of the poorest and dirtiest" in the city, *Sabʿoun* (Beirut, Dar Sadir, 1960), 9.

28. *Al-Jinan* (15 November 1880), 744. The title of the article was "Emigration to the United States."

29. Abdou, *Al-Safar*, 213.

30. *Al-Muqtabas* 5 (1910), 199.

31. *Al-Muqtabas* 5 (1910): 195–201.

32. *Al-Muqtabas* 3 (1908): 337; 2 (1907): 58 n.

33. *Arab Representations of the Occident: East–West Encounters in Arabic Fiction* (London and New York: Routledge, 2006), 3.

34. *The Syrians in America* (New York: George H. Doran Company, 1924), 58.

35. W. F. Lynch, *Narrative of the United States Expedition to the River Jordan and the Dead Sea* (Philadelphia, 1858).

36. As Karine Walther notes, "By 1872, American Protestants had extended their presence throughout the [Ottoman] empire and were able to spread their beliefs to more than 8,000 Ottoman students at hundreds of missionary schools," *Sacred Interests: The United States and the Islamic World, 1821–1921* (Chapel Hill: University of North Carolina Press, 2015), introduction. See also Jacobs, *Strangers in the West*, 29.

37. Ibrahim Matar, *Haʾulaʾ khadamu al-Sharq al-Awsaṭ*/Those served the Middle East (Beirut: Maktabat al-Mashᶜal, 1969), ch. 1. Interestingly, the Arabic translation of the Bible was not only used in Beirut and other parts of the Middle East, but also sold in the United States to the Syrian emigrants: see also Orfalea, *Before the Flames*, 53–6, and for detailed studies on the American missions: see A. L. Tibawi, *American Interests in Syria, 1800–1901: A Study of Education, Literary and Religious Work* (Oxford: Clarendon Press, 1966); Ussama Makdisi, *Artillery of Heaven: American Missionaries and the Failed Conversion of the Middle East* (Ithaca: Cornell University Press, 2008); and Samir Khalaf, *Protestant Missionaries in the Levant: Ungodly Puritans, 1820–1860* (New York: Routledge, 2012). For the reference to Van Dyck, see Adnan Abu Ghazaleh, *American Missions in Syria* (Vermont: Center for Arab and Islamic Studies, 1982), 26–7. While many of the scholars are critical of the American role in the Middle East, Abu Ghazaleh celebrates the positive side.

38. Quoted in Stefan Wild, "Negib Azoury and his Book, 'Le Reveil de la Nation Arabe'," in Marwan R. Buheiry, ed., *Intellectual Life in the Arab East, 1890–1939* (Beirut: American University of Beirut, 1981), 99 in 92–104.

39. See Naomi Jingled, "One of America's first Syrian immigrants helped conquer the West – with camels," *PRI's The World*, 15 May 2017. I am indebted to Professor Michelle Hamilton for this reference. For some additional information, see the preface to Jacob Rama-Berman's *American Arabesque: Arabs, Islam, and the 19th-century Imaginary*

(New York: New York University Press, 2012). There are many others who are claimed as the first emigrants: see the reference to Habib al-Nashi who emigrated c. 1845, Rustum, *Diwan* (1909), 22, and the other names that he mentioned. See also Khater, *Inventing Home*, ch. 3, "Emigration," for references based on Alixa Naff's 1960s interviews with early Lebanese immigrants. In 1911, Louise Seymour Houghton published an article in *The Survey* (vol. XXVI) in which she identified the first immigrants as Sahli Sabrinji and Professor Joseph Arbeely and his family, 483 in 481–95 and 647–65.

40. *Al-Machriq* 1 (1898), 1105. The article is by Yusuf Effendi Dahir. As Jacob Norris notes, before 1914, about 40,000 Palestinians emigrated to North and South America, in "Return Migration and the Rise of Palestinian Nouveaux Riches, 1870–1925," *Journal of Palestine Studies* 46 (2017): 60, n. 4. For a description of Holy Land goods, see Jacobs, *Strangers in the West*, 201–3, 206–9, and passim.

41. I owe this information to Mr Mina Khoury of Carmel, Indiana, near Anderson, where Harroun was buried in 1968.

42. *Al-Muhajir al-Suri wa ma yajib an yaᶜrifuhu wa yaᶜmal bih* (New York: al-Hoda Publisher, 1909), 14. He credited the emigration of Muslims to the desire to avoid military service, 15. See also Jacobs, *Strangers in the West*, 113–16. Already by 1907, "al-Bakura al-Durziyya," the first Druze organization, had been established in Seattle.

43. Alixa Naff, "New York: The Mother Colony," in *A Community of Many Worlds: Arab Americans in New York City*, eds Kathleen Benson and Philip M. Kayal (New York: Syracuse University Press, 2002), 6 in 3–10. See the extensive discussion of literacy or lack thereof among the emigrants in New York, Jacobs, *Strangers in the West*, 128–33.

44. Maronite Christians, *Al-Hoda*; Orthodox Christians, *Mirʾat al-Gharb*; and according to Mikhail Naimy, the Greek Catholics had a newspaper, and so did the Druze and the Muslims: "I learned of a young Muslim man from Maᶜan [Jordan] who established a Muslim newspapers [sic], *al-Sirat*, but it did not last more than a few months," Naimy, *Sabᶜoun*, 2, 71.

45. Evidently, each copy of a newspaper was read and borrowed and exchanged and quoted by many – which reduced sales and income; on the front pages of his 1919 memoir, Jibraʾil Ward denounced anyone who would lend his book around instead of buying it.

46. *Al-Diyaʾ* (1898–9), 502.

47. See also Stephen Sheehi, "Arabic Literary-Scientific Journals: Precedence for Globalization and the Creation of Modernity," *Comparative Studies of South Asia, Africa and the Middle East*, 25 (2005), 438–48.

48. I wish to thank Professor Mohammad Shaheen for sending me the volume with the first 100 issues of the newspaper.

49. As Tyler Anbinder strangely does in his magisterial *City of Dreams: The 400-Year Epic History of Immigrant New York* (Boston and New York: Houghton Mifflin Harcourt, 2016).

50. Issam Mahfuz, *Hiwar maᶜa ruwwad al-nahda al-ᶜArabiyya* (Beirut: Riyad al-Rayyis, 2000), 174; *Al-Diyaʾ* (1898–9), 560.

51. Hilwa, *al-Muhajir al-Suri*, 6. See the detailed study by Marwa Elshakry, *Reading Darwin in Arabic, 1860–1950* (Chicago: University of Chicago Press, 2013).

52. One of the first Syrian emigrants to Minneapolis, Tanyos Habib Dawud, became the president of a Socialist Club in Rugby, ND: Kherbawi, *Tarikh al-Wilayat al-Muttaḥida*, 874.

53. Racial categories were used in census returns in America as early as the seventeenth century: see Robert V. Wells, *The Population of the British Colonies in America before 1776* (Princeton: Princeton University Press, 1975). Michael Malek Najjar emphasizes the "institutional and ideological nature of race in America and the systemic presence of racial dynamics in the social spheres of education, art, social policy, religion, and science": *Arab American Drama, Film and Performance, A Critical Study 1908 to the Present* (Jefferson, North Carolina: McFarland & Company, Inc. 2015), 40.

54. For a detailed description of the impact of the Exclusion Act of 1882, see Part 1 in Erika Lee's *At America's Gates: Chinese Immigration during the Exclusion Era, 1882–1943* (Chapel Hill, University of North Carolina, 2003).

55. *Al-Rihla al-Amrikiyya* (Cairo, 1913), 211. On the other hand, a *fatwa* by Rashid Rida had sanctioned the participation of Muslims in fighting with the Czarist army against the Japanese. But see Elshakry, *Reading Darwin*, for the elation about the Japanese victory, 91.

56. Anis al-Maqdisi, *al-ᶜAwamil al-faᶜᶜala fi-l adab al-ᶜArabi al-hadith* (Cairo: Al-Muktataf Press [sic], 1939), 16–18. See also the study by Masᶜud Dahir, *al-Nahda al-ᶜArabiyya wa-l-Nahda al-Yabaniyya* (Kuwait: ᶜAlam al-Maᶜrifa, n.d.).

57. *Al-Muqtabas* 1 (1906), 222 in 221–4.

58. Ibid., 222. Abdou, *al-Safar*, 283. For a study of the first Chinese workers, see ch. 3 in Ronald Takaki, *Strangers from a Different Shore* (New York: Back Bay, 1998).

59. Rustum, *Diwan*, 199–201.

60. See the article in *al-Jinan* which described lynching and racial discrimination in the South, June 1874, 363–4.

61. Frances Trollope, *Domestic Manners of the Americans*, ed. Elsie B. Michie (Oxford: Oxford University Press, 2014), 145.

62. *Al-Jinan* (15 March 1883), 367.

63. *Al-Jinan* (1 January 1884), 151.

64. *Al-Muqtataf* 18 (1893–4), 188. Established in 1876, *al-Muqtataf* was fulsome in its praise of the United States and appeared to advocate emigration; but *al-Muqtabas*, while praising the advancements in America, was less strident. The word *irtiqaʾ* is the Arabic translation of "evolution," which had been introduced by Shibly Shumayyil, a Darwinist, in *Falsafat al-nushuʾ wa-l-irtiqaʾ* (1884)/Philosophy of Origins and Evolution.

65. Abdou, *al-Safar*, 5. He vilified the South Americans because their blood was mixed with the African and Spanish races – which was why they had become lazy, unlike the energetic White Americans of the north, 55.

66. Ibid., 38. The reference is to the Native American boarding schools that were established by the U.S. government at the end of the nineteenth century. They were run by missionaries.

67. *Al-Muqtabas* 2 (1907), 153–5. See also the reference to the "stupidity of the Indians," 410.

68. *Al-Muqtabas* 5 (1910), 705.

69. *Al-Muqtabas* 5 (1910), 582, 583.

70. Kherbawi, *Tarikh al-Wilayat al-Muttahida*, 396.

71. Quoted in Maḥfuz, *Hiwar*, 126. See the letter below by Sakakini on 3 August 1908 where there is a reference to Antoun's visit. As Jurj Saydah noted, the article about Niagara Falls made Antoun famous, *Adabuna wa udabaʾuna fi al-mahajir al-Amrikiyya* (Beirut: Dar al-ʿIlm li-l Malayin, 3rd ed., 1964), 373. I am grateful to Professor Terri Deyoung of the University of Washington for this reference. On Antoun, see Bawardi, *The Making*, 72–3. Paradoxically, Antoun tried to convince the Syrian emigrants to settle homesteads – on Indian lands that the American and Canadian governments were freely offering. Earlier, in 1904, *al-Muqtataf* published an article encouraging Syrians to buy agricultural lands – which purchase the American government facilitated, 29 (1904), 841.

72. For a discussion of de Tocqueville's views on the Indians, see Nolan, *What They Saw in America*, 59–62.

73. *Al-Machriq* 16 (1913), 132.

74. *Al-Jinan* (January 1875), 43–4; (1 July 1881), 329.

75. Abdou, *al-Safar*, 141.

76. *Al-Muqtabas* 6 (1911), 255.

77. Kherebawi, *Tarikh al-Wilayat al-Muttahida*, 420–1

78. See Jacobs, *Strangers in the West*, 357–63.

79. Ward, *Kitab al-jundi al-Suri*, n.p.

80. See the publication history in his *Diwan* (1909), 7.

81. Literally translated: Africans, slaves, blacks.

82. Many graduates from these schools as well as from the Syrian Protestant College emigrated to the United States. The Syrian Protestant College included Bible study in its curriculum, Zeine Zeine, *Nushuʾ al-qawmiyya al-ʿArabiyya* (Beirut: Dar al-Nahar, 1968), 51.

83. Rustum, *Diwan*, 140.

84. *Al-Muqtabas* 1 (1906), 185 in 184–92; see also 6 (1911): 789–90, and *al-Muqtataf* 36 (1910), 98.

85. *Al-Muqtabas* 2 (1907), 365.

86. The word translates as black in the plural; thus the name of the country of Sudan in Arabic.

87. *Al-Rihla al-Amrikiyya*, 75.

88. Kherbawi, *Tarikh al-Wilayat al-Muttahida*, 743. For discussions of anti-Syrian racism, see the essays in *Crossing the Waters: Arabic-Speaking Immigrants in the United States before 1940*, ed. Eric J. Hooglund (Washington, DC: Smithsonian Institution Press, 1987), especially "'Colored' and Catholic: the Lebanese in Birmingham, Alabama" by Nancy Faires Conklin and Nora Faires, 69–84; and Sarah M. A. Gualtieri, *Between Arab and White: Race and Ethnicity in the Early Syrian American Diaspora* (Berkeley: University of California Press, 2009), especially ch. 2. See also Najjar, *Arab American Drama*, 35. Rustum explained where the term *dako* came from, *Diwan* (1909), 170.

89. See for more details the chapter on "Law and Order" in Jacobs, *Strangers in the West*.

90. Quoted in Khater, *Inventing Home*, 87.

91. The title of the *New York Times* piece was: "Is the Turk a White Man?"

92. By November 1909, the racial designation of the Syrians was still under consideration by the attorney general assistant for naturalization, William H. Harr: Joseph Haiek, ed., *Arab-American Almanac* (Glendale, CA: News Circle Publishing House, 5th ed., 2003), 24.

93. Rustum, *Diwan*, 86.

94. Hilwa, *al-Muhajir al-Suri*, 3.

95. See Elizabeth Boosahda, *Arab-American Faces and Voices: The Origins of an Immigrant Community* (Austin: University of Texas Press, 2003), 132–6.

96. Ameen F. Rihani, *Letters to Uncle Sam* (Washington: Platform International, 2001), 14.

97. *Al-Rihaniyyat* (Beirut: Dar al-Rihani, 1968), 1:40–63.

98. *Kawkab America* opened its first issue with praise for "H.I. Majesty ᶜAbdul Hamid Khan, the 'Great Prince of the Faithful'" (15 April 1892) and whenever occasion arose, it praised Ottoman rule in "our country"/*biladuna*. When an earthquake devastated Istanbul in 1894, the names of dozens of Syrians in New York who had sent money to the victims were listed in the newspaper.

99. *Tarikh al-Wilayat al-Mutahida*, 1910. The "bad treatment" refers to the 1911 flight of large numbers of Christians from Homs and Aleppo to eastern Lebanon, 743–68.

100. Muhammad ᶜAli, *al-Rihla*, 125, 133, 145. See the detailed study of Father Serra by Gregory Orfalea, *Journey to the Sun* (New York: Scribner, 2014).

101. The official/legal term for Jews in the Ottoman Empire.

102. *Al-Jinan* 1 (1870), 176–8; 1 May 1872, 328; *al-Muqtataf* 6 (1881), 529–34. For the role of some Jews in the Arab *Nahda*, see the discussion of Yaᶜqub Sannuᶜ, Esther Azhari Moyal, and others in Moshe Behar and Zvi Ben-Dor Benite, *Modern Middle Eastern Jewish Thought: Writings on Identity, Politics and Culture, 1893–1958* (Lebanon, NH: Brandeis University Press, 2013).

103. *Al-Manar* 1 (1898), 53–5.

104. *Al-Bayan* 1 (1897–8), 55–7. A year later, *Al-Machriq* published an article about the European origin of this "fabricated story," 2 (1899): 496–8.

105. Radwa ᶜAshur's novel *Qitᶜa min Awrubba*/A Piece of Europe describes at various points the Jewish community and its activities in Cairo at the turn of the twentieth century.

106. *Nafir Suriyya* (19 November 1860).

107. *Al-Manar* 6 (1903), 196.

108. See also Jacobs, *Strangers in the West*, 302–3. He lived and worked in the Syrian Quarter in New York.

109. *Al-Manar* 3 (1900), 34.

110. *Al-Hilal* 17 (1908–9), 4–5. See Amaya Martin, "Reflecting his Time: Nineteenth-Century European Anti-Semitic Stereotypes in Jurji Zaydan's 1903 Arabic Novel, 'The Conquest of the Andalus,'" *Journal of Jewish Identities* 6 (2013): 25–40. Martin does not explain what the Western term "anti-Semitic" would have meant to Zaydan; the Arabs are Semites.

111. Ward, *Kitab al-jundi al-Suri*, n.p.

112. Rustum, *Diwan*, 22.

113. See Houghton, "Syrians in the United States," *The Survey* (1911), 662, 663, and elsewhere in her reports.

114. For religious institutions among the Syrians in New York, see Jacobs, *Strangers in the West*, 90 ff.

115. See Jens Hanssen, *Fin de Siècle Beirut: The Making of an Ottoman Provincial Capital* (Oxford: Clarendon Press, 2005), ch. 6, where there is a discussion of the sectarianism of the American missionaries at the Syrian Protestant College, their opposition to Darwinism, and the inter-religious concord in the "national" schools.

116. See his biography by Donald M. Reid, *The Odyssey of Faraḥ Anṭūn: A Syrian Christian's Quest for Secularism* (Minneapolis and Chicago: Bibliotheca Islamica, Inc., 1975).

117. Abdou, *al-Safar* (1907), 231.

118. The article had been earlier published in *al-Muqtataf*.

119. *Al-Hoda* (4 December 1908).

120. *Al-Hoda* (9 November 1908).

121. *Al-Hoda* (19 October 1908).

122. *Al-Hoda* (9 November 1908).

123. *Al-Muqtabas* 1 (1906), 241–2.

124. *Al-Muqtataf* 31 (1906), 848.

125. See also Jacobs, *Strangers in the West*, 51–2.

126. For a general description of women peddling, see Boosahda, *Arab-American Faces and Voices*, 65–73; for peddlers in New York, see ch. 6 in Jacobs, *Strangers in the West*.

127. *Al-Hoda* (15 January 1908).

128. Houghton, "Syrians in the United States," *The Survey* (1911), 648–50.

129. The *kushé* was the hallmark of the peddler, although later it was changed into the more sophisticated *jizdan*/ large bag, Hilwa, *al-Muhajir al-Suri*, 10–12. See also a description of the *kushé* in Saᶜadeh, *Dalil*, 55, n. 1.

130. *Kawkab America*, 21 December 1894. The report was sent to the newspaper by the court translator, Jiryis Yusuf Faᶜour.

131. *Al-Hoda* (21 December 1908). For a rare photograph of a Syrian woman peddler, see Jonathan Friedlander, "Rare Sights: Images of Early Arab Immigration to New York City," in *A Community of Many Worlds*, ed. Benson and Kayal, 51 in 46–53.

132. A view he continued to advocate for decades. See his article in 1933, *al-Riḥaniyyat*, 2: 92–3.

133. *Tarikh al-Wilayat al-Muttahida*, 788.

134. It is possible that he recalled the thousands of Syrian women who were employed in the silk trade in Lebanon, sometimes even side by side with men, Khater, *Inventing Home*, ch. 2, "Factory Girls."

135. *Diwan*, 82–3.

136. Ibid. (1909), 96.

137. Prince Muhammad ᶜAli, *al-Rihla*, 74.

138. Ibid., 70–1.

139. Ibid., 92.

140. Ibid., 236. The husband, Qaysar, had been a member of the com-
    mittee that assisted the Syrian survivors of the *Titanic*: see Leila
    Salloum Elias, "The Impact of the Sinking of the *Titanic* on the
    New York Syrian Community of 1912: The Syrians Respond," *Arab
    Studies Quarterly* 27 (2005): 82 in 75–87.

141. Prince Muhammad ᶜAli, *al-Rihla*, 270–2.

142. See Elsa Marston, *The Lebanese in America* (Minneapolis: Lerner,
    1987) for a study of emigrants/immigrants from Lebanon.

143. *Diwan* (1909), 66.

144. See the discussion of *tafarnuj* in Nicole Khayat, *Historiography and
    Translation during the Arabic Nahda: European History in Arabic*
    (PhD dissertation, University of Haifa, 2016), 191–3.

145. *Tarikh al-Wilayat al-Muttahida*, 786, 823. For Alixa Naff, however,
    the "Americanization" process "advanced most rapidly after World
    War 1": "The Early Arab Immigrant Experience," in *The Develop-
    ment of Arab American Identity*, ed. Ernest McCarus (University of
    Michigan: Ann Arbor, 1994), 31 in 23–35.

146. *Al-Hoda* (22 March 1898).

147. Carol Fadda-Conrey, *Contemporary Arab-American Literature: Trans-
    national Reconfigurations of Citizenship and Belonging* (New York: New
    York University Press, 2014), 5.

148. Rustum, *Diwan*, 162–3.

149. Ibid., 163–4.

150. Ibid., 42.

151. Ibid., 164.

152. Ibid., 54.

153. *Al-Hoda* (22 March 1898). This sentiment regarding language/
    identity would change later, see Mikhaᵓil Wadiᶜ Suleyman, "Tajribat
    al-muhajirin al-ᶜArab," in *al-ᶜArab fi Amayrka* (Beirut: Markaz
    Dirasat al-Wihdah al-ᶜArabiyya, n. d.), 26–30.

154. *Al-Machriq* 5 (1902), 576.

155. *Al-Machriq* 3 (1900), 429.

156. *Al-Machriq* 5 (1902), 570. See also Philip M. Kayal, "Religion and
    Assimilation: Catholic 'Syrians' in America," *The International
    Migration Review* 7 (1973): 409–25.

157. See the references to the missionary sent by the American Coun-
    cil to Homs, Maᶜlouf, *Dawani al-qutuf*, 438. For Muslims in New
    York, see Jacobs, *Strangers in the West*, 113–16. By the first decade

of the twentieth century, there were various Protestant Arab clergy in North and South America: the United States (14), Canada (1), and Brazil (1): Abdou, *al-Safar*, 328.

158. Ibid., 434.

159. See Kamal H. Karpat, "The Ottoman Emigration to America, 1860–1914," *International Journal of Middle East Studies*, 17 (1985): 182–3 in 175–209 for Muslim emigration and conversion.

160. Ahmad Mruwwat, *Al-Nasira, ʿalam wa shakhsiyyat, 1800–1948* (ʿAkka: Muʾassasat al-Aswar, 2009), 36.

161. *Al-Muqtabas* 2 (1907), 57–61; 3 (1908), 60. Emerson had visited the Middle East in 1872.

162. *Al-Muqtabas* 2 (1907), 58.

163. Quoted in Mahfuz, *Hiwar*, 178.

164. *Diwan*, 246. It does not seem that writers knew of Twain's sarcastic views on the Middle East in *The Innocents Abroad, or the New Pilgrims' Progress* (1869). But in 1910, a review of the book appeared in *al-Muqtataf* which praised its humor, without commenting on its negative view of the Arabs (10 July 1910): 581–2.

165. Jacob Norris, "Return Migration and the Rise of Palestinian Nouveaux Riches, 1870–1925," *Journal of Palestine Studies* 46 (2017): 60–75.

166. Nolan, *What They Saw in America*, 212.

167. *Diwan*, 84. In 1899, the *New York Times* noted that over twenty years earlier, Syrians had brought with them "Jerusalem goods", 5 November, 17.

168. *Khizanat al-anam fi tarajim al-ʿizam*, published by the Arabic newspaper *al-Ayyam* in New York, 35–49.

169. *Kitab dalil al-musafir*, 2.

170. *Al-Machriq* 1 (1898), 1113.

171. *Al-Muqtabas* 5 (1910), 765. While *muhajir* means immigrant, there is no Arabic equivalent for emigrant.

172. *Al-Muqtabas* 5 (1910), 772–4.

173. *Tarikh al-Wilayat al-Muttahida*, 774.

174. *Al-Hoda* (12 November 1908).

175. Hilwa, *al-Muhajir al-Suri*, 13.

176. Trollope, *Domestic Manners of the Americans*, 193–5.

177. Mikhail Naimy, *Gibran Khalil Gibran* (Beirut: Dar Sadir, 1964, 5th ed.), 207.

178. Naimy, *Sabʿoun*, 2: the last chapter, "Tasfiya."

179. Houghton, "Syrians in the United States," *The Survey* (1911), 487. See p. 657 for the first generation of dentists who returned

to Lebanon. The advertisements ran without interruption in the newspaper. See also Jacobs, *Strangers in the West*, 21–2.

180. *Diwan*, 64.

181. *Majallat al-Jamiᶜah*, 7 (1909), 30–8.

182. Kherbawi, *Tarikh*, 823.

183. Ḥanna Asᶜad abi Tuma and his friend near Pax River, and Yusuf Mutran in Mississippi, Saᶜadeh, *Dalil*, 81.

184. *Al-Hoda* (22 October 1908).

185. Title of a book by Hassan Farid (Cairo, 1945).

"OUR UNCLE, UNCLE SAM"[1]

What do you think of our uncle, Uncle Sam,
His body taller than others?
Although he is imposing,
He is cheerful and full of smiles,
With a beard nearly blown away by the wind
Like a spear, pointing forward.
And his coattail behind him,
He is a knight charging forward.
His attire is woven,
Not of silk or broadcloth
But with imprints of planets
And fabric of flags.
The stripes on his trousers appear
As if drawn with pencils.

There he is: he cares about work
Not about bearing arms,
But if necessary,
He does not fear the fray.
Yesterday he brought down the soldiers of Spain
Who tasted the bitterest of defeat.

He is as tall as ʿAwaj,[2]
While others are like pygmies;
And although he appears humble in attire and looks,
He continues to command the admiration of all
For wealth, work, and daring.

Mikhaʾil Rustum, *Diwan* (1909), 183–4

1. This poem is attached to the illustration shown opposite.
2. ʿAwaj ibn ʿInāq was a mythical figure in Islamic literature, based on the figure of Og the Amorite king in the Hebrew Scriptures. He was 3,330 and 1/3 cubits tall. I am grateful to Professor Asfour for this reference.

PART II

The Texts

The translations that follow are from works by travelers and emigrants who were sometimes confused, at other times gossipy, accurate in description but not lacking in fantasy: was the journey into the Klondike real or a re-make of an *Arabian Night* tale? How much did Ward embellish his war record? The texts combine the argumentative with the instructive, the bigoted with the compassionate. These *Ur*-narratives present the first images of a complex but alluring country, and as they were disseminated in print and by letters, in newspapers, periodicals, and books, they offered to their readers the first Arabic descriptions of America.

Minorities

1. From *The Book of the Description of Kingdoms in which there are accounts about Europe, the United States, Tunisia, Algeria, the Balkans (i.e. Rumania, Serbia, and Bulgaria), Greece, Syria and Mount Lebanon* by Idwar Ilyas, 1876 (published 1910)[1]

[*Kitāb mashāhid al-mamālik: wa-fīhī waṣf Awrubba wa-Wilāyāt Amārka al-Muttaḥida wa-Tūnis wa-l-Jazā'ir wa-l-Balqān (ay Rumāniya wa-l-Ṣirb wa-al-Bulghār) wa-l-Yunān wa-Sūriyya wa-Jabal Lubnān* (Cairo, 1910)]

EDITOR'S NOTE

*Ilyas was sent by Khedive Isma*ᶜ*il with the delegation that represented Egypt at the Philadelphia Exhibition in 1876.[2] Besides Egypt, Tunisia and the Ottoman Empire also sent delegations,[3] but only Ilyas wrote about his experience. As he mentioned in his account which he published in 1910, he had published an earlier Mashahid Awrubba wa Amayrka/Descriptions of Europe and America, but no copies of it have survived: in the 1899–1900 issue of the periodical, al-Diya', the editor mentioned receiving a copy of the book by "Idwar Bayk Ilyas, official in the Egyptian Ministry of the Interior." He praised the book and encouraged readers to learn from it.[4]*

Ilyas left Alexandria on 8 November 1875, arriving a month later in New York. He spent fourteen months in the United States and Canada and because he had an official function, he was able to visit New York, Philadelphia, Lancaster (PA), Landisville, Jackson, Altona, Pittsburgh, Lake Erie, Oil City, Buffalo, Niagara (i.e. the Great Waterfall), Rochester, Harrisburg, Washington, DC, and Canada. In writing his account, Ilyas drew on his personal observations, on information from Baedeker's guide book (for all the numbers and measurements he cited), and on what he heard from those around him. At that time, there were few Arabs in America, which may explain why he never mentioned meeting fellow countrymen.

One recurrent theme in his account was the superiority of the Americans to the Europeans. In his view, the United States had established a "marvelous system" of government and had become "without a rival, the richest country on earth, with power to stand next to the greatest of European monarchies" (470 and 471). He was also very impressed by American modesty: seeing President Grant walking around Washington, DC without guards or fanfare was unforgettable – as was the dinner he had in the "White Palace," which, notwithstanding the name he used for it, was, in his view, by far less opulent than the mansions of the Carnegies and the Rockefellers.[5] The visit enabled Ilyas to include some challenging remarks to his readers about the need for limits to political authority and about the civility of power. Ilyas praised the technological and industrial advancement of America and the different social and diplomatic codes that governed the relationship between men in power and the rest of the populace.

Although the book was published in 1910, the account about America belongs to the year after his return to Egypt in 1877, which he did not augment later: there is no mention, for instance, of the Statue of Liberty as he described his arrival in New York (the Statue was dedicated in 1886). His book, along with the earlier one, was the first "advertisement" for America in Arabic, serving the same role that Rifaʿa al-Tahtawi's pioneering work on Paris-France (Takhlis al-Ibriz fi Talkhis Bariz) did after its publication in 1834. Perhaps because he was a Christian, Ilyas took note of the Quakers, making him the first Arab visitor to the United States to do so. At the same time, he picked up and reiterated the racist discourse about the Native Americans: it is not clear why he singled them out since it is not likely he met with any – at least he did not mention any meetings. Interestingly, Ilyas mentioned his visit to the Metropolitan Museum, four years after it had been opened – the first in Arabic.

* * *

"QUAKERS"

The city of Philadelphia was established in 1682 by people belonging to the denomination called Quakers or the Society of Friends. This denomination is famous in Europe and America, although it is not known in Egypt. It is a Protestant denomination with numerous qualities that distinguish it from others.[6] First, it forbids taking oaths completely: its members never swear an oath by God or any other, even at court, to the point where in England, laws had to be legislated in courts and in Parliament to accommodate them. Also, they are pacifists and do not join the military or take part in wars; they never imbibe alcoholic drink or go to dance parlors and entertainments nor do they wear fancy clothes. The most famous Quaker was the minister John Bright, the

Free Englishman [in Britain's House of Parliament, 1843–89] whom the English consider one of the greatest in the English renaissance of the modern age. He took part in several of [William] Gladstone's cabinets but resigned in 1882 because he opposed his colleagues in their decision to invade Egypt.

Members of this congregation do not use names of months or weekdays. Instead of Sunday, they use first day, and for Tuesday they use third, and sixth for Friday, and so forth. The same for months: they say the first month or the fifth month instead of January or May. They are widely known for this trait. They also differ from all other Christian denominations in that they do not practice baptism or take Holy Communion. They are famous for their honesty, nobility, and adherence to honor and dignity. No people on the face of the earth are more famous than they in virtue and truthfulness.

Everyone admits to that.

They live and worship simply, never spending money on mundane goods, nor do they drink alcoholic beverages or frequent riotous or dancing parlors. If you tell anyone in America or in England that you are a Quaker, you will be immediately recognized for your high values. (486–7)

"INDIANS"

[I visited] the museum which held a large number of unusual Chinese plates, made in India and China, Japan and France. There was a wing which included more than 600 paintings that depicted the Indians and their customs and leaders. We mean by Indians here the native inhabitants of America: they are a race apart and are characterized by their height, pointed noses, sharp eyesight, and brass skin color which distinguishes them from others. They used to be numerous at first, and they had wide knowledge of some sciences, especially of astronomy. Their ruins in Mexico and other countries to the south witness to their advancement in past ages. But they are sly, deceitful, and dishonest, and Europeans who have built up America are repelled by them. Many wars took place between the two peoples that led to the near extinction of those natives.

In the United States, there are now about half a million of them in far-off states, but they play no role at all in the country's administration nor do they wield any power. Most Americans hate them intensely and if an Indian is imprisoned for a crime, they try to punish him quickly without waiting for the legal sentence to be passed. Indians are infamous for attacking American girls and so, Americans hold them in contempt: and whenever one of them is imprisoned for committing such an offense, some Americans disguise themselves and attack the prison at night and drag the offending Indian and hang him by their own authority without awaiting the judgment of the court. This custom is strange and peculiar to the United States and is practiced only on Indians, especially if their crime is the torturing of girls. This American custom is known as *"lynch"* and it is one of the strangest things reported about Americans.[7] (518–19)

2. From *Kawkab America* by Abraham Arbeely (published 1893–5)

EDITOR'S NOTE
Ibrahim/Abraham Arbeely was born in Syria and arrived with his parents in the United States in 1878. With his brother Najib, he established in New York the first Arabic newspaper in the United States, Kawkab America. *Starting in 1892, it consisted of four pages, three in Arabic and one in English, and served as a medium by which Arabic-speakers communicated their news and opinions from all parts of the country. The newspaper closed in 1908. In his Diwan, Rustum described Arbeely as "the Bismarck of the Syrians" (285).*

See Akram Khater's essay: https://lebanesestudies.news.chass.ncsu.edu/2016/11/30/arbeely-family-pioneers-to-america-and-founders-of-the-first-arabic-language-newspaper.

* * *

"A CHINESE MAYOR IN NEW YORK CITY" (PUBLISHED 27 JANUARY 1893)

Ḥākim Ṣīniyy fī madinat New York

Our honored readers might be pleased to learn about the Chinese and their customs, which albeit oriental in origin, are different in many ways from Ottoman customs.

The Chinese man is known for keeping his customs and clothes wherever he goes and emigrates; neither derision nor necessity can change him. He keeps his body in the manner to which he has been used and so his stomach has remained Chinese/oriental, eating what his fathers and grandfathers ate. By so doing, he economizes and saves money and grows rich in whichever foreign country he settles and works. He is never short of money and sends what he saves to the land of his ancestors, after which he turns to make more money.

This is the main reason why the Americans have prevented Chinese immigrants from coming to their country. They photographed the Chinese in the States and harassed the others whose pictures were not kept on file by the police.

Not only did the Chinese preserve their bodies and the habits of their stomachs, they also preserved the religious laws of their nation. They set up governors everywhere in the United States in accordance with agreements between them and their country. They revere their governor as if he were a goodwill sheikh who solves their problems and reconciles their differences: they obey him and defer to his judgments thereby showing their sense of patriotism to their nation. Individuals do not claim that theirs is the right opinion: they submit to reason and consider the welfare of the whole and choose the one who is best suited to look after the affairs of the community.

One of the founders of this newspaper decided to visit the Chinese governor in this city and so, at the end of last week, he hired a Chinese guide and followed him to an old brick building. The guide led him to the entrance and to a wooden staircase where there were horrible odors of opium rising from the chimney inside. The staircase was bare and not carpeted, except for the dust that had accumulated for days. In the lower floor, the visitor saw a grocer selling strange groceries grown in Snitway [?]. The herbs looked foreign although planted in America: for it is a Chinese who grew them and, as it were, irrigated them with his water and cultivated them under his sky. The visitor asked the guide about what he had seen in the first floor. In the east, this [first] floor is called the second.

The guide shrank his neck and pulled his shoulders until they touched his ears and then straightened and said: "I don't know."

The two then climbed the stairs and the visitor saw an open door. Inside the room, there were Chinese men playing, and he heard the tinkling of money among gamblers. A man came out and glared at us but said nothing; he was shocked to see us and dashed away quickly. The guide was asked about the reason, but he shook his shoulders and smiled – that was his only answer. On the second floor, there was the odor of opium, truly disgusting, and the guest saw that the doors had small windows through which the residents could see guests without bothering themselves to open the doors. The two climbed from the third to the fourth floor, reeking with opium, until they reached the top fifth floor in the building where the odor of opium was less strong. The guide knocked on the outside door and entered without asking permission, as is the oriental custom. The guest followed him into a square room, 15 feet in length with two windows overlooking shacks in Dobers Alley; you could also see something of the rear of shacks in Mott and Dobers Alleys [?], full of filth and garbage.

Three Chinese men were sitting cross-legged in this room on a bench covered by three mattresses, with silk decorations. They were facing the two windows and each held an opium pipe and had a plate in front of him with a lantern, a syringe, and an opium flask. The man in the middle sat on a high cushion, a sign of honor and preeminence among them. The three had braided their hair like the tails of pigs and were dressed in their national clothes. The man in the middle wore a silk shirt decorated with flowers; it was flowing loosely, just like pajamas among Americans. He looked important and his fingernails were long, each about an inch. In the middle of the room was a table with tea cups and some linen, and on the wall, something made in China, which is already known to readers. There was also a stove in the corner and the floor was without a carpet.

When we entered, the three men did not pay any attention to the arrival of a guest. The guide walked hurriedly to the man in the middle, showed him signs of submission and spoke to him in Chinese. The man was stingy in his answers, unlike the one to his right, who was quite garrulous. The guide told the guest that the man in the middle was the governor and so he nodded to him and the man nodded back and bowed in respect. He pushed the others gently away and put down the smoking pipe while the others continued to smoke and blow and shift about, like lethargic animals.

The governor then spoke to the visitor in English because he knew a little and said: "How are you?" He did not add anything and whenever he was asked about his role in the community, he smiled with his friends and added nothing to the words he had said. But then he explained that the one to the right was his confidant and so, the latter repeated the words of the governor: "How are you?" The guide told me that the man helped the governor. I told him to ask him what the duties of the governor were. He nodded and smiled and the guide translated my words. But I got no answer except nodding and smiling. I repeated the question to the governor and he nodded numerous times – and that was the answer.

I thought I was dreaming or in the presence of deaf-mutes, and so I stood up to bid them farewell. The governor stood and bowed and his shirt slid off his body and he appeared like a naked piece of clothing covering a bean stalk. His silk shoes under him looked like an old pirate or Roman ship, curved like a bow. His eyes shone and rolled showing submission and he clutched his ruffled hair in his hand. The way he and his companions looked was neither tidy nor clean and there were no papers or notebooks in his office to show the importance of his position. What I learned from the guide after I left was that the governor was an arbiter among his compatriots and nothing else.

I left, saying: "There is no power or succor except in God." I did not find out if that governor was a politician who wanted to keep his position secret for some personal reason or out of fear of the laws of the land; or else, there was nothing in his position that was worth talking about and so he kept quiet.

The Chinese are not an ignorant nation devoid of knowledge and shrewdness, for among them are learned ones and well-trained religious leaders – perhaps this elected governor is one of them. But because they have preserved their principles for nearly three thousand years, they have cut themselves off from the human family and stopped developing, thereby growing distant from modern civilization. That is why, and notwithstanding their numbers, they are unable to defend themselves and they play no role in the world at the same time that their land forces falter before a battalion of Western-trained modern soldiers – just like what happened thirty years ago between them and two battalions of the modernized French and English [armies].[8]

It is unfortunate that millions of people from the East remain asleep, burying their potentials under past traditions and customs, thinking that turning against traditions would be a sign of disbelief. They defeat themselves by ignorance and kill their numbers by illusions.

"LIBERATION OF A CAPTIVE FROM AMONG THE INDIANS" (PUBLISHED 26 JULY 1895)

Khalās asīr min qabḍat al-Hunūd

In 1861, Charles Lisinard was six years old and playing with his friends in the streets of New York when an Indian kidnapped him to Cortland, Indiana. He kept [Lisinard] on a farm and ordered him to work in his fields. The boy submitted obediently, but the Indian treated him cruelly and oppressively (think of Pharaoh's oppression of the Israelites). When the boy was nine, he tried to escape from that oppressor and so he took one of the Indian's horses and rode away for thirty miles. The Indian chased after him and when he caught him, he tied his neck to the tail of the horse, got on its back, and cantered away with the boy hanging on the tail. He returned to where he had come from.

On his arrival, he tied the boy to the stable door and went home. Soon, a storm raged and heavy rain started to fall. It so happened that four hunters who had sought shelter from the rain under the trees saw the boy tied by his neck to the stable door and felt deeply sorry for him. Taking pity on him, they untied him and let him go. He wandered aimlessly in the wilderness and then went in the direction of this city [New York] and reached it after much effort and pain. He had spent most of his life in the wilderness but he still wanted his mother. He searched for her in this city but could not find her, and so he went to Brooklyn where he found his mother whose sorrow had nearly killed her.

When she saw him, she thought him a ghost of her son returning from the land of the dead and was unable to speak. He approached her very slowly and she screamed in terror: "O God, why this torment? Is what happened to me not enough that I am now being reminded of my only son whom I lost in his childhood – and now he returns as a young man as if he is happy in the hereafter? By God, O ghost, go back to where you came from and do not stir my emotions and sorrows for him whom I lost a long time ago and because of whom I lost all peace and quiet."

The boy went up to his mother and took her hand saying: "I am your real son, mother, I am Charles Lisinard whom you lost in such-and-such year and today, I have returned. Hold my hand and look at it carefully, for I am still alive."

The mother knew for certain he was her son and was so indescribably joyous that she fainted. In a while, she rose and started kissing and hugging him, wishing she could squeeze him into her heart, afraid that she might lose him again. As she wept, he told her what had happened to him, from beginning to end.

The mother then became somehow crazed and started screaming and crying and then laughing. No sooner had the day ended but she had died, clinging to her son.

Many of the neighbors were deeply moved and started talking about this boy and his mother.

"CHINESE WEDDING" (PUBLISHED 6 DECEMBER 1895)

Zafāf Ṣīnī

Last Sunday was a day of celebration in the Chinese colony and neighborhood on Mott Street in the city of New York.

As soon as the sun rose, you could see men and women walking in droves to the house of the Chinese Mr Tom Bin Huways who had sent for a girl from his country to marry in this city. His fellow countrymen came to share in his festivities and spent the day in merriment, singing and playing music that was unfamiliar to our ears or to the ears of Americans. They continued for the whole day, and when evening came, they all went to the Chinese temple that is located at 16 Mott Street to complete the nuptials.

A large crowd of the couple's compatriots was waiting for them there. Led by the priest and temple servants, they entered the temple quietly and reverently, and the bride and bridegroom walked slowly until they reached the altar where they stood, with not a small crowd behind them.

Accompanied by four priests, the high priest began to pray and bow before the idols on the altar, which had very funny shapes. Some were idols of cats and others of dogs, and behind them idols of monkeys and in the middle of the altar was an idol that looked like a gorilla with a high dome above its head. Anybody who sees it cannot but repeat the verse of repudiation: "I seek the protection of the God of the dawn from the evils of the creation."

The priest then turned to the bride and bridegroom and handed them a very old book said to have been written on vellum in 160 BC, and he asked them to kiss it. They did what they were told and swore that they worshipped the heavens and the earth and would perform all the duties of worship towards their ancestors. At that moment, the bridegroom removed the veil from the face of the bride.

Everybody said "Amen" in the Chinese language and then walked to the bridegroom's house where they resumed what they were doing earlier. They filled their bellies with confectionaries and alcohol; the smoke of opium was so thick in the house that the police thought there was a fire, but then they discovered what was going on and turned a blind eye – they did not want to spoil the merriment and left the celebrants alone.

As for describing the feet of the bride, you can speak freely and not be ashamed! They are very small, perhaps the smallest among her com-patriots. They are perhaps not more than four inches, although she is quite large.

Mr Tom Huways is one of the few rich men among the Chinese in this city. He used to be a laundry man but now he is a salesman of all kinds of Chinese goods, clothes, and commodities which he imports from his country. He is among the prominent Masonic youths in the city, and many of his friends and local newspaper editors attended his wedding.

3. **From *Alaska and the Klondike: Land of Gold* by Jibraᵓil ᶜAssaf Mirᶜi, early 1890s (published 1909)**

[*Alaska wa-l-Klondīk: arḍ al-dhahab* (Tripoli of Sham: al-Hadara Press, 1909)]

EDITOR'S NOTE
Mirᶜi was from Duma, Lebanon.⁹ His name indicates that he was a Christian and he wrote with pride about the Phoenician forefathers of his Syrian brethren (223). He spent, as he explained in his preface, a long time in the United States,

and after he mastered the language and began reading "their [American] books and newspapers," he learned about Alaska and its gold mines. And so, he joined the prospectors during the gold rush of the mid-1890s: in 1895, it was reported in Kawkab America that the gold collected from the Yukon River had amounted to three million riyals (20 November 1895).[10] After returning to Lebanon, Mir^ci wrote his book describing all that he had seen and read, and he published it in 1909 to inform his compatriots about "the land of gold"; it is not clear, though, why he waited that long since by that time, the gold rush had long been over.[11] Mir^ci felt that the book was his "patriotic gift" to the readers of Arabic. He anticipated a prosperous future for Alaska and prophesied that within a short time, it would become the destination of many. But, he warned, while some returned with millions, others returned empty-handed (3).

Mir^ci collected information from government records, geographical compendia, atlases, and histories, but an extensive part of the text was based on his personal observations and adventures that ended in 1907, the last date mentioned in the book. He told of the early Russian presence there, the sale of the region to the United States, the cities and rivers and mountains, and the vast natural resources – not just gold, but also copper, oil, coal, seals, furs, livestock and agricultural products. Importantly, in writing about the Native Indians, he relied on personal experience, becoming the first Arab writer to spend time in contact with them.[12] As he pointed out, the Alaska census showed that half the population was Native American, the "wataniyyin"/ native inhabitants, as he called them. His descriptions of them were positive: they were hospitable, treated guests well, and made wonderful handicrafts. This depiction is very different from the one that appears in the 1898–1900 serialized novel (in the Lebanese periodical Al-Machriq) al-Safar al-^cajib ila bilad al-dhahab/The Wondrous Journey to the Land of Gold, which depicted Indians as strange, devious and murderous. In 1912, when Prince Muhammad ^cAli visited Sitka, Alaska, which had been mentioned in the novel as a departure point for the gold rushers, he commiserated with the Native Americans and wondered how they had contracted the venereal disease that was killing them. Mir^ci had given the answer: the Russians (114), who had settled in Alaska in 1799. In 1867, the United States purchased Alaska from Russia and in 1906, only a few years before the prince's visit, moved the capital from Sitka to Juneau.

* * *

"CONVERSION OF THE INDIANS OF METLAKAHTLA"

Today, the city [Metlakahtla] has become a marvel for visitors. Practical and reflective men look at it and wonder not only because it has risen on the ladder of civilization and urbanization, becoming prosperous and rich, but also because its inhabitants are Indians who, just decades ago, used to be at the lowest rung of savagery. Now they profess Christianity and labor to enlighten their minds while working in trade and crafts. They have beautiful houses and spacious markets: all in all, they have become urbanized and are marching toward civility.

You see ships entering the harbor unloading passengers and merchandise on a well-built pier. If the visitor wanders in the streets, he will find them dotted with attractive buildings and a grand church. On the seashore, there are factories for drying fish, sawing lumber, along with depots for storing goods. There are also schools for boys and girls, and a big hospital, too – all attesting to the progress of this people. He who can recall that these barbaric native/*wataniyyin* Indians wiped away their savagery and rose on the ladder of civilization cannot but pause and wonder.

This ascent would not have occurred to a people who had no way of knowing about change had it not been for a wise leader who transformed them: the good man, William Duncan [1832–1918].[13] The story of this great reformer needs to be told because it offers an example to all who undertake reform. Although he was not a man of the cloth, he was sent as a missionary to the city of Port Samson in 1857. At the time, the city was full of traders but the most important citizens were Indians from a local tribe known as Tsmishan. Its people were some of the most depraved and savage to the point that they did not refrain from eating human flesh. He turned his efforts to Christianize them and to teach them enough to enlighten their minds and raise them from barbarism. He dedicated all his efforts to that goal and brought all their men, women, and children around him and started instructing them about the value and worth of Christianity. He taught them reading and writing, offered them some elementary education, and slowly trained them in various crafts. He persevered with patience and dedication until he succeeded in Christianizing them and leading them out of the darkness of ignorance and paganism and savagery to the light of religion and piety and civility. He turned them into a working people who relied on God Almighty and on themselves.

And they have succeeded.

The difficult road he took led him to a big confrontation. The established church [Anglican/Church of England] saw that those people who had renounced superstitions and myths and had become civilized should not be confined to the rudimentary Christianity that Duncan had taught them, which ignored doctrines and fundamental rituals that he feared would confuse them. When the established church heard about this [delinquency], it sent an inspector to investigate the matter

and to ensure the implementation of all doctrinal Christian requirements. Duncan vehemently opposed the inspector, refusing to impose
church rituals on a people who had not been long in the [Christian]
religion. The people supported their mentor and so, when a break
occurred between the official church and Duncan's men, the latter
started worshiping God separately.

The Indians [who joined him] were some of the most important citizens who had planned the city and raised its buildings and constructed
its church. But they were all under the jurisdiction of the government
of Canada which had authority over all their lands. Their opponents
appealed to the government which supported their position and so,
they brought legal action against the Indians in order to deny them the
right of property possession and construction. At that point, their mentor [Duncan] appealed to the government of the United States and was
granted the island of Alt [Annette Island, Alaska] for his people. And so
he made them leave their city, which they did not mind even though they
had spent thirty years in establishing it: they went to the aforementioned
island where they built the city of Metlakahtla, leaving the old one in
ruins. In the new city, they built houses and stores and factories, along
with churches and schools.

Their labor was a struggle for retaining their religion in the manner
that they understood it. They developed great interest in Christianity
and its literature and changed from being a savage people to one that was
orderly and law-abiding with a government established according to the
American model.

From 1887 onwards, they left the region of Canada in which they
had lived and settled on the island. Everyone should be indebted to that
venturesome Duncan and the plans he made to change those savages
and bring to them the light of civilization. For he had set his sight from
the start at not only guiding them to Christianity but also at making its
adoption associated with the acquisition of the knowledge of useful crafts
that would refine their morals and teach them the value of life and of
self-reliance.

Duncan's efforts did not just start after the immigration to the
American destination, but from the very beginning when he took on the
responsibility of civilizing those people. In 1870, he realized that he did
not know certain crafts and so he traveled to England where he acquired
the knowledge he needed. In Yarmouth, he learned rope-making and
spinning and then he went to another place where he learned about
smithies and then to a third place where he learned brush-making. He
did not stop but continued and learned how to build a carpentry shop

with all the necessary equipment. He spent all his time in learning about small industries and then returned with gems of knowledge which he distributed to those in need, steering them out of the darkness of ignorance and poverty into the light of knowledge and prosperity.

What should be mentioned about the new city is that it is well-built and that its church can accommodate all the population – about 800 or more. It was built with their own hands in accordance with their own design; no outside hand assisted them. And so was the case too with their schools, their municipality, and the rest of the factories. All are local.

The carpentry machines are run by water. When the building was completed and the equipment was installed and water ran through pipes from a nearby hill, it is said that Duncan said to his people that he would send the water through the pipes to activate the machines and saw the wood. They were stunned and could not believe what he said, even though they had full confidence in him. An old man from among their elders shook his head and said:

"I don't believe you."

"Be patient with me and you will see water saw wood."

Soon, water poured into a wheel, and so he placed a large wooden board near the saw which sawed through it, in sight of the old man. When the latter saw that, he exclaimed:

"Yes, Mr Duncan. I have seen water saw through wood. There is nothing left for me but to die."

"Why do you wish to die?"

"Because I have seen water saw through wood. If I die I can carry this information to the elders who preceded me to the grave because they died without seeing what I have seen."

In short, Duncan performed wonders because he ventured on his own and struggled like a hero to eradicate superstitions and fables and replace them with what is better and more lasting. He relied on God Almighty and on his own effort and the plan he had set for himself. People are hopeful that the government of the United States will adopt plans similar to his in its attempts to improve the condition of the Indians who live under its flag. For those people who were changed had been the most savage among their brethren and the farthest from accepting modernity.

In truth, the Indians of Alaska generally prefer the Americans because they are simple, honest, generous, and hospitable. But they cling to old habits and antiquated beliefs and do not see the difference between kindness and harshness, honesty and deceit. What made them cling to their values was the abuse, cruelty, meanness, brutality, and rapine they encountered at the hands of the [so-called] civilized traders; they see no dignity in those traders. But this statement does not apply to all [white traders], for there are millions among the civilized who take pity on the Indians and wish them well. Many of them mention and praise their virtues, especially, as it is said, their deep compassion which none of the other barbarians have – as one oft-repeated story confirms.

One day, an Alaskan Indian went into a city and saw in an American store a picture depicting America as an old man called Uncle Sam. The man in the picture was bare-footed and so the Indian stared at him and then asked the storekeeper:

"Is this the picture of the great white father in Washington?"

"Yes."

"I see that he is bare-footed."

"That is so."

"He has no shoes."

"He has no shoes."

The poor Indian was confused and left feeling sad. A few days later, he returned to the store with brand new shoes saying to the American:

"These are shoes. Please send them to Uncle Sam."

These are the sentiments of the barbaric Indians!

No wonder that many people admire their conduct and hope that by educating the Indians, humanity will gain a people that will be among its very best. The civilized who insult and tyrannize over them are not, as we have said, everyone who deals with them or lives next to them. For as mentioned above, many of the inhabitants of Alaska take pity on those savages and wish them well, and whenever the Indians meet with straits and difficulties, as they often do because they have little means of warding off poverty, the civilized help them and send them supplies. The charity of the whites is not confined to food donations but extends to actions that improve the Indians' conditions.

One of the strange customs of the Indians is that when they are exposed to famine, disease, or epidemic, they do not complain to the world about their suffering: rather, they endure with admirable patience. They might die in droves, but they remain silent because they have grown used to ill conditions and know that they cannot change anything. Even now, when they live so near to civilized society, death might devastate them and famine might destroy them, but their neighbors would know nothing about them. But when they do, those neighbors will help them as best they can. Not long ago, a story was told of an Indian village near

St Michael which was overcome by famine during winter. Accompanied by fierce cold, it killed a large number of Indians before the villagers found out what had happened. Immediately, they started sending them what they could to help those who were still alive and save them from the jaws of death.

But the United States government did not develop a plan for such a situation nor did it try to save the survivors from disaster. (54–61)

"THE SECOND JOURNEY"[14]

One of the characteristics of gold seekers is that if they spend their time in one part of the world they begin to desire more and they stretch out their necks to learn about new discoveries. They want to find gold dust in every land and they "want to be part of every wedding," as the proverb goes. So, they never settle down in one place even if bounty pours down on them and fills their pockets with wealth and riches.

I was no exception to this rule which governed nearly all those searching for gold dust. I was greedy and wanted to explore, and so the two desires pushed me to take on dangers. I would not rest from one journey and settle down in a job before I started thinking of venturing into a new region. But I was not one who could walk in heavy snow and frozen water, and so I decided to imitate the rich tourists and travel on a sled pulled by dogs. I prepared all I needed of food and clothing along with a tent to protect me from the freezing cold. I also took enough food for my dogs so they would have strength to pull the sled.

I then started crossing those icy regions, prodding the dogs to pull and go forward.

I ventured into a wilderness in which I did not see a single human being. There was snow and ice as far as the eye could see, hills covered in white, and spacious plains that were made level by the snow, even though there were undulations in them. There were no elevations or declines except for valleys and hillocks: everything was bright and white which dazzled the eyes. There was neither man nor domestic animal, only ferocious beasts, and in the air, birds of prey.

I would continue on my sled until I saw the dogs growing tired, whereupon I would pause for them to rest and eat their food, and then I would start again until I saw that the day was drawing to a close. Fearing darkness and travel by night in such unknown parts of the world, I would halt and untie the dogs from the sled and feed them. Then I would choose a spot and set up my tent to shelter from the biting cold. I would let darkness engulf me as much as it wanted and I would sleep comfortably after the fatigue of travel. At dawn when all the beautiful sights could be seen again, I would return to my sled and continue.

One day, after crossing a long distance without meeting a single human being, I saw smoke at a distance rising from the ground and disappearing into the clouds. I was relieved because I knew that I was near to people. At first, I was taken aback by their looks, but then I remembered that they could be from among the native Indians – which I did not confirm until I prodded my dogs and reached them. I left my sled at a distance and walked in the direction of what I had seen: it was the house of an Indian, made of tree branches on the inside and plastered on the outside with earth mixed with water. Around it was a moat five feet deep. When the people saw me, they rushed to welcome me, expressing happiness and confidence and invited me inside to sit and meet with them. I acceded to their wish and entered their cave and found that they were around fourteen persons – men, women, and children. Some of them sat cross-legged while others were squatting or stretching on the ground; I saw others who had nothing under them while a few sat on fur skins. As soon as I was inside, I greeted them and they stood up and welcomed me with friendly smiles. More than one of them went out to bring me a big thick skin, just like fur, and they spread it on the ground, gesturing to me to sit down.

I cannot but tell the reader how happy I was to see these natives[15] and find company in that forlorn place. I started talking to them in the common language of people, by which I mean signs, because their spoken tongue was difficult for me to understand. This people have a language with which they communicate but it is so different from the language of other Indians that the outsider cannot comprehend what they say. It became apparent to me that the words they used to convey their meanings were few and terse – barely enough for them to explain their needs, even though their needs are very few because of their debased position in comparison with other societies, their distance from civilization, and their limited exposure to outsiders. They compensate for the inadequacy of their language by using gestures. Whoever has such a language cannot but be closer to animals than to humans.

Although I have described them in such a manner, I saw that they were great craftsmen, able to carve delicate and beautiful things, as is common among all such natural people. As soon as I sat among them, I signaled that I would like to see their handicrafts: they happily complied and fetched some of their carvings. They were made of animal, fish, and whale bones, on which they had carved exquisite designs of various creatures. If a stranger saw these handicrafts and did not know their origin, he would think that they were made by a people high on the ladder of civilization. For it is not likely that he could imagine that a simple native can so design and carve that not the slightest detail is missing. The arti-fact looks exactly like the object in nature.

I learned from this people and from other Indians and their commu-nities that if a man wanted to work in order to pass the time or to show his skill, he would spend one or two years, perhaps even more, until he perfected his carving after which the piece would be kept with the family as an heirloom.

I continued looking at their handicrafts and wondering at them until it was time for their supper. I said to myself: This is an opportunity for me to see them eat their food in their house, an opportunity that rarely occurs to the likes of me. I remained in my place whereupon they brought some dried fish and laid it in the middle. They then brought a large pot filled with whale oil and gathered around the food: they took a piece of fish, dipped it in oil, and ate it. They continued eating until they were full after which they brought a land herb like tea which they boiled and drank until they quenched their thirst. Once supper was over, they left the food and returned to their former seating places.

When I finished watching them at their meal, I left and returned to my tent, prepared my own food, ate, and slept soundly until dawn. After I got dressed, I returned to visit those friends and was welcomed by them. Using signs, I asked them to show me again their handicrafts because I thought of selecting some as souvenirs to take with me to the civilized world. I knew how much civilized people appreciated these valuable pieces because they were rarely available, given the difficulty of reaching the Indians. Eagerly, the community brought me all their valuable pieces. I looked and studied them until I spotted a piece of excellent ivory, exquisitely carved with images of animals, fish, birds, and some houses. I gestured that I would like them to gift it to me and that I would be willing to pay whatever price they asked. A man from among them stood up and indicated that it was his but that he was very sad he could not gift it because the piece had been carved by his father, chief of the tribe, who had spent twenty years on it, and which he had left to him as a bequest.

On hearing his words, I expressed my disappointment and offered him more money, but he replied by laughing. I thought he found the sum too small and so I increased my offer, but he laughed even more and signaled to me that whatever money I offered him was worthless because he had no need of money – which he had never seen before. But then he saw my hunting rifle, which he liked very much. He did not know anything about it, but when a bird flew past, I shot it down. When my friend saw what I had done, he was thrilled and started dancing in joy. He asked me about it and I showed him the secret of firing a rifle and how to aim the shot at the target: he was so amazed and excited that he hastened and brought me what his father had crafted, along with other objects, and laid them in my lap signaling that he would give them all to me in return for the rifle. I agreed and we completed the profitable exchange.

This episode shows that when natives barter, they deceive themselves more than they are deceived by swindlers because they become attracted to unusual objects more than to money. Take note that the money I had offered for the handicraft was at least three times the value of the rifle. The Indians then started offering me gifts of fur in return for the gunpowder and bullets that I still had. I agreed.

Later, the community told me about a distant location, beyond the frozen northern zone, that was full of gold. And so, I started on my sled until I reached the northern zone. The earth in front of me was flat with dazzling white snow, but then, on the side of the road, I saw a man sitting motionless and so I immediately stopped my sled and walked towards him. The closer I got to him the more he appeared to me to be exhausted and sitting down to rest. I drew near him and saw that he was a young man under thirty years of age, and so I called out to him but got no answer. I moved up, and lo, he was dead.

I was truly sorry for him and said: O God, how toil kills many people before they achieve success. Then I said to myself: What can I do for this dead man and what service can I render mankind, having no one to help me carry him? And even if I did have someone to help me, I was at least 300 miles away from civilization: is it possible to carry him? Do not ask about my sorrow when I had to leave him in that dreadful condition and prod my dogs to my destination, which was still about 400 miles away.

I left the man and started thinking: he had ventured after what I was seeking but he died without reaching his goal. But these thoughts did not deter me; on the contrary, they gave me impetus and determination, and I continued, marveling at the magnificent scenery around me until I had crossed vast distances and reached my destination, or somewhere close to it. Because it was getting dark, or just about, I pitched my tent and slept till morning after which I finished the last miles and arrived safely. I started looking around and found gold dust and so I laid claim to that piece of land, in accordance with the established rules. I stayed there for a month searching and panning – alone without any fellow worker except for a Norwegian man who had reached that spot first and had been successful.

When I was ready to leave, I prepared provisions and started on my journey to civilization. Putting my trust in God, and pleased with my success, I traveled until I had crossed nearly one third of the distance, but the food supply I had carried was all but depleted. I hurried on, afraid that the snow would melt and I would not be able to reach my destination – and be trapped and die as that poor man had died, martyr of the snow. But then, and as I was pushing on, I saw a group of white men searching for gold. They were delighted to see me and welcomed me, and I learned from them that they were planning to stay and not leave their work and that, as a precaution, they had brought food supplies on sleds that would last them for a whole year. They gathered around me asking me about where I had been and so I told them what I knew and stayed the night with them, all of us enjoying each other's company. The next morning, I prepared to leave but they urged me to stay another day so I could rest from my travels – at the same time that they would learn from me about the new location I had found. I agreed since one of them decided to join me.

I spent that day there and on the following morning I loaded as many supplies as I needed to reach the station – which, like many others, is about fifty miles apart from other stations. The station furnishes provisions to travelers, and so it does a booming business. It has restaurants where people can eat and pay five dollars for a meal, and five dollars for lodging, too. Whenever a traveler reaches one of those stations, he buys all the supplies he needs till he can reach the next one.

We left at the appointed time after bidding farewell to the new friends and for three successive days, we climbed hills and crossed plains – but we could not find the station we wanted. What I need to explain is that the places which I thought I remembered were different from before because the snow had melted in certain areas, leaving the ground exposed. The big disaster, however, was that our provisions were growing slim and we had lost our way. We became afraid of either starving to death or getting lost in this vast region.

As we were in this dire condition, we saw an Indian house at a distance and so we turned our sleds in its direction. We sped on until we reached it with high hopes of finding relief and salvation from disaster, but our disappointment was great when we realized that it was dilapidated and empty. I feared that death was drawing closer and closer and that we were about to drink from its bitter cup in that desolate place.

And none would know about us or weep for us in lamentation.

I thought of all that as we stood near a high mountain covered in snow. I decided to climb to the top and look to see what is around, all the way to the horizon, in the hope of finding people or of spotting a camp or a house. Quickly, I left my companion at the sled and went on my way, carrying half the provisions that were left, and leaving the other half for him. I struggled up the mountain until I nearly fainted, but I pushed on until I reached the summit. For a while, I stopped to catch my breath and then straightened to look around: I saw magnificent vistas that enthrall the heart, but these were not the sights I wanted, for at that moment they were like instruments of torture or chalices of deadly poison. I strained with all my might in the hope of seeing some sign of people so that I and my companion would escape the claws of death, but I saw nothing except the sword of the cruel executioner wielded at my neck to sever it without compassion for my youth. As I reflected on this disastrous disappointment, I became terrified and nearly gave up hope of salvation and [a line is missing here] from returning to him and conveying news of his death to his relatives. He declared to me that he had a sweetheart whom he missed and wished that she would say one word to him from her charming lips to revive his spirits, or that he could see the redness on her cheeks and gather roses and posies from them. He then sighed recalling her groans for his departure and how she had bidden him farewell, urging him to return quickly without ever realizing the extent of his greed.

Suddenly, he started talking to her as if she had appeared to him, afraid that she would waste her beauty and youth on the altar of his love – and other such words of besotted lovers. I felt sad for him and grieved at his condition, thereby adding to his bleak feelings, as if that were possible. I could have continued in my commiseration for him had I not said to myself that lovers are like poets: they wander in every valley and clothe their lovers in all the perfection that their passion-inflamed imagination can conceive. Strangest of all is that they obey the sultan of love even in the last moments of their lives – but, then I thought, why should I bother with what they say when our condition was so wretched?

And so, I started grieving for my ill fortune in word and thought. I sat down and invoked God in His mercy to forgive my sins and spare me.

Not a moment had passed when I felt as if I had been granted a ray of hope that made me stand up and look again, forgetting the four hours I had spent earlier in climbing the mountain. I started striding to and fro, from one spot to another, staring and gazing intently, but I saw nothing and grew despondent again. I felt my eyes growing tired of staring and straining and I became impatient and nearly lost hope.

But then, I regained my senses and sought again the mercy of God.

The sun was setting, and so I went down the mountain to my friend. I continued walking until I reached him: he was sleeping, completely unaware of our ominous condition. I woke him up and told him about disappointment and hopelessness and that all my climbing and looking and searching had been fruitless. My words had such an effect on him as if I had come to pronounce death on him and he started crying and bewailing his youth. As he continued crying and moaning and recounting his sorrows and calamities, I started crying too, having held back in submission to the will of Almighty God. We continued shedding tears and moaning until my senses returned to me and I determined to be patient, and so I wiped my tears and turned to console my friend and to calm his fears until he took control of himself. We then finished whatever food we still had and slept till dawn.

We distracted ourselves from our misery by preparing the sled as if the hope we had lost yesterday had returned to us, even if briefly. "How tough life is without the aperture of hope."[16] We decided to persevere and confront every disaster with all the courage we had left in us, enduring the horrors of hunger without giving up until death became inescapable. I do not claim that this decision was a result of courage: it was of necessity. Whoever faces such dangers and everything else that we had encountered: his courage will not be a matter of choice but of necessity. It fits the Arabic proverb which says: "Done not because it was desired, but because it was unavoidable."

We trudged on, moving away from the mountain; we saw no living being as if we were in an endless desert. The day passed and our remaining food supply was finished, but we still did not find what we needed. After another day and half of the next, we decided to return to the mountain and take another route in the hope of finding some reprieve. We decided on that course because we knew that our destination could be reached by either route, and so it was better to take the straight one that would get us to our goal. We turned the dogs around and they pulled us back the way they had come, struggling with our sled despite their hunger. Starving, we reached the mountain after having left it three or four days earlier.

As soon as we returned to the spot which we had left, we collapsed in exhaustion, and the signs of starvation began to appear on us. Our legs became weak, our hearing grew feeble, and we could barely stand or speak because all our energy was gone. Our tongues were stuck motionless and our mouths were dry; we started feeling the cold even though our clothes were impenetrable by the wind. Now we realized that our remaining hours were few.

We sat at the foot of the mountain, totally exhausted, but then our only option was to push on: there was more chance of escaping the claws of death by walking than by sitting and waiting. We decided to continue and immediately got on the sled and took the same route we had initially taken. O God, what endurance the dogs showed in this grueling trail for they sped on as if they did not feel hunger and exhaustion – even though we did not allow them rest by day or night. We wanted to reduce the time of our hunger and so we struggled on until two more days passed and we had nearly expired, for our fast had started six days earlier and there was no hope in patience.

As we were at our last gasp, having lost all hope and having failed in all our attempts, we looked in the direction of another mountain and saw a tree at its foot. We were surprised and said: How could this tree stand in this wilderness? So, we turned in its direction and when we reached it we found that it was huge. We stared at is trunk and branches and quickly got off the sled and as we walked around it, we noticed a hole in the trunk with a cloth covering it. We lifted the cover and entered inside, one following the other, and we saw that the trunk was hollow and spacious and full of provisions of wheat, cans of dried meat, and other foods. We solved its mystery: those who own lands or are searching for gold dust are compelled, once in a while, to leave their treasure. Being in far-off regions, away from human habitation, they need provisions that can last them for a year, but rarely are they able to carry those provisions in a single journey to their camps. And so, they carry provisions for part of the road and stash them in safe places. When the depot is full, they go to their work and when they are short of food, they return to the depot.

This tree that stood alone in that place, away from all other trees, had been hollowed by the hand of time and became a depot in which some workers stored their supplies – which saved two young men from the deadly claws of starvation. Glory be to the Great Creator.

My friend and I looked at the supplies and touched them with our hands, unable to believe our eyes, for salvation after hardship had come suddenly to us:

Things may get increasingly tight but lo, succor came when least expected.[17]

We went on the attack, opening the cans and nearly swallowing them, tin and wood and all. But we ate only a few mouthfuls afraid that the long fast, if followed by excessive food consumed quickly, could be harmful. So, we restrained ourselves and did not fill our stomachs and confined ourselves to sampling: we thanked God Almighty for His bountiful mercy.

Because we had been exhausted, we found it necessary to wait in that place until we regained our strength. We stayed for a few days in which time we wandered to nearby regions and then returned to the hollow tree until we were strong again and all signs of fatigue and hunger had left us. After two weeks, we got ready and took supplies to last us for a month: we calculated the price of what we had consumed and what we were taking, added a bit more, and left the money there. We got on our sled and herded the dogs: they were strong again after all the hunger and exhaustion they had endured.

We were back on the snow but it was not hard because it had started to thaw and the sled did not slide quickly. In the daytime, when the sun shines, its heat melts the snow, making travel difficult. But at night, the cold winds do the opposite and the snow freezes. And much as in winter, night is long and very dark, full of dangers, in spring, night poses less danger because the snow is hard, unlike in the daytime when it cracks.

So, we started traveling at night and resting and sleeping during the day.

We continued crossing distances, seeing rivers and rivulets, hills and hillocks which sometimes blocked our path, leaving us with no choice but to go around them. But soon, we were back to the earlier miserable situation: twenty days or more passed and disaster dogged us. Our supplies were again about to be depleted and if God Almighty saved us once by what we found in the hollow tree, could we hope for that again?

After much struggle and exertion, we saw a wide river which we could not cross. We made a raft from tree barks and jumped on it, but before we continued, I fell in the water which pushed me toward a tree standing in the middle. I clung to its branches and was saved. We then continued on foot until we saw a station, the one we had sought at the start. We were extremely happy but when we drew near it, we discovered that the current was very strong, preventing us from reaching it. We started looking for a way to reach it but could not think of anything. At last my companion said that he had been an excellent swimmer since his youth, and so he took a rope and tied it to a tree and held the other end of the rope in his hand: he then threw himself into the water and reached the other bank. He ran to the station but soon returned saying that he had found the door locked and that he had forced it open. He told me to throw myself in the water after tying the rope around my waist and he would pull me to safety. I did.

We walked into the station and lit a fire, warmed ourselves and waited until our clothes dried. Then we went looking for something to eat and found some flour. We mixed it with water and baked it on the fire and ate it. Very hungry, my friend over ate, which caused him such a stomach ache that he fell into delirium. When he started getting better, he told me in great detail about a dream he had. After he recovered fully, and having spent the day at the station, we looked in the direction of the door and saw an aged man walking towards us. He was surprised to see us but then greeted us and asked about us and how we had reached that place safely, since it was not easy for a passer-by to do so because of the river. As for him, he had a boat and had just returned from transporting a man after which he had gone to check on his property. How did we get there? We told him our tale but he kept on asking for more details and clarifications so much so that whenever we paused in recounting our tale, he would grumble and ask us for more. When it was time to sleep and we had not finished our tale, we rose to leave but he groaned and sighed and said: "I will not be able to sleep tonight. How will I close my eyes while your story is in front of me with its wonders which have enthralled me?"

At night, two hours after midnight, and while we were sleeping we sensed the man's insomnia; he was walking and giving no rest to his body, and so we sat up and told him the rest of our tale.

When we got ready to leave, he joined us, and we got into the boat and crossed to the other bank of the river. We then bade him farewell and started crossing distances, carrying on our shoulders all the supplies he had given us because the sled and its load had disappeared. Then, from afar, we saw two men hurrying towards us, and so we went over and found that they had been returning to the city from their place of work but, like us, had lost their way and run out of food. So, we gave them some of our food and together we continued walking until one of the men collapsed in exhaustion. He was an old man and his strength failed him. We felt sorry for him and we did not want to leave him there to die alone in that wilderness. We called on God and slowed our pace in consideration of him, but he kept on getting weaker and weaker and we alternated in carrying him. Days passed and the food supply ran out – and we had no idea where we were in the world or how far we were from civilization. We became afraid that we would starve to death, but we pushed on because man, even after despairing of life, continues to persevere, consoling himself with hope even if it is very faint.

We were losing our strength and could no longer carry the man when we saw an Indian house. We reached it and found it empty but for a few pots that were useless to us because there was nothing to cook. After resting for a short while, we wandered around hoping to find something to eat. We were not disappointed because we found a frozen pigeon which we brought to the house – only to find that the old man's condition had worsened and he was on the verge of dying. We started a fire and boiled the pigeon but verily, we did not wait till it was cooked because hunger drove us to eat it quickly. Small as it was, the pigeon soothed our bellies. After consuming it, we went out again and found a big river flowing in the middle of the snow. Its water was too cold for us to cross: no human could endure its temperature for more than a few minutes. And we had no boat.

We returned to the house and found the old man crying and moaning, but when he saw us he stopped. We sat down to discuss our situation and after some time, we realized that we had lost our way and if we did not find food, sooner or later, we would face a bitter death. Since we were to die of starvation, with no choice left for us, we thought it better to stay in the house until death came to us. Why add to our miseries?

We stayed there that night and on the following morning, grew weaker and fainter.

The old man tried to speak but his words choked him. He then strained himself and said something to the effect that we had been kind to him and he was on his way to eternity. "I have no more than a day or so left of this life so full of tribulations. Sacrificing the few remaining hours of my life to save you will demonstrate to you my gratitude: if you want, slit my throat and eat my flesh, perhaps you will gain some strength. Slitting my throat will be beneficial to you and to me: it will end my suffering and it will give me the best opportunity to prove to you that I appreciate your kindness and care. At the same time, by eating me you will fortify your bodies and revive your faltering spirits."

We thanked him for his offer but refused to commit such a ghastly deed. By then we were so depressed and despondent that we started weeping and wailing from the bottom of our hearts. The *shaykh* [the old man] started talking to us and comforting us, telling us to be patient and persevere. We turned and went to sleep and on the following morning when he did not wake up early, we left him and went out to explore the region. When we returned to have some rest, we found him still asleep, but after looking at him closely, we discovered that he had died hours earlier. We sought mercy for his soul and rejoiced for his rest. I remembered the words of the poet: "In dire sickness, you will see death as cure."

After we made sure he was dead we carried him outside the house and laid him on the snow. My companions then started talking about the need to eat his flesh, horrible as that was since eating human flesh was never practiced by those with religion, piety, and civility. But necessity overrides proscription and if man finds no other food but the flesh of his fellow man, what can he do when he is in need and in danger of dying by starvation?

Suffice it to say, we agreed to eat the flesh of the dead man. One of the two men among us, Andrew and Nelson, took out a knife from his pocket and began cutting the corpse. He sliced a large piece from the thigh and we carried it into the house and threw it into the pot on the fire. It boiled for six hours, but the flesh remained uncooked and hard. We were unable to wait any longer and so we took it out of the pot and sat looking at it. When we saw the color of the boiled meat, which looked as if it had been dyed in dark saffron, we could not touch it and sat undecided for a while, some willing to eat, others not. Finally, Nelson took a piece from the pot and stuffed it into his mouth as we looked to see its effect on him. He immediately started chewing but it was quite hard; he kept on chewing and tried to swallow it but his throat would not allow him. We decided to follow suit and stretched our hands to the pot – when a man suddenly appeared at the door.

He walked in as we were sitting at that abominable meal and paused, confused and shocked. As for us, we were happy to see him and hoped for the best. He came close and stared at us and then spoke to us, but we could not answer because we were totally exhausted. We tried hard and answered him. He relaxed when he realized we were humans because, as we learned from him later, we looked more like savages than people – or like jinn mentioned in tales. And why not? Our hair was down to our shoulders, our eyes hollow, and everything about us wild.

After he sat down and heard part of our story, he comforted us by telling us that he had food and that he would share it with us. He was not long gone and returned with food of which we ate our fill and regained our strength and resolution. He told us that he had arrived by a boat which could transport us all. Joyfully, we went with him and got into the boat and sailed on the river for three days without any difficulty or hardship, eating and drinking to our hearts' content until we reached the city.

People assembled around us from every corner and started asking us about our journeys and what gold-filled regions we had discovered. Because I was the only man who had returned alive from those regions, the prospectors crowded around me more than any other man and listened to the information I relayed. I still had not regained my strength fully and was not able to speak for long periods of time: I set a special time in the morning and in the evening to meet with them.

Days after my return, I was strong again and wandered around the streets and neighborhoods of the city. I noticed that the population was quite active in trade and other forms of work, especially in panning for gold dust near the sea coast and in streams and on hills. I was impressed by their energy and labor and decided to join them in the hope of meeting with success. I agreed with one of the workers to use a pan of the kind called Rox (*al-hazzaz*) but we could not find it on sale and so we had to make it ourselves. We took a wooden box and carved it the way we wanted and then bought a pickaxe and shovel. We hauled sand from the sea shore which was mixed with gold dust, then washed off the pebbles and the sand so that gold sank to the bottom. We continued doing that for a month gaining a daily profit between twenty-five and fifty riyals.

But that which does not regenerate goes empty. And that is what happened: on every foot of the shore which was glittering with gold, a greedy man toiled, turning the coast upside down. Profit thus started to plummet until it reached near nil and at the end of a day, even the hard worker could not make more than five riyals. So, people moved away in search of new locations.

The reader shouldn't think that those panners who are after gold are all poor and struggling to eke out a living. The majority are rich with big fortunes who view the world as a house of strife and struggle, where the one who perseveres most earns most.

When people left the gold-filled sea shore, they turned to look for their lost goal in the mountains and hills, and on the banks of streams. Their work made it possible for many to prosper but hundreds and thousands of others returned with the shoes of Ḥunayn.[18] Glory to Him who has power and who gives without accounting to whomever He chooses. (121–37, mispaginated).

4. From *Instructive Travels in the New World* by Dr. Naguib Abdou (published 1907/1908/1909)

[*Dr. Abdou's Travels in America*. Al-Safar al-Mufīd fī-l-ᶜĀlam al-Jadīd (Washington, DC, 1907, 1908, 1909)]

EDITOR'S NOTE
Naguib Tannous Abdou was born in Lebanon in 1876 and moved to Canada where he received his MD in 1900. In 1904 he worked for the Immigration Service in New Orleans and later for the State of New York's Department of Health at the Port of New York. Abdou practiced as a private physician on Greenwich Street, near Manhattan's Syrian Colony. Sometime before the 1920 census, Abdou married an Irish immigrant named Anna. Little is known about him after 1922.

His almanac contained detailed information about the professions and addresses of emigrants, divided according to states, as well as names from outside the United States, particularly from South America. There were also advertisements for businesses, often in the traditional rhetorical flourish of Arabic. Abdou added a few passages in English translation, but his volume (448 folio pages, plus 8 more at the end) was in Arabic and for Arabic-speakers – although he explained in English that the book was also "of great value to American and English Merchants dealing with Arabian and Syrian businessmen at large" (449). He included an English "Index to Advertisement of American, German, French, Armenian, and Jewish Merchants."

Abdou established an office on 54 Washington Street, New York City and started collecting information about the Syrians in the Americas and in all other parts of the world. In his mind, the Syrians/Arabs were one, unified community and so he wanted them to know about their compatriots in order to cooperate with them in business. He published the book in 1907 and promised to revise it every year (449). It sold for "5 American riyals."

The piece below reflects Abdou's adoption of the American racist discourse about the Chinese who were part of the mosaic of races and ethnicities whom the emigrants met for the first time in their lives. Abdou is vitriolic in his racism, reflecting the hostile mood around him in New York as well as the vicious literature that was published against the Chinese after the San Francisco earthquake. He mentions nothing about their background and repeats the false arguments of how immigrants take jobs from Americans. Chinese men and women were brought as "cheap" laborers to build the transcontinental railroad in the second part of the nineteenth century, but then, they began to be denigrated as the "yellow peril." Abdou's text reflects the ongoing American – and Arab emigrant – antipathy to the Chinese over a quarter of a century after the Chinese Exclusion Act of 1882 and the 1892 Geary Act which was to ensure that Chinese men, who were already living in the United States, would not be permitted to re-unite with their wives and children.

* * *

"THE AMERICAN EAGLE AND THE CHINESE DRAGON: A POLITICAL TALE"

Uncle Sam closes the door of immigration in the face of the children of the sky; and those of the braided hair are angry with the citizens of Uncle Sam.

[This report] had appeared on the pages of the newspaper, Mir'at al-Gharb, and the author returns to the subject again and summarizes it. Consider:

Since 1883, the American government has completely closed the door on the immigration of Chinese laborers to the United States. It granted those who were already resident a whole year to register their names before expelling the delinquents. Since that time, every Chinese who does not carry a registration certificate is considered to be illegal, and so is arrested, tried, and sent back to his country till whenever God wills.

All expenses paid by Uncle Sam.

If a Chinese man claims that he has lost his certificate for whatever reason, he will have to offer proof by bringing witnesses from the white race after which their testimony is compared with the certificate. And if the Chinese wishes to visit his homeland and return to the United States, he needs to leave in the city of his immigration either his wife, or legitimate children, or 1,000 riyals in the custody of the customs officials. He is not permitted to absent himself for more than one year, and before returning, he has to inform the American customs authorities of his travel plan and to send a photograph of himself so it can be compared with the one he deposited before his departure to China. His return must be approved by the government of the Son of the Sky and of the United States consulate in that kingdom. To avoid fraud, he is required to enter at the same port from which he had departed because it is difficult to distinguish among the Chinese who all look alike. The Chinese man is not permitted to give or loan his certificate to another and before he is allowed to return, the American government examines his conditions and if they meet with the requirements of the law, as mentioned earlier, it allows him to return. Otherwise, he remains in exile forever!

A Chinese may cross United States territory if he is transiting from a foreign country back to his homeland: for instance, if he arrives from Havana to New Orleans and then travels to San Francisco to board a ship to Hong Kong. But every Chinese has to put down a deposit of 500 riyals and should not remain in the United States. The Chinese can only be in transit if he is free of contagious diseases; otherwise, he will be denied transit and will be turned back – forever. He will be deported to wherever he came from after penalizing the [shipping] company that had brought him 100 riyals for every Chinese with a dangerous disease. Chinese sailors are permitted on the wharfs as long as they are watched by American police and after depositing 500 riyals per head as guarantee. And if the winds cast a ship with Chinese passengers onto the shores of the United States, they would have to leave as soon as possible; and if a ship captain or any other tries to unload the Chinese without the approval of the customs authorities, he will be fined 5,000 riyals or jailed for three years. As for Chinese workers and salesmen who bring goods to display at United States fairs: each has to deposit 500 riyals as surety after which he goes directly to the fair, and under police custody, stays there until the end. Afterwards, the Chinese has to return promptly to his country, also under custody. If he leaves the fairgrounds and stays off the premises for more than 48 hours (unless he is sick and has to stay in hospital under medical and police supervision), he will be arrested and deported to his country of China for the rest of his life!

All the Chinese and those of their race are treated the same way: nor can the children of the dragon come to the United States from its colonies, such as the islands of Puerto Rico, Hawaii, Honolulu, or the

Philippines. In those regions, they are governed by laws specific to them which also threaten them with deportation. Meanwhile, agents on a diplomatic mission are recognized officially and are allowed into the United States on condition that they not carry contagious diseases and that they carry out diplomatic duties and nothing else.

Chinese merchants are allowed into the United States only after they present certificates notarized by the government of their country and by the United States consulate: all their documents have to be sent before-hand to the customs authorities. They should enter at ports designated by law. Also, they should only practice the trade that involves buying and selling: they should not open a saloon, a hotel, or a game parlor, etc. And if God misguides a Chinese and he washes a shirt by hand and collects 10 cents in pay, or if he repairs manually some of his own merchandise such as filing a piece of wood to craft something: it is a black hour if Uncle Sam's *dewetlu* [Turkish for government] finds out about this work: he will be immediately arrested and tried before the commissioner. He will then be handed over to the marshal who will see to it that he is deported from the United States back to China, from the moment his braided hair is caught by the police until the end of time!

Registered Chinese merchants can visit the land of the dragon on the same conditions that apply to laborers, but they are not required to pay 1,000 riyals or more, or to leave legal wife or children. Still, they have to leave their stores under the scrutiny of an American worker, who, prodded by his uncle, Sam, walks around those stores like a wolf stalk-ing a sheep pen. This civilized employee can check for anything amiss in the Chinese store during its [the owner's] absence and investigate if the owner had done anything more than buying and selling, as mentioned earlier in regard to the law. If so, the American worker promptly informs the Chinese [owner], already terrified and reprimanded by his conscience, that he cannot return to the United States and is expelled from the lands of Uncle Sam for all time! The reason is that after careful investigation, he – that is the Chinese – was discovered to be doing manual labor, which categorizes him as a laborer and not a merchant!

The Chinese who are born in the United States are not treated in that manner and enjoy all the rights of Americans. And if one of them is lucky, or if he is like others who have acquired citizenship before 1883, he can become the vice president in the capital, Washington. On those, the laws governing Chinese immigration do not apply, but no Chinese was naturalized after the aforementioned date.

Such strict laws on immigration were imposed to reduce the impact of the Chinese because they fell on the United States like locusts. They spread vice in the cities, and because of the degraded and cheap way of their lives, you see them working for very low wages thereby undercutting American workers. In order to eliminate their bad influence and to protect the rights of the local workers from their invasive infestation, the United States government legislated laws to curb their immigration. It is enough for the land of Uncle Sam to have to cope with the evil of 60,000 of those braided-haired [people], both men and women, with tails of hair that begin in their heads and end at their feet. These are the ones who continue to commit iniquities in the alleys and side streets of San Francisco leading to the earthquake and fires that destroyed the caverns of the dirty Chinese living in them. But so too was destroyed the rest of the beautiful city: the virtuous paid for the crimes of the sinful and all became homeless on that coast. (282–4)

5. From *The American Journey* by Prince Muhammad ᶜAli Pasha, 1912 (published 1913)

[*Al-Riḥla al-Amrīkiyya* (Cairo, 1913)]

EDITOR'S NOTE
Muhammad ᶜAli Pasha (1875–1955) was a member of the royal family and grandson of the famous Muhammad ᶜAli (d. 1849). He decided to visit the United States after the sinking of the Titanic *in 1912, in which over 100 "Syrian" emigrants drowned.[19] The sinking had been widely covered in Arabic newspapers and periodicals, sometimes giving rise to reflections about human hubris and the need for ever thinking on the vanity of this world; Louis Cheikho, the editor of* al-Machriq, *described the sinking as the* masraᶜ *jabbar al-bihar/ destruction of the giant of the seas (9 [1912], 425–31).*

In his three-month sojourn, the prince visited more cities in the United States and Canada than his earlier countryman, Ilyas; he also wrote at regular intervals thereby producing a travelogue about North America over five times the length of his countryman's. By the time the book was published, about 90,000 Arabs had emigrated from Syria to the United States,[20] although he thought they and the Egyptians counted in the hundreds of thousands.

From his youth, the prince had loved to travel. He was highly cultured, spoke perfect English and French (he was shocked at the sloppy French of the Canadians in Montreal), and he traveled in style. Cook Travel agents handled all his reservations and he stayed at the best hotels, accompanied by aides who did everything for him, from bargaining about the price of souvenirs to conveying messages and even assuming his name when he did not want to be bothered.

He traveled incognito so he could enjoy his tour without harassment: as he noted, the United States was a country of newspapers, and reporters were ever eager to write about visitors whom they relentlessly pursued. He was a very curious man and did not hesitate to visit and see everything around him, and in writing, he was precise and detailed (frequently using the royal we), adding that the goal of travel was to learn and to return to one's country with new ideas and values. He admired much in what he saw, especially the organizational skills of the Americans and the innovations in technology and means of transportation, but he was not sympathetic to their "populist" mode of government. He also thought the middle class was vulgar and uncouth, the general populace prone to deceptive exaggeration, and the industrialists so greedy as to destroy whole forests for their lumber, unlike the Europeans who were cautious and respectful. Often, he noted how the natural scenery in Europe was more impressive than in the United States, how Americans were as foolish as Egyptians in running after planes in flight, and how the tramways in New York were just like those in Cairo.

Muhammad ʿAli showed tremendous interest in the Arab community in the United States, mentioning numerous specific persons and praising many others. Strangely, however, he did not take interest in (was he aware of?) the literary revolution generated by the periodicals that were circulating between New York, Lebanon, and Egypt. Also, Gibran's Broken Wings *had been published in 1911 to wide local acclaim, as well as Rihani's* Book of Khalid; *in fact, Rihani had been busy publishing poems and articles in English in American journals and newspapers for years.[21] Rather, Prince Muhammad ʿAli was deeply interested in Ibn Khaldoun and found his theory of the rise and fall of dynasties quite useful in interpreting the plight of Indians in America. He also had read Alexis de Tocqueville's account about America,[22] and like him, he reflected about human nature and society, comparing and contrasting Europe with America, without, however, forgetting Egypt, and more generally the East/mashriq. While he used terms like Syrians and Egyptians and Arabs, he emphasized the term sharq/sharqiyyin/East/Easterners because he viewed the numerous religious and ethnic communities of the region as victims of western colonialism. The prince was privy to the political tensions in Egypt, between the Khedive and the British administration, and he understood the dynamics of foreign domination that started with commercial advantages to the Europeans, to the exclusion of the locals, after which they turned into control of the country. In his 20 July 1912 speech in New York, he called on his Arab audience to fight colonization and defy "the avarice of peoples that want to extort our national resources" (158). Repeatedly, he emphasized how Arab-Islamic history was by far superior to that of America, adding numerous poems in praise of the Egyptian Khedive (who* was his brother), but at the same time commending the Arabs in America on their success and prosperity and urging them to return because "our country needs working men" (258).

From de Tocqueville, the prince learned to appreciate philanthropy and to understand how American hard work, unfettered by class or social limits, was at the basis of the country's wealth.[23] But Prince Muhammad ʿAli denounced European colonization of Muslim lands, unlike de Tocqueville who had supported the French occupation of Algiers in 1830. Although he was, like de Tocqueville, an aristocrat, he was sensitive to the suffering of the poor, but while the Frenchman situated poverty in the context of the polarization between master and laborer, the prince did not seem to have an understanding of the ravages of capitalism; and while de Tocqueville praised the egalitarianism of Americans, Prince Muhammad ʿAli tolerated mixing with the hoi polloi only because he was a temporary visitor. Unlike the French aristocrat who met with important dignitaries and politicians, including John Quincy Adams, the prince avoided them although like de Tocqueville enjoyed meeting the French communities in Canada, he felt most at home among the Arab communities he met.

Both he and de Tocqueville decried the condition of the Native Americans, and although the prince spent less time in America and Canada than the Frenchman, he wrote more about them. But de Tocqueville's work was by far more sophisticated than the prince's – and of course while the former was dissatisfied with politics at home, the latter was worried about political criticism being voiced by emigrants in America who were beginning to discover an Arabism that separated them from the Turks. The French text is nearly three times as long as the prince's, but it may not be unfair to see the Egyptian author as the first Arab who tried to come to terms with the mystery of the United States and its rise to power.

* * *

I woke up on Wednesday [22 May 1912] and it was not yet 6 am before I was fully dressed. I went out and found my two companions, reading in their seats. I inquired about the previous night and they told me they had not slept a wink because of the illness of Mustapha Bayk.

At seven o'clock, breakfast was served in the [train] cabin and so we went to have coffee and noticed that we were crossing a plain where the local population was quite poor. Their houses were contemptible, built of mud, similar to the houses of the poor peasants in Egypt. When I inquired about them, I was told that most of the people in this region were poor.

The train arrived in Albuquerque where the railway separated in two – one going to the border with Mexico and the other to El Paso.

Here, the carriages that were going in each of the different directions were separated. There was nothing worth noting about this city, but tourists on board the train seized the opportunity of the half-hour stop to go to a store near the station where there were exhibits by the old inhabitants of America. It is called the Indian Museum. What shows that this city was not big was that its residents were barely 8,000. We joined the other tourists and saw the wives of those Americans (Indians) squatting on the ground and selling hand-made trinkets. Their red faces, which had no beauty in them, were unveiled but they wore head scarves.[24] They had shoes on their feet tied with cords. We surveyed the trinkets and then went to the Indian Museum where we found various rugs on sale, made by those Indians, along with different bracelets and earrings, some made from old Mexican coins. There were also stones from these regions with which rings and brooches were decorated: people bought them to offer as gifts and souvenirs to their relatives and friends after returning from their tours.

We looked at everything there but bought nothing. We selected a few postcards (*cartes postales*) which we bought and returned to our passenger car and no sooner had we sat down but a newspaper reporter showed up and asked me which one of us was the prince (*al-prins*). So, I told him that I was Khayri Bayk, designated aide to the prince, and that His Highness had gone to rest now and did not wish to meet any newspaper reporters because he had been irritated by all the interviews, having read what they wrote about him and having found much that was different from what he had told them. He started asking me about what we had enjoyed in America to which I offered cautious answers, saying that the country was vast. He then told me that he knew of a certain Syrian in town, called Monsieur Khoury, and another, a Turk whose name was Salamon, who lived in El Paso and was very rich. This last must be Jewish.[25] He then left me after thanking me for the interview and being impressed with my mastery of the English language to the point where he thought I had learned it in England. So, I concurred.

After I got rid of him, I went to Khayri Bayk and asked him not to leave his cabin until the train has departed. I then told him about all that had happened between me and the reporter, mentioning how I had borrowed his name and position and how I had talked to that reporter as if I were Khayri. In order for my ruse not to be exposed, I asked him not to leave his cabin but stay there because if he left and met the reporter, he would have to talk with him the way I had – which would expose our trick.

Our train was full of peddlers selling Indian goods along with others who were advertising and encouraging the tourists to visit the Grand

Canyon. Two stations earlier, and before we had reached this town, we had seen those Indians and had recognized them from their features even though they were wearing European clothes. Their skin color revealed their race and origin. As for their women, they wore head scarves/*khumur* on their heads which drew attention to them. We noticed that the region which these miserable Indians inhabit is wet and full of swamps that bring killer diseases, reducing their numbers year after year. As for their lands, they are not properly cultivated and because of their poverty, they use old agricultural tools and only reap the fruit of their labor after great hardship. We saw some horse-breeding ranches but most ranches there were for raising cattle. We learned that all animals there belonged to a few [white] merchants and not to American Indians who were just the hired hands watching over the grazing animals. In truth, the huge profits that are made go to the European and American capitalists [*arbab mal*] while those Indians get nothing other than their small wages. If one wanted to inquire about their [capitalists'] wealth, it can be calculated by the number of cattle and horses they own, just like among Arabs. Their grazing grounds are full of wild grass that grows naturally: we saw their horses grazing on weeds that grow in the middle of the swamps, on the surface of the water, or near the swamps.

The train continued near the Rio Grande which is a long and wide river that stretches to Mexico. It was beautiful with green trees growing on both its banks. Occasionally, we saw attractive little islands in the middle of the river covered in vegetation and trees. We passed by numerous small Indian villages which reflected the poverty of the inhabitants and their miserable condition. Here, let me give the reader a description of these village houses: most of them are one floor and are characterized by not having any doors on ground level because the doors are in the roofs. Each house has a ladder which a person uses to enter during daytime; at night, it is pulled up for fear of enemies. But what good is that: the houses are not high and a man on horseback can easily jump to the roof.

There are many tribes among the Indians. In the region we were crossing, there were the tribes of the Mokis, Zunis, Navajos, Apaches, and Pimas. But the reader should not imagine that these tribes live in large cities: rather, they live separately in small villages where the maximum number barely reaches 100 families. Nor is it true, as we had heard before, that each tribe has a chief who is absolute in his authority: for everything of what they used to have has disappeared, including many of their customs and clothes. The tourist no longer sees Indians in strange outfits with different colors or with hats decorated with bird plumes of various hues or painted with their favorite colors: everything is gone and the European style prevails, and if the tourist wants to see something different, he can only find that in historical dramatization performed in front of him – on demand.

"To God is dominion, and everything is transient except the Almighty."

On the road, we passed by many villages, some teeming with Indians while others were full of Mexicans or immigrants from European countries and elsewhere. The tourist will find no difficulty in distinguishing these villages: let him just look at the doors to know whether the inhabitants are Indians or others; and it is enough for him to observe the poverty of some of them to know whether they belong to Mexican or European immigrants. If the latter, they are cleaner in their way of life and more sophisticated than the others. But if he wants to distinguish them on the basis of race, there is no difficulty in that either: the color of the American Indian is red, his head is large, and his hair is black; he has a strong build and is of medium height. As for the Mexican, he looks like a Sa'idi from Southern Egypt, but he is darker in color and physically weaker, not possessing the strength that the latter has.

We passed by the two cities of Isleta and Laguna [?] which are inhabited by American Indians, but there was nothing to write about. Perhaps I need to make myself clear to the reader: generally, the lands in which the European immigrant or the American conquistador settled are rich in mineral resources and the soil is fertile. Such lands go by right to the whites while the arid and swampy lands are allotted to the Indians or the Mexicans.[26]

Here is enough proof that even when man reaches the highest level of civilization, injustice cannot be removed from his nature:

Injustice is a human trait,
And he who does not practice injustice
Must be suffering from some malady.[27]

[Williams, Arizona] This house was a commercial store run by the hotel to sell Indian crafts. It is open to the public at no charge. We entered and saw there numerous precious stones, such as turquoise, and a very large number of American Indian rugs, many bracelets, silver earrings, and baskets of various shapes and sizes. There were also Indian clothes, hats, and horse saddles, bows and arrows, spears and shields, and other things.

The storekeeper was energetic and he took us around explaining all that we inquired about. We chatted with him until we came to the question about the origin of the Indians and so I asked him his opinion and whether he thought they were natives to America or had migrated from other lands. He answered that he believed them to have come from Asia. I was pleased with his opinion because it supported mine: before leaving the United States, I had included this same opinion in my Japan travelogue. When I was in Manchuria, I had seen the Uighurs and had compared them with the American Indians whom I had seen in pictures and in the post cards I had bought in Magden. I then realized that the Indians of America could not but have been part of those Uighurs and of the peoples of north Asia. It is not inconceivable that in the distant past they crossed via Kamchatka [Western Russia] – which means that the Asians were the first to discover America, before Christopher Columbus. But because their conditions were savage, their knowledge limited, and their correspondence with the rest of the world nearly nil, and since they neither mixed nor made contact with the Europeans, their discovery of the continent remained unknown. Still, it is not possible to corroborate this opinion with any information from the Indians themselves because they do not know their origin and do not recall their history. The only definite proof I can offer of my view is the conclusion I had reached while visiting Manchuria and comparing its inhabitants with these American Indians.

One strange thing caught my eye: among the objects that were exhibited was a Mexican bridle decorated with a crescent, and the ironware was Arabic. I thought it a remnant of the Arabs: for we know that the Spaniards were the first people who came and fought the Mexicans. Spain had been an Arab possession, and although it was taken away from the Arabs, some of the Arabs' military artifacts could not but have survived. It is also possible that the Spaniards who came and conquered Mexico included some [men] of Arab descent – or some who admired this military gear and brought these historic remains with them – after which the gear traveled from Mexico to here, where it is sold as trinkets to tourists. What further confirmed my opinion was the presence of full Arab saddles for sale – doubtless remains of the Andalusian Moroccans. Also, surprisingly, there were similarities between the bamboo crafts of those Indians and the crafts of our Sudanese or the *zunuj*/Africans of central Africa. People's ideas and handicrafts reflect the level of social progress or primitiveness: and if two groups of people are similar in their progress or primitiveness, their handicrafts are bound to be similar even if they live far apart. The condition of the blacks is no less primitive than of those Indians.

After we finished visiting all the sections in this antiques store, and as we were leaving, we saw an announcement in English on the wall stating that there was going to be an Indian dance at eight o'clock that evening.

So, we decided to return and watch something we had not seen before. We left and strolled around the hotel for a while after which we returned to my room so I could write my travel diary. At seven o'clock, we went to eat in the dining hall, and no sooner did it strike eight than we went to watch the dance. We found many tourists there and the chairs were arranged in a semi-circle around the space designated for the dancers. Two Indians walked into the center, each holding in his hand a small hollow reed to which was attached a wooden ball with small pebbles: when shaken it produced a sound just like that of the rattle of the *zunuj*. They started dancing and shouting at the top of their voices, just like dogs barking, lifting one leg and then the other and so on. Indian dance is similar to the dance of the *zunuj* of Africa, but their voice is shriller. When they finished, the store owner threw at them some American coins of five or ten cents so that the tourists would do the same – which they did, each throwing what he wanted, while the two dancers hurriedly collected what was thrown at them.[28]

Their act finished, the two left the dance floor and five Indians entered who lined up in single file and started dancing and shouting, just like the black/*zunuj*. Afterwards, money was thrown at them and they picked it up. Then they left the floor and were followed by two barefooted Indian women, each with a piece of cloth on her shoulder, and they started to dance, and were followed by three children who brought the show to an end. After each dance, coins were thrown on the floor and the dancers, males or females, hurriedly collected them. As for the tambourine they were beating, it was very similar to the *dalluka* of the blacks. I could not figure out the mystery of these similarities between those Indians and the inhabitants of central Africa. What is even more surprising about those similarities was that in the past the Indians used turquoise and shells and other things for their transactions: earrings and bracelets made of these were sold for many heads of sheep, cattle, or horses. As for their colorful clothes: they decorate them with multi-hued beads, which, as among the blacks, are of great value.

Such was their original state but then they slowly changed after the discovery of America and the arrival of the Europeans. They started making their earrings and bracelets from silver and gradually, they changed their clothes and started wearing European clothes, confirming [Ibn Khaldoun's] dictum that the conquered emulate the conqueror.

[The next day] After lunch, I decided to rest a bit but I developed a terrible headache, the severity of which I did not get rid of until around 3:30. So I decided to go out and take a walk in the fresh air to overcome this debilitating pain. My two companions joined me and we wandered until we approached the huts of the Indians who worked in the hotel or in the aforementioned store. We saw a woman skinning a sheep hanging in front of her hut and as we tried to go near her to see what she was doing, she disappeared into the hut. We continued towards the hut to see what was inside, but she shut the door in our faces. We walked by the other huts near the one into which the Indian woman had disappeared, but we met with the same treatment and were not able to find out what was inside. Every time we got near a hut, a woman or a child would hurry and shut the door in our faces, not wanting any outsider to know anything about their private affairs.

These incidents, insignificant as they are, impressed me, because I am one who cherishes the preservation of old customs. I found myself so pleased that the headache left me. Perhaps the reader might think that I am a fanatic, one of those who do not want to improve conditions by discarding old, useless customs that lead to stagnation and choosing the best ways leading to true civilization. Experts claim that old customs are the reasons why eastern nations remain underdeveloped: they are the obstacles that prevent these nations from reaching the great levels of progress that the West has attained.

By God, far be it that such is my way of thinking – I who love my country and the rest of the East so deeply. But my many wanderings, my mingling with civilized peoples and others, and my careful study of their customs have enabled me to distinguish between the good and the bad. So frequently have I heard from civilized [people] the bitter complaint about how hurriedly we have imitated their customs without knowing the consequences or reflecting on where the [new customs] will lead us.[29] (142–8, 158–63)

"CHINATOWN, SAN FRANCISCO"

[Wednesday, 5 June 1912] We reached Polk Street, finished our errands, and continued to the Chinese city which lost much of its glory after it burnt down during the Chinese revolt.[30] We were told that before those two incidents, the Chinese population numbered 40,000; now it is not more than 20,000. As for the buildings that were restored after the fire, they no longer exhibited the cheerful character of oriental Chinese houses.

We walked to a street leading to the Chinese stores which was at the entrance of the city. An American came up to us and showed us a license that authorized him to accompany tourists who wanted to visit the city, saying that he knew all the city's secrets and every strange thing worth seeing in it. He offered us his service, charging one dollar per person. We agreed and he told us that he had been a guide for twenty-three years.

First, he showed us a Chinese butchery, then a pharmacy with dead snakes and chicks, all kept in fluids inside flasks. We learned that the Chinese still used traditional medicine, believing it efficacious. We then visited a jewelry store and realized from what was on exhibit that the Chinese do not know of jewelry except gold and *jade*.[31] We then left and headed to the domestic quarter of an old Chinese woman and her ten daughters: they lived under street level and, for very small pay, they worked in mending and washing clothes. We saw where they slept: on a few wooden planks lying next to each other and covered with a single large blanket.

We pitied their plight which bespoke dire poverty.[32]

We then visited the rest of the rooms in that place, fifteen in number, each 3 x 2.5 meters, inhabited by one or more people.

How miserable.

Our guide told us that the American police find great difficulty in arresting Chinese murderers and cutthroats because the Chinese all look alike. Also, Chinese houses have many doors which open on winding streets. A Chinese can kill a person and then hide in a house and escape through the back door and the police will never find him. Fearing revenge, the Chinese never help officers in arresting criminals even if they know the culprits.

We then went to the house of an old musician who played on an instrument that resembled a dulcimer. With two short bamboo sticks, he struck its chords; then he played on a guitar and a violin, which was not dissimilar to a rebec. After listening to him, we gave him a dollar and went into the house of a poor Chinese family where we listened to two little girls, singing first in English and then in Chinese.

Reader, do keep in mind that all the houses were below street level.

After that, our guide wanted to take us to other Chinese houses. But as he was about to open a door and enter, the owner charged out and pushed him away. We learned that the wretched people inside were opium addicts. The government treats opium use as a crime and fines the culprit fifty dollars. I think the man, along with his friends inside the house, was using this deadly poison, and when we opened the door, they became scared and thought the police were charging in to arrest them. So, the house owner furiously came out and slammed the door in the guide's face. The reader should not be surprised: these addicts are like our hashish users who, when the men of Harvey Pasha try to apprehend them, flee in different directions.[33] They know many ways of escape. Do not forget how terrified they become when they suspect that the police are at the door.[34]

After this incident, we went to a Chinese temple on the first floor of a building and found it beautifully decorated with gold-colored wood. We met the priest who promised to tell us our fortunes after he finished performing the necessary prayers. We let him do what he wanted and then he said what all those who claim to know the future tell you – the same cryptic words everywhere in the world. We went on to a large store that sold clothes and Chinese silk and viewed the trade room where judges, chosen from among their prominent merchants, resolve disputes. They arbitrate civil cases and examine the needs of the poor and of relatives in the homeland.

After we had had enough of the Chinese City, we paid the guide his fee and returned to our hotel, not far from there. (233–6)

"INDIANS IN SITKA, ALASKA"

[Thursday, 27 June 1912] We reached the city of Sitka which used to be the capital of Alaska when it was a Russian possession. We found a large number of Indians [the Tlingit], men and women, selling their handicrafts. We surveyed their goods and lo, they were exactly like other goods we had seen everywhere else: shoes made of deer skin, wooden spoons, bracelets, Indian ornaments, animal skins from here and there.

We continued on our way until we reached a forest-turned-park full of densely planted trees with many carved Indian totems (which had been described earlier), all carved differently because they are considered by the Indians as emblems of each family's lineage. After we wandered around in this forest, we crossed a bridge and returned to the city where we visited its general exhibit. There was nothing new there that we had not seen before. Then we passed by a school where Indian girls were taught washing, ironing, cooking, sewing, and everything else needed to run the household. The girls were wearing European clothes. We then entered a Russian church, one of the oldest as we were told, and one of the most beautiful [Cathedral of Saint Michael]. We paid half a dollar in entry fee per person, but we did not see anything of what we had been promised other than two paintings, one of Lord [al-Sayyid] Jesus and another of the Virgin, truly the finest that the human hand can paint. A third painting was of the first Russian priest who had reached Sitka, but it was less impressive than the other two . . .We wandered around town and bought some Indian wares, and then surveyed their miserable houses and blighted condition. We saw that many of them were suffering from deadly diseases, some having gone blind because of not paying attention to eye hygiene. We were deeply moved at the sight of an old blind Indian sawing a plank of wood.

How cruel the heart of man: this Indian was not left to spend the rest of his days in peace even though he was in the worst condition. Old age made him shake, and poverty added to his wretchedness. I walked up to him and gave him something to alleviate life's crushing suffering and noticed by his looks that he did not expect anyone to give him anything to silence his hunger. We learned that those Indians used to be Christians according to the Orthodox rite when their lands were occupied by the Russians, but then they changed and now they follow Protestantism, the denomination of Americans. No wonder: people are of the religion of their kings.

Afterwards, we decided to go to the Russian and Indian gravesites. We walked up to a native girl [wataniyya] and asked her for directions but she refused to tell us, saying she did not know. We noticed from her facial revulsion that she hated the white race – and perhaps she is justified. Finally, an aged Russian showed us the way and we climbed a high hill until we found ourselves among the graves, but there was nothing unusual there except an empty spot surrounded by tree trunks and stumps. We climbed further and saw the beautiful vista of Sitka. We liked the location of those graves because they were in the most scenic spot in Sitka.

When it got cold, we decided to start back and soon met Mr Doman in front of a store who said to me: "The store is run by one of the educated [Indians] and has objects worth viewing." So, we entered and noticed intelligence on the face of its young manager. I inquired about the number of the Indians on Baranov Island [named after the first Russian governor] where the city of Sitka is located. He answered that they do not exceed five hundred and are divided into three groups under three different leaders.

He then gave me a container with very fine sand saying that it was from the sands that blew after an earthquake and the eruption of the volcano that occurred not too long ago [6 June 1911] in the region of the Kodiak, which is 600 miles away. The wind carried the sand and darkened the sky, covering all the houses and workers and other things. I had noticed that the trees which had been exposed to this sand were lifeless and so I collected some of the sand to analyze its components. It is thought that it came out of the depths of the earth when the volcano erupted. He gave me a small quantity of sand so I could examine it in Egypt and identify what components in it are deadly to plants.

Then he continued about the Indians: that in the past, they used to live under the domineering rule of their princes who were reverently obeyed. In those days, it had been natural for them to help the poor and the blighted as much as they could. The able one among them used to work to help the disabled or the sick or the aged. But now, all those good qualities are gone and every Indian cares just for himself. They no longer obey their age-old leaders; even so, they still have some upright qualities. They love each other and do not steal from other Indians; all dealings among them are honest unlike their dealings with the white race – as if they reckon that everything that the whites own is licit for them [to seize].

He then continued about Indian knowledge saying that those savages knew that fish laid eggs long before they encountered Europeans! That is why they used to throw tree branches into the sea near the shore and tie them down with stones. When the time came for the fish to spawn, they swam to these branches and laid the eggs there after which the Indians collected them and dried them, to keep for times of food scarcity. Since they did not know how to use metal in making their utensils, they wove baskets from tree leaves which they covered in mud and left to dry, after which they poured water in them to submerge the egg-covered leaves. They then heated rocks that were mixed with metal and threw them into the baskets: the hot water separated the eggs from the leaves. They then removed the leaves and the rocks and were left with the eggs, which they ate like caviar. This was the ancient way for cooking their food which required water.

It is very strange.

I asked him about the cause of the prevalence of eye disease among them. He answered me that most of them suffer from venereal disease, but he did not know where they contracted it. Also, they do not pay attention to bodily or domestic hygiene. In winter, they burn wood to warm themselves, but as they sit near the fire, the smoke gets into their eyes and blinds them.

Where are the lovers of humanity to save them from this deadly disease? Where is the learned one who will instruct them in the good and help them avoid the bad? The word humanitarianism does not exist in this world, except in the imagination of philosophers who believe that man should love his fellow man and help him during times of distress. But sadly, we see the opposite as if the progress of the children of Adam in science and civilization leads the strong to tyrannize over the weak and to trample on their rights.

There is no strength or power except in God. (324–9)

NOTES

1. Where authors spelled their names in English, I have followed their spelling.
2. The Centennial Exhibition took place between 10 May and 10 November 1876.
3. See Orfalea, *Before the Flames*, 63; Kenneth J. Perkins, *Saudi Aramco World*, November/December 1976, 8–13; Jacobs, *Strangers in the West*, 139–40; James McCabe, *The Illustrated History of the Centennial Exhibition* (Philadelphia: National Publishing Company, 1876), 436–41 for the section on Egypt.
4. *Al-Diyaʾ* (1899–1900), 566.
5. Similar modesty on the part of an American president was reported later in *al-Jinan* (6 June 1885), 356–7.
6. It is interesting that the other Egyptian traveler, Prince Muhammad ʿAli, was suspicious of the Protestants who had "intruded into our land to denigrate the noble religion of Islam," *al-Rihla*, 231.
7. On 6 August 1892, *Kawkab America* reported on lynching. See also the account on the lynching of an Arab, Nola Romey, in Lake City, Florida, in May 1929, in Gualtieri, *Between Arab and White*, ch. 4.
8. This is a reference to the Second Opium War between Anglo-French forces and the Qing Dynasty, 1856–60.
9. A review appeared of the book in *al-Muqtataf*, but it did not include information about the author, February (1911), 187–9.
10. Most authors used riyal and dollar interchangeably.
11. That was why Alaska may not have been a destination for the Syrian emigrants: between 1899 and 1907, only one of the 41,404 Syrian arrivals declared his intention to go there, Houghton, "Syrians in the United States," *The Survey* (1911), 488.
12. See also the Turkish account that had appeared in a journal of the Ottoman royal family in *al-Muqtabas* 5 (1910), 581–9, based on information from Russian sources. It was summarized in Arabic by ʿAbdallah Mukhlis from Haifa.
13. For his biography, see Jean Usher, *William Duncan of Metlakatla: A Victorian Missionary in British Columbia*, Publications in History 5 (Ottawa: National Museums of Canada, 1974).
14. The text includes descriptions of three journeys.
15. The word is *fitriyyin*: living naturally.
16. An Arabic proverb.
17. Quoting al-Imam al-Shafiʿi, d. AD 820.
18. A common saying indicating failure.

19. See Leila Salloum Elias, "Alien Passengers: Syrians aboard the *Titanic*," *Palestine Quarterly* 52 (1999): 51–67 and the numerous references in the endnotes.

20. Bawardi, *The Making of Arab Americans*, 13.

21. In 1904, Rihani translated (à la Edward Fitzgerald's extremely popular translation of Omar al-Khayyam) the *Quatrains of Abu'l=Ala* [sic] to introduce American readers to the "Lucretius of Al-Islam, the Diogenes of Arabia, and the Voltaire of the East" (New York: Doubleday, Page & Company, 1903; London: Grant Richards, 1904), vi. Muhammad Rashid Rida had already praised Rihani, "that resident of America and one of the advocates of nationalism and an enemy to bigotry," *al-Manar*, 7 October 1903, 838.

22. Reference to de Tocqueville appeared in Arabic in *al-Muqtabas* 1 (1906), 186. It appeared in one of six articles about the "Renaissance [*nahda*] of America". The author was translating from French and introduced de Tocqueville as a lawyer who had written about the United States. See also the study by Ariel Salzmann, *Tocqueville in the Ottoman Empire: Rival Paths to the Modern State* (Leiden: Brill, 2004).

23. See chs 30–2: *Democracy in America*, trans. Henry Reeve (New York: D. Appleton and Company, 1904), vol. 2.

24. The prince uses the Arabic word *khumur*, sing. *khimar*, and in parenthesis a transliteration *shilan*/shawls.

25. The Arabic word is *Israi'li*, the official Ottoman designation for Jews.

26. The Allotment and Assimilation policy of the nineteenth century (Act of 1887) continued into the twentieth century thereby leading to the further loss of land by the Native Americans.

27. From a poem by al-Mutanabbi, d. AD 965, the greatest of Abbasid poets

28. The little "show" that Prince Muhammad ʿAli saw coincided with the demeaning shows that were performed nationwide, especially the "Buffalo Bill Wild West Show": see L. G. Moses, *Wild West Shows and the Images of American Indians, 1883–1933* (Albuquerque: University of New Mexico Press, 1996).

29. The prince echoes the discussions that had been going on in Egypt since the last quarter of the nineteenth century about the advantages – and disadvantages – of modernization. See Hourani, *Arabic Thought*, the chapters on Abduh and other reformers.

30. The "Chinese Revolt" was actually a riot against the Chinese carried out by the white population of San Francisco between 13 and 24 July 1877. It resulted in vast destruction of Chinese immigrant property.

31. Written in English after the Arabic *yashb*.
32. Had the prince visited Arab immigrants in New York, he would have found many of them living in similar conditions: see Khater, *Inventing Home*, 82–4; Jacobs, *Strangers in the West*, 56–65.
33. Sir George Harvey Pasha, Colonel, Chief of Cairo Police.
34. Muhammad ʿAli transliterates *police* in Arabic, having also used the Arabic term *al-shurta*.

Women and Gender

1. From *The Book of the Description of Kingdoms* by Idwar Ilyas, 1876 (published 1910)

[*Kitāb mashāhid al-mamālik* (1876, published 1910)]

EDITOR'S NOTE
Although Ilyas came from a sophisticated social background, he still found some aspects of women's behavior in America intriguing. He admired the modesty and conviviality of the president's wife as she toured the Egyptian section: coming from a political and courtly culture where rulers were supercilious, he saw in Mrs Grant's demeanor a lesson for all men and women in power. But at the same time, Ilyas found the mixed swimming of men and women extremely objectionable. As he noted, this custom had been exclusively American but it had been adopted by Europeans who seemed to enjoy it tremendously.

* * *

"AMERICAN WOMEN"

Rich American women are nearly crazy about spending money on clothes. Sinclair, a noted expert on these matters, stated that a woman can spend on a silk-woven *jilbab* [dress] from Paris around 300 guineas. The hat that matches costs 50 guineas while spring hats cost about 200 guineas. Women buy shoes made of deer hide with buttons of pearl shells, costing twenty guineas. Clothes for dancing parties are embroidered with flowers made of silver, with shawls that are studded with precious stones, costing 1,200 guineas – excluding other jewelry. A handkerchief costs ten guineas and silk stockings are ten guineas too, while an umbrella with a gold and pearl handle costs fifty guineas. Some women wear their clothes once or twice and then discard them. It was calculated that the jewelry worn by a certain woman was worth 50,000 guineas – which is why she needed to have police escort to and from the gala she attended. Because the wealth of Americans is widely known in Europe, every man with a title such as "prince" or "lord" or "count" or "baron" has sought to marry an American woman: Lord Curzon, the previous governor of India [Governor General and Viceroy of India, 1899–1905],[1] the Duke of Marlborough,[2] Mr Chamberlain,[3] and the Duke of Manchester,[4] and other Englishmen. Besides these Englishmen are the many French, German, Magyar, and other men who have married the daughters of Americans to the point where it is said that Europe has gained no less than 50 million guineas from rich American women. (482)

"MRS GRANT VISITS THE FAIR"

We received a letter from the aforementioned Mr Child informing us that the wife of General Grant, the president of the republic, wanted to visit the Egyptian section in the Fair. We were asked to prepare to meet her and to take her on a tour and to answer all her questions. I got ready and stood at the entrance at the appointed time, eager to meet this distinguished woman.[5]

She arrived with her daughter and son-in-law and I took them around, explaining everything about the archeological objects. For a whole hour, she was deeply involved, asking about everything she saw. When she admired some ebony spoons that were beautifully crafted, I offered them to her as a small souvenir from the Egyptian section. She accepted them graciously, along with a few other objects. As she was leaving, she invited me to her palace in Washington,[6] the capital of the republic, and so I thanked her and promptly sent a report to his highness, the Khedive, informing him about the visit that had raised the profile of Egypt.

Thus you can see the difference between republican governments that are based on the decisions of the people and the consensus of the citizens and the hereditary governments where princes remain aloof from people and behave very haughtily. The president of the republic of this great country views himself as one of the people: he is willing to visit the house of a friend and accepts invitations from others to attend their meals and celebrations. There is no difference between him and them, even though he is the president of a nation at the highest level of civilization whose population exceeds all the populations of the kingdoms of Europe, except the kingdom of Russia. (510–11)

2. From *The Traveler's Guidebook: And the History of America* by Saj‘an Effendi A‘raj Sa‘adeh (published 1896)

[*Kitāb dalīl al-musāfir: tarīkh Amāyrka* (Ba‘abda, Lebanon: Ottoman Press, 1896). Published by Ibrahim Effendi Sadir]

EDITOR'S NOTE

A ͨraj was a Maronite Lebanese who returned to his homeland from South America and published Dalil al-Musafirin in 1896. As he explained, many of his friends had urged him to write a book about North, Central, and South America, to help both travelers and emigrants living there "even temporarily." A ͨraj was a well-read man: he cited Arabic poetry, conducted careful research about the regions he described, kept abreast of news, and wrote in fluent but simple Arabic. The book was the first of its kind to combine practical advice with general information. Travelers, he advised, should sail on French ships because they were the cleanest, should not carry too much luggage, should drink Syrian arak in order to avoid sea sickness (only if the person was not an alcoholic), should tour around the "great city" of Alexandria, the first stop after Beirut and Jaffa, and should watch out in Marseille for the gangs of Syrian crooks, who "climb the ship like pirates" and entice their gullible compatriots with false promises and services. In his Diwan, Rustum frequently denounced those Syrian ruffians who cheated passengers: they were abominable ͨifreets (317).

The book opens with a description of various countries in the world (England, France, etc.); the United States; Central America; and South America. The last is the longest unit, with an extensive section on Venezuela, where A ͨraj had spent most of his years: by learning about Venezuela, he wrote, the reader will learn about the rest of the countries in the region. A ͨraj described social institutions, history (the discovery of America by "the late Christopher Columbus"), opportunities for work, and political structures. He praised Syrians who raised the profile of their countrymen – such as the late Dr. Yusuf Effendi Arbeely, who died "in New York on 12 August 1984," and Colonel Salim Naffa ͨ in Venezuela. A ͨraj wanted his countrymen to aspire to higher goals than peddling, which he denounced because, on arrival, most Syrians gravitated to that "wooden box, two thirds of a cubit in height, with three drawers, a mirror at the bottom, and a string attached to the shoulder."

The book combines raw facts with excerpts from newspaper articles and oral accounts of Syrian experiences, both good and bad. It ends with words of advice to the reader: imitate Gladstone (the British prime minister), that grand shaykh, who always kept a book in his pocket so he could make use of his time when free; read the essays of that "famous scholar Franklin" and learn the rules of hard work and perseverance which are the markers not just of Americans, but also of all successful nations – after which A ͨraj proceeded to summarize them. The last words in the book are in praise of Ottoman sultan ͨAbd al-Hamid II (reg. 1876–1909).

*　*　*

The pen cannot sufficiently describe the insults that our wandering peddler women encounter in all the regions of America – offensive to good taste, objectionable to noble spirits, and unacceptable to the worthy. Far be it that the men of my country should lose their honor, pride, chivalry, and inherited integrity, but they have driven some of their women to a base degree of humiliation, disgrace and shame over and above the encumbrance and strain of carrying that *kushé* on their chests. It is these actions that have demeaned our status and brought shame and indignity on us from Americans who have shot us with arrows of blame and culpability, saying in their conversations: "You Syrians, look at your women as they wander around the streets, going from one house to another, knocking on doors." Where is the Syrian honor when such scathing remarks are made and where is that honor which we have had of old? How can we accept seeing our women in this condition which can melt stone, and what is the value of the money if honor is lost? Perhaps the sons of our dear home country will pay heed to this matter and abide by the noble [Maronite] patriarch's injunction forbidding Syrian women from traveling to America and Australia if they have no pressing reason. Wish that this injunction would be accompanied by binding orders to those in charge of such matters so as to preserve the honorable name of the home country.

I would have described the behavior of some of these women but I have limited myself to allusions rather than to details, hoping that national pride will compel those with responsibility to lift the burden of shame and insult from the shoulders of the gentle sex lest they should become a target of strangers' abuse. And so, I will recount an incident about a woman who was killed in the hope that it would be a warning to whoever wants to be warned.

The incident occurred in the city of Kumnah in the Republic of Venezuela and involved Elisha᷾ Shina Kayruz from Bsharri of "Lebanon" and his wife Tsiya. The incident resulted in the murder of the latter and the imprisonment of the former. Here are the details:

Elisha᷾ left his house at the beginning of December in 1893 carrying his *kushé* to peddle around the markets and streets. At home, he left his wife, whose name was Tsiya and his son, Murshid, who was three years old. Soon, he returned, to find his wife carrying the child in her arms and still in the same room. He started cursing her for not having left quickly that morning to go out peddling like him. He abused her verbally, threatening and bullying her. As for her, her tender and sweet feelings, or rather her "newly acquired" *tafarnuj* [becoming Western/Frank-like], which some Syrian women acquire as soon as they leave their home country, did not allow her to stay quiet, composed and restrained. She countered with the same rough language whereupon he threatened her with his authority and his "holy" will. But she snapped at him and turned her back, which made him so angry that he took a revolver and shot her thrice, hitting

her first in the right shoulder, and aiming the second and the third bullets into her belly – "to send her to the hereafter." The wretched woman
fell down on the spot, covered in blood, and cried out a farewell to her
beloved and supporter, meaning her son, imploring him to spare "nothing to avenge her." She said to him, "*Mi esperanza* Murshid. Murshid, O
my son Murshid, take revenge on your cruel father who denied you my
maternal love. O my hope, Murshid, do not spare him who denied you your
protection and nightly care."

As for Murshid: his poor mother, and just before the first shot was
fired by the barbaric father, had thrown him from her arms to the floor
for fear that one of the bullets of "kindness and compassion" might hit
him. Young as he was, he cried: "*Mi papa nu mata mi mama.* My father,
do not kill my mother. *Mi papá si oste la mata mika de solo.* O father, if
you kill her, I will remain alone," and other such injurious words that
make hard hearts melt in the chest. But the sword had already preceded
justice, for this evil murderer did not think of what punishment he would
receive until the *police* arrived after they had heard the shots. They tied
him up and whipped him and dragged him to jail. The woman was buried
after a medical autopsy. That murderer received a stiff sentence for what
he had done in killing one whom God had made a productive member
in society who contributes to advancement and improves civilized life,
even if nature made her lower than men in regard to the weakness of her
constitution, her emotional uncontrollability, and her inability to perform, like him, the same great actions and other things which need not
be mentioned here. (86–90)

3. From "The [female] Syrian Emigrant" by Miss Wadiʿa Faris Rashid (published in *al-Hoda*, 1908)[7]

[Al-Sūrīyya al-muhājira (*al-Hoda*, 1 October 1908)]

* * *

The more the Westerner respects women, the less the Syrian [male]
respects them and, instead, usurps their rights, mocking them and turning them into a toy in his hands. The exception to this practice is among
the well-mannered people, but how many are these in comparison to the
others? I once heard a man excoriate his wife, demean and insult her,
because after she went out peddling, she did not bring in much money. In
vain did she try to explain to her husband that people did not open their
doors to her.

A woman arrived to live with her brother-in-law who owned a small shop. She had arrived by land on Saturday evening and so on the following morning, he told her to prepare her merchandise so she would work and not miss half of Monday. The woman refused and so, the kindly brother-in-law did not hesitate to swear at her and to threaten that he would write his brother about her, because, according to him, she was in America to work night and day and send money back to her husband.

It is clear that I am writing about none other than the class of women who peddle from one place to another. Among this class of women, the number of newspaper readers is very small because, as the excuse goes: she is a wandering peddler, or, Americans do not like to read foreign newspapers. But on many occasions, and while visiting my brother who is a lawyer and head of the "Tribe [sibt] of Joseph" Society, I receive Arabic newspapers which I proceed to read in the office, in the presence of Americans, high and low. They do not scoff at me because they recognize the value of knowledge.

I hope some Syrians will stop insulting women and start reading so they can improve themselves.

4. From "Who has Precedence: Man or Woman?" by Mrs Asma Sabir (published in al-Hoda, 1908)

[Liman al-awlawiyya a-lil-rajul am lil-marʾa? (al-Hoda, 28 October 1908)]

EDITOR'S NOTE
A reader of al-Hoda, *Sabir entered the fray after reading a demeaning article about women – although she admitted that she was unprepared for the task of writing a rebuttal. Her piece was published in a special section in* al-Hoda *that focused on* al-mabahith al-nisaʾiyya, *women issues.*

*   *   *

I read in *al-Hoda* newspaper an article by Nimr Effendi Ruhana, the honorable writer, under the title "Who has Precedence: Man or Woman?" and so my womanly zeal and literary solicitude prompted me to refute what the gentleman had said about the female sex. He insulted women by ascribing to them weakness in mind and intelligence. It is offensive that in this age, there are those among our writers and literary figures who continue to uphold the opinions of our grandfathers' grandfathers even after all evident proofs and testimonials.

One of the views that the gentleman upholds is that "if a woman cannot perform the tasks of a man, how can we treat her as equal?" Heavens, Sir, don't you see among the civilized nations that have granted woman her rights, how she is equal to the man in mental capacity and physical strength? Do you not see her standing in commercial stores next to men, shoulder to shoulder, so much so that she competes with them in making a living? You see among them writers and saleswomen and workers, too. How many people have complained to their governments because of women's admission to work which reduced the number of jobs for men? In truth, if the woman was less mentally capable than the man, would she have taken his place and blocked his chances for earning wages?

Walk into any office in this great country and you will see that the number of female writing staff is equal to that of men. And if you say that writing or trade or industry requires little knowledge, and that we should look at positions where there is need for sharp insight, accurate perception, and wide-ranging imagination, I will answer you: Did you not hear what the women in the English nation did last year when they protested to the government, demanding the right to vote and to have a say in politics?[8] Don't you know how much they persisted in their demands that they compelled the government to threaten them with the use of force? Had they not been certain about their abilities to perform difficult tasks they would not have persisted in making their demands with such audacity; and had men not been certain of women's competence to perform such tasks, they would have retorted that women were incapable and not sufficiently intelligent to fill such high positions. For if women were given the right to participate in political action, but were unsuitable, their entry through that door and granting them that request would be like the letter *waw* in the name of ʿAmru.[9] In fact, it was because government members were convinced of the capabilities of many of these women that they refused to grant them those rights, fearing for men's jobs; they knew for certain that women possessed the same abilities as their male counterparts.

Don't you see how much England progressed under the rule of its Queen Victoria? Had she been of little reason, how could she have governed her country with that wise sagacity? And there are many like her in all countries and nations, and even if they are not queens, they are capable of fully performing the responsibilities they are given.

You say that woman is weak-willed and add that she will do anything and everything to get what she wants: here you contradict your first view with the second. Don't you think that her persistence in trying to achieve what she wants demonstrates strength of perseverance that should be noted and applauded? According to you, she always sticks to her views so much so that she does not care, even when she should, about the destruction of a kingdom or the defeat of an army. By my truth, this is a false accusation, as evident as the sun in daytime. Don't you see the peace that prevailed in the dominions during the reign of the queen of England: how can you say that she did not care about the destruction of a kingdom and the defeat of an army – she who was endowed with gentility and sincere compassion by the Almighty Creator?

It saddens us to tell you, Sir, that you accuse our sex of all that is demeaning and insulting, making no difference between light and darkness. You accuse us of weakness while showing off your strength, and you accuse us of degeneracy instead of extending compassion: if the Almighty Creator assigned to woman child-bearing and domesticity and to man work and remuneration, and if He in His praiseworthiness has given each their position, could He have desired to insult woman?

The Almighty has assigned us honorable tasks of which we are proud and which we wholeheartedly fulfill. If you consider them lowly, I will show you proofs that demonstrate that when we choose and are permitted to, we can do what men do. But our foremost duty is to complete our honorable mission which is ours alone, and even she who refrains from pursuing her mission continues in her dedication. But if you want us to undertake the two tasks at the same time so you can then honor our dignified status or lead us away from the degeneration into which you pushed us, I say: No one can serve two masters. Either [we serve] the domestic, or the ethical, or the material.

We are, Sir, guardians and cultivators of ethics and of the planet.

5. From "The need to put a limit on or to pass a law prohibiting the Syrian woman from emigrating to America" by Yusuf Effendi Ilyas Yuwakim and Yusuf Effendi Jirjis Zakham (published 1908)

[*Wujūb waḍʿ ḥhadd aw sharīʿa tamnaʿ muhājarat al-marʾa al-Sūriyya ila Amāyrka* (al-Hoda, 12 January 1908)]

EDITOR'S NOTE
Zakham lived in Omaha, Nebraska, and regularly wrote articles for al-Muqtabas about U.S. history, economics, immigration, and other topics. He also wrote for al-Hoda, but the editor, Na'um Mukarzil, told him not to bother with writing for newspapers and to concentrate on literary works that

would prove "useful." His friend, Yuwakim, however, wrote urging him to participate in a discussion about husbandless Syrian women who were arriving as emigrants in the United States. Zakham agreed because he knew that Yuwakim was a man deeply concerned about "Syrian honor." In his Diwan, *Rustum praised Yuwakim for being foremost in writing about the conditions of emigrant women; he also included a photograph of him (333).*

Zakham started the "Proposal"/iqtirah, which was the heading given by al-Hoda, by quoting Yuwakim's letter. Writing from Pennsylvania on 3 January 1908, Yuwakim stated that he had the support of the Women's Society in New York and "our Arabic newspapers." The Women's Society had prepared an open letter to be published in all Arabic newspapers listing the necessary qualities for Syrian women in the "New World." He had traveled widely around the country and had found "important secrets" which he wanted to expose in order to preserve the dignity and ethical status of the Syrian emigrant. He then continued:

* * *

"PROPOSAL" BY YUSUF EFFENDI ILYAS YUWAKIM

The Syrian emigrated with his brother or sister or wife or mother or relative or in-law, say what you want. He stated to the immigration officer that she was his wife and the rest his sisters and brothers. He then went up and down in the New World where he met with great success. Afterwards, he returned to the homeland to tell his community about what he had seen, experienced, and learned about in America. He praised the success of women in making thousands of dollars, whereupon stupid/ *mutakhallifat* women deserted their husbands, either by their own choice or at the insistence of their husbands, and they sailed across the dangerous seas, heading to the land of Columbus. They did not seem to regret leaving their husbands or the Old World.

After grueling labor crowned them with success, some of the emigrant women returned to Syria and to their husbands, having sworn, however, that they would not return to America unless accompanied by their husbands and children. They had met with all forms of humiliation, difficulty, and trouble in the foreign land – all in order to make money and support their lazy husbands who were born for indolence and inactivity and idleness. And, do not forget that they returned to find their children having lost their good manners and all that goes with proper behavior.

We cry out from the New World saying: Where are our men? Where are the men of the future? Who are they?

At the same time, because of the cruelty of their "sweet and tender" hearts, some women divorced themselves from honor and stomped on chastity. They took up new partners forgetting, or feigning forgetfulness of, their children – those small children awaiting the return of their mothers by the minute with what is needed to feed and clothe them. Of women from this second group, large numbers have emigrated to America and the Office of Immigration, believing what these women tell them, continues to accept them.

The depravity that is running in the veins of the Syrian community will have dire effects on the morality of the Syrian nation, especially if this depravity reaches the Old Country. We already have enough there of ill conditions and failure, and if we allow that depravity to grow in the hearts of those with hearts [women], there is no doubt it will undermine the morality of the nation and its strong foundation.

"RESPONSE" BY YUSUF EFFENDI JIRJIS ZAKHAM

[The response of] Yusuf Effendi Jirjis Zakham: Limiting the number of Syrian emigrants cannot be effected by the local governors or by the Washington or Ottoman governments. It has to be done by our Arabic newspapers and all our merchants, writers, and societies, different as they are, who are concerned about this matter. For the government that prohibits the emigration of men cannot prohibit the emigration of women, although the Ottoman government prohibits the emigration of both men and women. But Beirut sailors do not care and allow the emigration of men and women, nor do they care if Syrian women emigrate on their own.

Therefore, the best way to prevent women from emigrating alone is for the Syrian press to rise up and denounce and humiliate every Syrian man who gives his wife or his daughter permission to come to America on her own. The correspondents of the Arabic newspapers, along with their agents and readers in all the lands of immigration, should expose every immoral woman and publicize the name of her husband and her family along with her place of residence . . . Also, they should scandalize every man who helps the Syrian woman continue in her immoral deeds and who trades on her honor.

If worse comes to worst, it might be necessary and essential for the government of Uncle Sam to apprehend every male and female offender.

15 December 1908

6. From *The Stranger in the West* by Mikha'il Rustum Shuwayri, 1895 (published 1909)

[*Dīwān al-gharīb fi-l-gharb*, vol. 2 (New York: al-Matbaʿa al-Tijariyya, 1909): Al-Gareeb fi-El-Garb, copyright February 16, 1909, in the United States of America.]

EDITOR'S NOTE
Rustum wrote his books to show the links between the "Syrians" and the "Americans" in their cultural histories and identities. He fully realized the advantages offered by the United States – thus his numerous short anecdotes and jokes about the tensions, confusions, but also the successes of the Syrians in their new environment. His books were full of poems, anecdotes, brief news accounts, humorous disputations, histories, and some illustrations.

Volume 1 was published and praised by Kawkab America in August 1895 and was sold for one half of a riyal, "and 12 [copies] for 5 riyals or 1 English pound sterling." It was sold at 40 Washington Street in New York or by the author himself in Philadelphia, "south of 10th Street, number 225" (Kawkab America 2 August 1895). Rustum published later editions – the second in 1909, the third in 1921 – and was active in the Syrian community of New York; when Prince Muhammad ʿAli visited the city in 1912, Rustum was among the guests whom the prince mentioned.

"STORY OF A SYRIAN WOMAN WHO LOST HER SON
(A REAL STORY)"

Fifteen years ago, a Syrian woman lost her son and after failing to find him, and satisfied with the amount of money she made, she returned to the homeland. She stayed there for five years and then returned to this country and lived in the same city in which her son had been lost. One day, a few years later, she saw a youth of about sixteen years of age and her heart took to him. So, she followed him whereupon he started running and so she ran after him until they reached a house. After he had entered, she rang the bell and the lady of the house came and asked her what she wanted.

She said: "I want to look at this youth who just entered."

"What do you want from him?"

"I just want to look at him."

So she let her into the house and she started examining his features. She asked him what his real name was, whose son he was, and where he came from, all the time staring intently at him. Her heart took to him and she started kissing him saying:

"You are my son."

Then she told her story to the lady of the house: how she had lost him ten years before and never saw him again until she spotted him in the market and followed him to the house. The lady said:

"My husband is a police officer and he found the boy lost and brought him to our house and we have raised him all this time."

The boy deliberated for a while about staying, but then returned with his mother (the world is your mother and you return to your roots). In him the verse of the gospel was realized: "He was dead and now lives, he was lost and now is found" [Luke 15:24]. She had left him with little understanding and now she found him well-mannered and polite. Here is his description in verse:

> She lost him while he was unable to distinguish right from wrong,
> And when she found him, he proved to have followed the right
> path.
> Many a youth went astray, but he ever remained safe and sound.
> (121–2)

NOTES

1. He married Mary Victoria Leiter, daughter of an American millionaire.
2. Charles Richard John Spencer-Churchill, 9th Duke of Marlborough, married Consuelo Vanderbilt.
3. Joseph Chamberlain, a statesman, married Mary Endicott, daughter of the U.S. Secretary of War.
4. William Montagu, 9th Duke of Manchester, married Helena Zimmerman, daughter of an American railroad president.
5. The entrance to the Egyptian section showed a temple with lotus-leaf capitals. The motto was: "The Oldest People to the Youngest."
6. Julia Grant was known to invite guests frequently to the White House.
7. Among the "exotic" newspapers at the time, the Arabic dailies had a higher circulation than the Chinese, the Greek, or the Yiddish dailies, Robert E. Park, *The Immigrant Press and Its Controls* (New York and London: Harper & Brothers, 1922), 302.
8. In 1906, the Women's Social Political Union had lobbied Parliament for the right to vote. When women representatives who met with Prime Minister Henry Campbell-Bannerman realized that he would do nothing for their cause, they organized in 1907 the first of what they called "Women's Parliaments."
9. ʿAmru ends with a letter *waw*, which is not pronounced.

Identity and Americanization

1. From *The Book of the Description of Kingdoms* by Idwar Ilyas, 1876 (published 1910)

* * *

"DINNER WITH PRESIDENT GRANT"

One day [during the Philadelphia Exhibition], Mr Paul, a dignitary, invited President Grant to dinner, and he extended the invitation to us, too. So, I went to his house at the appointed hour and found the president of the republic and his wife and others in a magnificent hall, waiting for dinner. The gracious lady told her husband about our reception when she visited the Egyptian section and so His Highness [sic, President Grant] extended a special welcome to me. We then sat down to dinner at a magnificent table and after we finished, we walked over to the smoking parlor, as was the custom of men. The women went into the reception hall, where they waited for the men to finish smoking. As we were sitting in that parlor, the president of the republic told me of his desire to tour Egypt in the following winter. I quickly asked him if I had his permission to convey his wishes officially to the Egyptian government. He answered affirmatively, showing a gentility not to be expected from a leonine hero like him who had been in wars and had fought thousands and defeated great armies. For it is known that he had been the commander of the northern soldiers during the Civil War between the people of the north and of the south. He had been victorious in all the decisive battles.

He was known for his reticence and thoughtfulness, but when I had the honor of meeting him, he was quite garrulous. I remember that when the word "tourism" came up, he turned to me and said: "It would be quite tiring for him to go on a tour in France or Austria or Italy because he was a man of one tongue, and that was the tongue of truth." Everyone laughed at his joke. He loved smoking and did not put his cigar down unless he had to. He is considered one of the greatest and the finest presidents of the American republic. (496–7)

I already mentioned how the wife of President Grant invited me to the "White House" in Washington after her visit to the Fair. This is the name of the magnificent palace in which the president of the republic and his family live during the term of his presidency. It was built with public funds, and most of it is of white marble. It has everything that is needed for domestic life and servants are paid by the government. The president needs do nothing more than bring his own possessions and private servants, and when his term ends, he makes way for his successor. There are spacious rooms in this palace, full of expensive furniture, also paid for by the government, and they are used for hosting delegations of people, ambassadors, emissaries, and men of authority whom the president cannot but meet. Every week, he meets whomever he chooses from among the people, and shakes hands with the high and the low, and walks among government ministers and laborers so much so that you will not be able to distinguish him from others – unless someone points him out to you. The term of presidency [in America] is four years but the president could have another term although, since their independence, people have become accustomed to not electing the man more than once so that he will not be able to control government. They fear that such re-election will take them back to monarchy which Americans absolutely despise.

The president is equal to a prime minister and king in constitutional monarchies. He enjoys wider power than the king of England or of Italy and he has the authority to appoint ministers exclusively from among his own party. He also appoints ambassadors and consuls from his own party. His salary is 75,000 riyal per year – that is 15,000 guineas only; it used to be 5,000. The Senate has the power to put him on trial and to remove him from office if he is found guilty. He has the power to reject legislation by Congress except in the case when Congress insists on it after his rejection – which has not yet happened. But one of the previous presidents, Andrew Jackson, was accused of many things and was tried by the Senate but was not convicted.

The vice president has very few powers but, every four years, he is elected just like the president. He is the presiding officer [President] of the Senate (which will be described below), and if the president dies, or is forced to leave office because of illness, no one is elected to the presidency, and the vice president will take over until the end of the term.

After receiving the invitation from President Grant and his wife, I took the train from Philadelphia, alongside the Delaware and Schuylkill rivers which surround the city, and continued in open fields until I reached Washington six hours later. I went directly from the train station to the hotel and spent the night there. In the morning, I took a coach to the palace of the president and after some time, the driver stopped and said, this is the "White House." I was stunned because I did not see any presidential signs of power around the house. There were no guards walking up and down, nor soldiers in readiness, nor men in flamboyant uniforms and regalia. Here, America shows its difference from all European kingdoms. I rang the bell, as the driver had told me to do, and a servant opened the door and asked me whom I wished to see. I gave him my name and my visiting card whereupon he asked me whether I wanted to see the president himself or his wife or his son-in-law, Mr [Algernon] Sartoris – because all were out.[1] I told him to present my card to His Highness, the president himself, and then I left, surprised at the modesty of the ruler of one of the strongest countries on earth. I could not but admire the stability of a system that does not need soldiers and that celebrates freedom openly, making the president of a great nation equal to the lowliest person.

I returned to the hotel and on the next day, the manager handed me a dinner invitation from General Grant, President of the Republic, for the day after at seven in the evening. I was told that one of the assistants at the White Palace had brought that invitation. So, I went to the White House at the appointed time and the servant admitted me to a glamorous reception hall where I stayed for a little while. Soon, the wife of the president came, accompanied by the president and General Philip Sheridan, Secretary of War and also a hero of the American Civil War. I joined them as we all went to the dining hall where we found the daughter of the president and his son-in-law. We sat at the table and had dinner while conversing about many topics including Egypt and its historic sites and present conditions. I saw nothing in the palace worth noting because in its furniture and design and appearance it was no different from the houses of rich Americans. Actually, many millionaires have palaces by far grander and more opulent on which they spend fortunes in decorations and renovations, many times more than the house of the president.

Frequently during my stay in Washington, I saw this great president leaving his white house or walking in main streets, on his own, just like other people, with his hands behind his back, as he was known to do. (513–15)

2. From *History of the United States Since its Discovery until Present Times, Followed by the History of Syrian Emigration and All That Pertains to It* by Basil M. Kherbawi, 1888 (published 1913)

[*Tārīkh al-Wilāyāt al-Muttaḥida mundhu iktishāfiha ila al-zamān al-ḥāḍir wa yalīhi tārīkh al-muhājara al-Sūriyya wa ma yataʿllaqu biha* (Printed by the "Printing and Publishing House" N.s. Badran Prop. 1913)]

EDITOR'S NOTE

Archpriest Basil/Basilius Kherbawi (1872–1947) was born in Tyre, Lebanon, and after studying at the American University of Beirut, he emigrated to North America where he became Dean of St Nicholas Syrian-Greek Ortho-dox Cathedral of Brooklyn, NY.[2] He was an active writer, authoring and publishing in 1911 a history of Russia in Arabic, and two years later, the longest book published in Arabic to that date about the United States, Tarikh al-Wilayat al-Muttahida, which he sent to subscribers from Florida to Mount Lebanon. To write about the history of the United States, Kherbawi read through a vast array of primary and secondary sources: his goal was to introduce a complete portrait of the United States that included records of past events, a survey of presidents, description of the laws that pertain to immigration, and other useful information. He was widely respected and in 1919, Jibraʾil Ward described him as one of the "eminent men of culture and knowledge in the mahjar." He wrote a moving article after the murder of Emperor Nicholas II and his crown prince and, eager to defend his Eastern Church which was maligned as "schismatical" in America (by both Protes-tants and Catholics), he translated the prayers of the Orthodox Church into English and in 1930 self-published a history of the Orthodox Church, The Old Church in the New World, for which he received commendations from the New York metropolitan as well as from the "Archbishop of Neapolis, Palestine"[Nablus].[3]

Although there are numerous claims about the first Syrian arrival in America, the account reported by Kherbawi was the first detailed and auto-biographical one.

*   *   *

"THE FIRST EMIGRANT ACCOUNT"

I will write down what Tanyus Effendi Tadros told me about his arrival in these lands.[4] He is the owner of the large Tadros & ʿAkkari store, famous in New York. His account shows both pleasure and humor and reflects the condition of the first immigrants.

He said:

I came to the United States at the end of 1884, accompanied by
Hanna al-A'qda and Jirjis al-Mukarbil from Tripoli, and Amin Salloum
from Kafr Sarun [both in Lebanon]. The reason I decided to emigrate
was that I used to own a small shop in which I sold, among other things,
Turkish tobacco wholesale. One day, a man came and asked me the price
of the ounce of the best kind of tobacco I had. I said: "Four piasters and a
half." He said: "Weigh me two ounces."

I did.

He slipped his hand into his pocket and pulled out a stack of *liras* and
started looking for a small denomination with which to pay me for the
tobacco. I was stunned how a man who did not look important could pull
out so much money from his pocket. When he saw my surprise, he said:

"Did you not recognize me, Khawaja Antonyos?"

"No," I said.

He said: "I am Ishaq al-Amyuni. I used to be a servant at the house
of Habib and you and others used to taunt me and throw stones at me
whenever I walked in the market."

I said: "And so, how did your condition change that you are now a
man of wealth?"

He answered, "I emigrated to Barcelona where I made a fortune in
less than a year and a half."

So, I asked: "O Ishaq, where is Barcelona?"

He answered: "It is in America."

And so, from that moment, I decided to go to America.

I started preparing myself and when I was fully resolved, I stuck 85
liras in my pocket and with my three aforementioned friends I boarded
a French ship from Tripoli to Marseille. On that ship, there was a man
called Arkilo who served coffee and he spoke many languages. I asked
him what he thought of emigration and where he advised us to go. He
answered: go to New York because there, people spend 100 riyals in the
way you spend your *matlīk* [small Ottoman coin].

When we reached Marseille, a Jewish agent who spoke little Arabic
saw us and asked us where we planned to go. We answered: "New York."
He said: "Four of your countrymen have been denied entry and sent back
because of their poverty and shabby clothes. Actually, had you seen those
four you would agree that not even Satan would accept them in hell
because of their filthiness and grubbiness."[5]

We shall not mention the name of the town from which they came in
order not to hurt anybody's feelings.

The Jew added: "I advise you to change your Arab clothes for European ones and to buy some merchandise and take it with you. Enter
like merchants not like beggars. I also advise you to get passports to

Philadelphia and not New York." He bought us passports to Philadelphia and we sailed from Marseille to the United States in December
1884 and reached New York harbor at the end of that month. The
immigration officials gave us passports to Philadelphia and so each of
us took the "little paper" and stuck it in his pocket, not knowing that it
was our passport. We stayed in the immigration center for twenty-one
days, eating and drinking and sleeping as guests of Uncle Sam. The
immigration center was then located where the fish market is today, in
the Patri Garden.

But we were more like captives than immigrants.

One day, I left the center and saw a garden where people were strol-
ling. I walked around until I found a shop selling tobacco and so I gestured
to the salesman that I wanted to buy some tobacco. He handed me a
sheet of Naifeh Tobacco which I took back to my friends, happier than
Columbus and his men at sighting America. When my companions saw
the tobacco, they were ecstatic.

Three weeks after we had been in the immigration center, I took out
from my pocket the "little paper" and showed it to one of the workers
there whose name is Mr Adams (he is still at the center today). He took
it from me and from my companions, gave us others instead, and sent
us with a man to Pennsylvania Train Station in order for us to travel to
Philadelphia.

The train left after 11 pm on the evening of 17 January 1885 and we
reached Philadelphia at 2:30 am the next morning When we walked out
of the station, there was snow on the ground and it was freezing cold. A
policeman saw us and signaled us to walk for about a mile where we would
find another policeman to whom we should give a paper he handed us.
Later we learned what was written on it: whoever knows where the (*arab*)
Arabs live, let him direct those foreigners there. As we started walking,
Jirjis Mukarbil slipped on the snow and started screaming for help. We
helped him up and walked slowly until we reached the location about
which the aforementioned policeman had told us. There we found the
policeman who advised us to walk another half a mile where we would
find another policeman who would tell us what to do. When we found
him, he gestured for us to follow him, which we did.

He took us into a shop owned by an Italian who seated us near the
fireplace for a little while. Then he made signs for us to follow him into a
room which had nothing in it to protect us from the biting cold, neither
furniture nor stove. We spread whatever blankets we found on the floor
and went to sleep, but soon we felt extremely cold and our bodies shook.
We woke up afraid and not knowing what to do, and so one of us, Amin
Salloum, stood up, kicked the door with his foot, and started cursing and

screaming. The Italian and his wife woke up terrified; the wife thought that thieves had broken into the store, but her husband told her that he had admitted four strangers who had arrived late into the empty room. She took up a cane and started beating him and scolding him for his cruelty in putting those "Catholic" foreigners in that cold place. She then opened the store and started a fire and moved us near the warmth.

We stayed there till morning after which we went out walking around the city looking for someone who spoke our language. After a short distance, we met a Jew whose name I do not remember who said in Arabic: "Where do you come from?" Do not ask how happy we were when we found someone who spoke our language. We clung to him and told him that we would not let him go until he either found us a place to stay or he led us to our own people. We asked him: "Who are you?" He said: "I am a Jew from Jerusalem." He then said: "Bring your luggage and follow me." We did and we reached a hostel owned by an Italian man where he rented us a single room with four beds, each for one riyal per night. For the next two months, we ate bread and milk in the morning and bread and sardines at noon and in the evening. In all that time, we could not afford to buy anything else.

One day, I left the hostel and saw people walking on the street, so I followed them, staring at them to find out if one of them was Syrian or Arab. I noticed that many of them went into a restaurant and as I passed by it, I smelled the cooking and became hungry; I had not had a cooked meal for months. I thought of entering the restaurant but hesitated fearing that I would break some of the customs of the people in this country. Finally, I sat down at a table across from a man eating *bif stu* – which is a stew with meat and potatoes. A waiter came up and asked me what I wanted to eat and so I pointed to the man across from me and said the same. He left and returned with a tray full of stew, bread, and a cup of coffee. He charged five cents for everything. I ate ravenously and as soon as I was finished I ran hurriedly to my companions and told them about my "new discovery." They were eating the aforementioned lunch of bread and sardines. When they heard what I told them, they left the food and hurried with me to the aforementioned restaurant where I seated them at a table and ordered for them the same kind of food that I had eaten. They ate and were overjoyed. We went back to the Italian's hostel where we stayed for five months until our money nearly ran out. Every night, we were like the Prophet David, drenching our mattresses with tears and composing with Jeremiah sad lamentations on our plight and our emigration.

One day, I was walking down a street when I saw a man selling baskets. I bought one and then on the following day, I put in it some of the merchandise we had brought from France and as I walked in the market,

I noticed there was no one else carrying a basket like mine. I thought that perhaps in this land they do not sell in markets. Then I saw the street tram (*strit kar*) and so I got on it and continued till the end of the line when the conductor told me to get off. I left and no sooner had I taken a few steps than I saw a Jew carrying a bag on his back. I thought him a salesman, which he was, and so I followed him. I saw him walking up to a house and after removing his hat, he greeted the lady of the house saying: "*Du yu want tobay ani thin to-day?*" I understood from his gestures that he had asked her if she wanted to buy anything. So, I sat down and started repeating that sentence, "*bayy som ting to-day.*" Then I wrote it in Arabic letters and memorized it and started going around houses until I sold for ten cents that day. I went back to the hostel and found my companions waiting to see how "I found America."

I told them that I had sold for ten cents. As soon as they heard that, they started weeping and lamenting, cursing the hour that I had met al-Amyuni and cursing the coffee man who had advised us to travel to America, the land of gold. We spent the night deeply dejected but in the morning, I took my basket and wandered in the market where I met a Jew who carried various scraps of metal on a flat board tied to his chest. I followed him until he entered one of the bars (*salun*) where he sold for four dollars and a quarter. After the Jew left, I presented my wares which were made of brass, *jewelry*, and I sold for two riyals and a half. I then left that bar and went into another and sold whatever I could sell and continued from one bar to another until noon. I sold for nine riyals and a quarter. Every time I was handed a paper dollar, I exchanged it with a silver one, fearing that paper currency was counterfeit. I ran back to my companions and told them the happy news that America was "fine."

When I told them of my success, they did not believe me until they saw the money and counted it with their hands, just as Thomas did. Then they believed what I had told them and asked me to buy each of them a basket. I did and spent all the night teaching them how to sell and sharing with them all that I had learned. First, you need to greet: "*kood mornin*" then "*bayy som tin today*" and I continued with them until they memorized the lesson.

In the morning, we separated and went selling and returned in the evening, each telling the others about his success. Every day, each of my companions sold for two or three riyals, while I never sold for less than seven riyals. But our luck did not last long because one of us, Jirjis Mukarbil, was arrested by the police in Germantown [PA] because he did not have a permit to sell, *lisen* [license].[6] He was thrown in jail and we cannot tell you the difficulties and obstacles we encountered in trying to find out where he was. A week later, we learned that he was in jail and that he had spent all the time eating and drinking nothing until he nearly starved to death. We took him away in a very sorry state and we spent our time looking after him because he was not even able to swallow the milk we poured down his throat and vomited it out. When he recovered and was strong enough to travel, we went to New York where we met many of our countrymen, all of whom were "merchants" selling rosaries, prayer books, crucifixes, icons and other things. The number of Syrian merchants in New York in 1885 was fifteen "baskets" including Salim al-Ghazz who carried coal. I suggested to him to join us, which he did.

From this report, the friendly reader can learn what tribulations and difficulties the first emigrants faced.

3. From *The Traveler's Guidebook: And the History of America* by Saj'an Effendi A'raj Sa'adeh (published 1896)

[*Kitāb dalīl al-musāfir: tārīkh Amāyrka* (Ba'abda, Lebanon: the Ottoman Press, 1896]

* * *

"SUICIDE"

People commit suicide either because they are poor or unemployed. In order to escape the fangs of hunger and the talons of poverty, many commit suicide, as you can see, without having any regrets about leaving this miserable world and its transitory possessions. Some commit suicide because of dire poverty, while others do so because of love that takes hold of them and controls their feelings; there are others who commit suicide after falsely being accused and in order to escape the punishment of the law. There are many other reasons, but nothing should cause the destruction of what God has made.

People commit suicide in many ways: either by poisoning or by shooting themselves. This is one of the evil customs that our countrymen have picked up from the Americans and which they have practiced. Would that we could imitate the Americans in their great projects and huge enterprises that have given them pride and brought them vast riches!

Some of our young men have committed suicide, and so, after asking for God's forgiveness, we have thought fit to publicize the news of their suicide so that others will learn and be warned.

The most unlucky Khalil al-Sawabini lived on 92 Washington Street, New York, with some other Syrian tenants. He was talking with one of them who was sitting next to him and in due course, he sighed and said to him: "Soon you will hear about what has happened to me because I am sick of this life. All my hopes have been dashed and I am now in dire straits in this foreign land. It is as if mountains have fallen on my head." As soon as he finished he left to his room, combed his hair, adjusted his clothes in front of the mirror, and returned to where he had been sitting. He was so despondent and depressed that he kept to himself. Then one of the people there started unburdening him of his morbid thoughts and hallucinations: he encouraged him with gentle words, commiserating on his tribulations. But the kindly words were useless and all of a sudden, Khalil said: "This is the last hour of a miserable life which I have endured in suffering and wretchedness and fruitless labor." He then pulled a gun from his pocket, the kind with six bullets, and he shot himself in the belly and died instantly.

No one sitting there had even thought he would commit suicide so abruptly and unexpectedly. He left behind him a riyal, four or five cartridges, two silk handkerchiefs, a freight invoice for a box of merchandise, a pocketknife, a stamp with his name on it, a briefcase with some documents, and a receipt from a Chinese laundry. The time of his suicide was eight o'clock in the evening of Thursday, 9 April 1894, in number 92 Washington Street in the city of New York.

He had been honest in his dealings, trustworthy in his business, gentle, well mannered, and kind to his friends. He was not over twenty-five and had been born in Damascus, Syria.

Not long after the suicide of Khalil al-Sawabini in New York, another disaster befell the Syrian community by the loss of another young man in the prime of his youth for reasons that need not be mentioned since they are unimportant. At one o'clock in the afternoon of Friday, 20 April 1894, news of the suicide of Yanni Mikhbat reached the Syrians in their stores and dwellings on Washington Street. It spread by informants as quickly as batting an eyelid. The Syrians had turned that street into their headquarters, and so it became known and associated with them.

He committed suicide at eleven of the above-mentioned day by shooting himself in the head which killed him instantly. As for the suicide of the son of ʿAbdallah Karam in Quarabu [Mexico?]: the reason was that the aforementioned young man fell in love with a girl whose father refused to her to marry him. After he failed in all his attempts, he turned to suicide by stabbing himself in the belly with a knife – bringing death on that unfortunate lover.

And there are many other disasters and calamities that have befallen our countrymen who have followed in the wicked tracks of the Americans: would that we could imitate their good deeds or at least preserve the honor of our name so that we do not tarnish it with shame. How many are the horrible deeds that have been committed by those who belong to our dear country! (82–5)

4. From *The Syrian Soldier in Three Wars* by Jibraʾil Ilyas Ward, al-Tarabulsi, 1898 (published 1919)

[*Kitāb al-jundī al-Sūrī fī thalāth ḥurūb* (New York: The Syrian-American Press, 1919) by Lt Gabriel E. Ward, S.A.W. V., G. E. W.V. M. C. – B. F. – C. M.]

EDITOR'S NOTE

Ward was born in Tripoli, Lebanon. His father was the first translator to the Russian consul – suggesting that he belonged to the Orthodox Christian community.

What is known about him appears in the account he published in 1919 which introduces him as a young man living in Springfield, Massachusetts. He had two brothers, Hani and Fuʾad, in San Paulo, Brazil. In 1898, he enlisted to fight in the Spanish–American War in Cuba and found himself advantaged for knowing Spanish, though at the same time disadvantaged because he did not look American and had dark skin (25). He was well read and wrote in good classical Arabic (although he made some grammatical mistakes).

After Cuba, he returned to New York and unsuccessfully tried to muster support among the emigrants against Ottoman rule in his homeland. He then worked as a translator (English–Spanish) to the government officials who went to Cuba to reclaim the bodies of the American dead. After reading an advertisement in Kawkab America asking for volunteers to fight in the Philippines, he joined as a translator for the military government there. In 1913, he returned to Boston, married a Damascene girl, and moved to Yarmouth, Nova Scotia, where he opened a "Dry Goods" store. Later he would describe himself as "Syrian by origin, Canadian by citizenship."

A fire destroyed his store in September 1914, and so he enlisted to fight with the Allied Forces in WWI (Canada being part of the Commonwealth). He traveled to London and from there to France and described the horrors of the trench warfare, along with the Battle of the Somme in 1916. During this time, he sent articles to al-Hoda about the course of the war that gained him the reputation of a heroic soldier, jabbar/mighty. Ward was wounded and moved to a military hospital in London, where he learned about the Syrian community in England: that some of the Syrian men who fought in the war and whose names Ward mentioned had had English mothers and Syrian fathers.

Ward promised another volume in which he would describe his service in the "secret police." But he never wrote it.[7]

In the selection below, Ward repeated the jingoism against Cubans that had inundated the American press; he also fell victim to the anti-Spanish racism that was widely expressed and disguised as patriotism. Ward wanted to present himself in the account as the great believer and defender of American values – although, curiously, he recorded the views of one of his workmates who explained how much the war was a capitalist ploy. Although anti-Spanish feelings were high, not all Arab emigrants shared in them: Ameen Rihani wrote a scathing attack on the newspapers that propagated falsities about the casus belli of the war (the sinking of the Maine): the war, he wrote on 10 May 1898, was unjust, and the goal was not to liberate the Cubans but to wreak vengeance on the Spanish, who were being derided in racist language in "all the newspapers of the republic."[8]

* * *

"THE AMERICAN FLAG"

This glorious flag of ours, the flag of stars and stripes, flutters above the celestial edifice of freedom which was built by the hands of its valiant heroes. It celebrates the great history of America and the greatness of the American and his achievements in religion and literature, commerce and industry, invention and science, and other areas of excellence. The flag has been enshrined since the beginnings and it will continue to be enshrined until the printing of this book: it will continue forever, with God's will and protection. It enshrines the noble ideal and honorable principle, I mean, "the divine right of freedom for man." Each of its three dazzling colors points to true freedom, and each of its shining stars and its straight stripes represents true freedom.

The freedom which the victorious American flag stands for does not include the chaos that results from adventurism and desecration and injustice; rather, it is the true, stable, and organized freedom that is protected by the constitution and by the just laws that ensure each person his right.

Long live America, the origin of freedom, the mother of justice, the cradle of the free, and the home of the reformers. May its victorious flag continue to flutter in the skies of justice and service to humanity forever and ever, Amen.

"ENLISTMENT, COMBAT IN CUBA, AND RETURN"

It is widely known that enlistment in America was, at that time, voluntary not compulsory, and there was no law to force subjects to enlist in military service at a certain age. And so, as soon as President McKinley announced his need for soldiers to fight Spain, thousands of young, sturdy men from all around the United States rushed to the enlistment offices to serve Uncle Sam.

At that time, the author was living in Springfield, Massachusetts, working in a telephone wire factory, and lodging with an Irish family.

One day, as I was having dinner with some fellow lodgers, we started talking about war and enlistment. One of the group by the name of John Maloney, who is Irish, said:

"You, young men. Your talk shows that you know nothing about war and its woes and calamitous consequences. As for me, I have read a lot about wars and their evils and devastations and I would be more than a fool if I supported war or enlisted in the army. War brings profit to the rich and the monopolists and woe and misery to the poor like us. Let the rich with profits and assets enlist first."

An Irish boy by the name of Edward Mahoney lifted his tea cup and said:

"If I were of the right age for the army I would not have let John finish his words, dripping with cowardice. I would have rushed immediately to enlist and fight under the honored flag of America. Ah, I wish I were over 16 years old."

His youthful face shone with excitement and disdainful pride. Everyone sitting there applauded him and praised his patriotism and enthusiasm. As soon as we finished eating, we went into the sitting room and continued talking and smoking. Then one of us said:

"We have declared war on the hot tamale eaters and there is nothing that stops us from going to enlist and heeding the call of our resolute president. In fact, I heard today that he is asking for 2,000 volunteers from our city. So, what do you plan to do?"

He then turned to the aforementioned John Maloney and said:

"Why are you quiet, John?"

John answered with a smile: "There are five young men here, all meeting the age requirement for enlistment. If you enlist, I will go with you," whereupon we all shouted, "*Hurray* John, *hurray!*"

We left the sitting room brimming with excitement and readiness to enlist. And then Thomas Sullivan said:

"Your commitment is great, all of you. But you should know that you cannot be soldiers unless you pass the physical exam. I am sure that we four will pass it easily, but what about this Syrian, Rose?"

John Parker turned and asked me: "Rose, how is your health? Are you strong enough and free of all bodily defects?" To which I answered that I was. Thompson turned to Sullivan saying: "And what about his poor command of English?" Edward Mahoney said to him: "Does the government need writers for the ministry of war or strong arms that can shoot at the enemy? Is it not enough that Rose is courageous, with a strong build? That is all that is needed in a soldier."

We walked to the enlistment office and when we got there we met an officer who asked us what we wanted. We told him we wanted to enlist in the army. He smiled and started writing down the name of each of us, his place of birth and age, and other information. Then he led us, one after another, into the medical exam room where we were examined, according to the rules. When it was John Malone's turn,[9] we heard the examining doctor say that the size of his chest was one inch less than what is accepted. Malone unsuccessfully pleaded with him to ignore the size and let him join his friends who had passed the exam.

Then it was my turn for the exam and I entered, whereupon the doctor looked me over, from top to bottom, and asked me:

"What is your race?"

"Syrian," I said.

"Take off your clothes," he said. I did, and he examined me more thoroughly than the others who had gone before me. When he finished, he gave his approval. I left the examination room and met with the question of the four friends: "Are you with us?"

"Yes," I said, "I am with you in body and soul and nothing will separate me from you except death."

They said: "We should agree that if they reject John Malone in the military, we will refuse to enlist." I agreed, "We shall do that."

The doctor heard what we said and came out and said: "I am sorry that your friend cannot be accepted because of his chest size." One of us, Thomas Sullivan, said to him: "If John is not accepted, we will not enlist." He turned to the rest of us and we all shouted in concurrence. When the doctor saw our determination to include John and our unwillingness to enlist if he insisted on rejecting him, he said: "Well, then, John will go with you," and he wrote down his name among those who had been accepted.

Then an officer approached us and said: "Each of you, raise your right hand." We did, and he started reciting to us the oath which we repeated after him: that we will be loyal to the American government and to the military institution, etc. Then he handed each of us the American flag and we swore loyalty and fealty to that victorious flag. He then dismissed us saying: "Come back tomorrow morning."

We left elated but the one who was the happiest was John Malone who thanked us for our true affection and he took us to a bar where he bought us beer. Then we returned home and spent our night merrily. In the morning, we collected all the belongings we did not plan to take with us and gave them to the landlady. John Maloney said on our behalf: "Keep those things, and if we return, we will take them back; if not, give them to the poor." We then bid her farewell and went to the military base where an officer met us and took us to the train station that transported us to the city of South Birmingham [Alabama].

It was teeming with soldiers from numerous battalions. A member of the military met us and asked: "Are you volunteers?" "Yes," we answered and showed him the documents which the officer who arranged our travel had given us. He signaled to us to follow him until we reached the camp where he said to a sergeant there: "Give these brave ones the honorable fatigues of the army." After we got dressed, we went out, each looking at the other and laughing – and what increased our laughter was the sight of John Maloney: his military outfit was too large and he wore the right shoe on the left foot and vice versa.

An employee led us to a tent and said: "This is yours. You are now Company B, Battalion 2 of the State of Massachusetts. When you hear the trumpet and see the soldiers going to eat, follow them." We entered the tent and were overjoyed to see it had everything the soldier needs: bed, mattress, covers and other things. As soon as we sat down, we heard the trumpet and saw the soldiers lining up, and so we joined them and did what they did. One of the officers shouted: "*Attention. Right. Turn,*" which means, pay attention and turn to the right. John Malone turned to the left and we followed suit whereupon the officer said: "Great to have such soldiers who do not know left from right!" We corrected our mistake and turned in the direction we had been told. The officer then called: "*Quick march,*" that is, walk quickly. We marched until we reached the dining hall and sat at the tables prepared for us. After we finished, we left the dining hall in single file and the officer shouted "*Dismiss,*" which means go, and so each went to his own place.[10]

South Birmingham was cold and so we had to squeeze together at night to stay warm. At five o'clock the trumpet sounded for reveille. One of us called: "Come on guys, time to rise." Maloney said: "How can we get up in this freezing cold? I swear by my pipe I will not. Go tell them Malone does not like this miserable way of life and will return to Springfield to the telephone wire factory. The weather there is nicer than here." We laughed at him and got dressed and left the tent to find a long line of soldiers led by an officer. We joined the line and the officer began to train us in athletic activities, after which a fat man with intimidating features and riding a black horse started sizing up the soldiers' movements very carefully. We found out then that he was the colonel of our battalion. He said:

"We need junior recruits, corporal and sergeant and such. Who of you had knowledge of the military before enlisting?"

John Malone raised his hand, indicating that he had. And so, the colonel asked him:

"Where did you learn about military training?"

He answered: "In the public schools and by reading various books."

"Fine," he said. Then he turned to the officer and said: "Write down his name so he can be tested." The colonel then turned to the soldiers saying:

"Whoever has any familiarity with the military, step forward. The rest go back to your tents."

Thomas Sullivan turned to John Malone and whispered in his ear:

"What do you think John? Do I know anything about the military?"

"Sure," Malone answered him. "Don't you remember we were at the same school and the teacher used to show us military maneuvers? Come along. You will get to be a sergeant."

We laughed at Malone and his stupidity and remembered how only yesterday he had not been able to distinguish left from right: no doubt he was a trained soldier! And so, the rest of us went back to our tents.

It happened that while I was sitting in front of my tent, the captain of my company came up to me. He had known me in Springfield where he had been chief of police. He asked me:

"Do you like the life of the military?"

I answered: "Yes, my friend."

He said: "I remember that you once told me you knew various foreign languages. Do you know Spanish?"

"Yes," I said, whereupon he smiled, saluted me, and left.

In the evening, after dinner, I wandered among the many battalions until I reached the 9th battalion. A soldier there was playing on a violin and I stood listening to the music. Suddenly, one of the officers put his hand on my shoulder and told me to follow him.

"Whereto, officer?" I asked, but he did not answer and instead ordered two soldiers to escort me to one of the tents. They did, and took me inside the tent. I could not believe what was happening to me, as if I were in a dream. Then I saw two other soldiers with rifles, each with a bayonet known as "*sinka*." The officer said to them:

"Watch this man very carefully and if he escapes, you will be severely punished."

I was totally bewildered at being treated in this manner; I could not understand why. I asked one of the soldiers who was guarding me why I was treated that way; he did not answer and just glared at me with hostility and anger. At that point, I started wondering and remembering the events of my life trying to find a reason for my arrest and close guard. But I could not think of anything at all that could explain this bad treatment. After two hours – and I leave it to the reader to imagine what my feelings and thoughts were – the officer who had arrested me returned and led me into the presence of the general, who looked very distinguished. He asked me:

"Do you speak Spanish?"

I nodded.

"What is your name?"

"Jibra'il Rose," I answered.

He stared at me, examining the emotions on my face. He continued: "Where did you get this military outfit?"

And immediately, I knew why I had been arrested: they took me for a Spanish spy who had secretly infiltrated the camp to pass on intelligence to the Spaniards about the movements of the American soldiers. To exonerate myself, I explained that I had enlisted in the American army in the city of Springfield. He sent a soldier to call the captain of our company who, when he arrived and saw me, was quite surprised:

"What brought you here?"

The general asked him if he knew me and if I was one of his soldiers.

"Yes," the captain answered, "I know him well and he is Syrian."

The general said that an officer had seen me wandering from tent to tent and from battalion to battalion and thought me a Spanish spy – which is why I was arrested. The officer was not in the wrong: Rose was the only soldier in all the companies whose skin color and features resembled those of Spaniards.

The officer smiled and said: "I assure you that Rose is not a spy."

The general and the officer who had arrested me apologized and released me. I walked with our captain to our tent and he urged me not to leave my company so I would not fall victim to suspicion again.

Four days later, the governor of Massachusetts [Roger Wolcott] came to bid us farewell. We had been ordered to leave for Tampa in the state of Florida. The Massachusetts soldiers lined up in front of the platform that had been erected especially for the governor and all the dignitaries with him. He stood on that platform and gave a speech full of advice and wise council. He said to the soldiers:

"You brave ones, you are going to destroy the yoke of slavery and remove the bonds of injustice from your brothers in humanity. I ask you to be courageous and resolute and redeem the American flag with your blood, and to prove to the world your loyalty, drive, courage, and nobility of goal. You will return with victory on your banners and your service crowned with success. And if you capture the enemy, be compassionate and merciful to him and remember that you are Americans and your duty is to care for the defeated and show clemency," and other such language that exuded wisdom and confidence. Everybody applauded him and bowed their heads in respect.

On 30 May 1898, we sailed from the port of Tampa. We were 15,000 soldiers under the command of General [William R.] Shafter. We continued at sea until 15 June when we reached Santiago in the island of Cuba. In front of us, we saw the famous fort of Morro Castile [Castillo de los Tres Reyes Magos del Morro]. The ship sailed around the island and we disembarked in a place called Jacqui, a large forest covered with thick trees and a sugar factory which uses the famous sugar cane. Our disembarkation was comic: they ordered fifty men of the infantry into a boat, but when the rowers could not find a good place to moor, they would stop in the water whereupon the men would jump out and walk for about 200 feet until their feet could touch the ground. As for the cavalry, they were even more comical: they brought vessels and forced the horses on them and headed towards the shore. Once they got to a certain depth, they would push the horse with its rider into the sea, after which the horse would swim with its rider to the shore. When we had all reached land, we marched in single files towards the port of Siboney during which time we seized carts full of rice. We arrived in Siboney hungry and exhausted and so we started eating everything we could find of fruit and other edibles. We felt revived and our knees stronger. We spent the night in Siboney in what is called Dog Tents (*Docket Tent*) – so named because they were narrow and low tents, each enough for only two soldiers. Each soldier had to carry half the tent and could not enter it except by crawling. We were protected from the sea by the [USS] St Louis, which shone projectors at night in all directions.

The next morning, we had breakfast – consisting of hard beans [navy beans] cooked and preserved in cans. They then distributed the rations to the soldiers: two cans of the aforementioned beans and two of tomatoes, twenty pieces of dried bread, known as *bixmat*,[11] half a *pound* of coffee, tea, and sugar and whatever was needed of salt, spices and other things; also, forty cartridges, and a *rubber* belt. The soldier had to carry everything on his back, becoming soldier and porter at the same time. This would not have been a problem had it not been so hot in Cuba. As soon as we started walking, you saw the soldiers' load of tomato and bean cans and the rubber blankets thrown on the road. It so happened that I had with me a pair of trousers I did not need and so I tied up its legs turning it into the saddlebag of Shaykh Hussayn when he goes down from the village to the city. I started picking up what the soldiers threw, putting everything in the saddlebag until it was full. In the evening, the soldiers became hungry and so I opened my saddlebag and started selling them each can and each piece of bread for an American riyal, and so I made sixty riyals from that blessed saddlebag.

In the morning, we continued the march but suddenly heard the whizzing of bullets that fell on us like heavy rain. An army of Spaniards had laid a trap for us. At the head of our American army marched

Colonel Theodore Roosevelt with his famous company "*Balruff Raiders*" [Rough Raiders; The 1st United States Cavalry Volunteers]; sixteen of our men died by perfidy and forty were wounded. In a twinkling of an eye, the Americans attacked, like a lion out of the den, and fell on the Spaniards, hiding like rabbits, who fled desperately, leaving their dead behind along with large quantities of food and ammunition. In that battle, six American men were killed among whom was the famous wealthy man Hamilton Fisher [Hamilton Fish II, d. 24 June 1898] from New York; all were from the valorous company of Roosevelt.

On 28 June, we reached near the fortified city of El Caney, only five miles away from Santiago. We started sharpening our weapons and getting ready for a tough day of fighting. As I was talking to a Cuban man, Colonel Roosevelt passed by and asked me what the man was saying. I answered that he had told me there were 6,000 enemy soldiers in the city and that it is defended by three front moats and that there is a machine gun in the church steeple. Roosevelt was pleased but also surprised and asked me:

"Soldier, to which battalion do you belong?" I told him.

He continued: "Would you like to accompany me as translator?"

I answered: "Colonel, that would be a sign of my good fortune."

Roosevelt asked permission of my commander to have me accompany him. He was granted what he wanted and so I became Roosevelt's private chamberlain/*yawur*. On that same day, I met one of the Turkish pashas who had come to Cuba to observe the battles that were imminent, and he spoke Arabic. After we were introduced, he asked me where I came from.

"Tripoli of Syria," I answered.

"Bravo," he said, "a Tripolitan?"

"Yes."

"And are there other Syrians in the army?"

I answered: "I know one more Syrian soldier, and I have heard that there were some Syrian volunteers in the American army but I have not been lucky to meet them."

We stayed in that location until 30 June. In the evening of that day, we marched to the city of El Caney and camped so close to it that we could see the lights in the houses. We were ordered not to set up our tents that night, or to smoke or to speak in a loud voice, rather in whispers so that the enemy would not detect us. We spent the night in total silence and at dawn, we the infantry advanced towards the city. We marched stealthily; none could hear us and the trees, full of delicious fruit, gave us cover. At 6 am, the first shell was fired from one of our cannons, signaling the beginning of our first battle with the Spaniards.

I will not hide from my good reader that when the first shell was fired, I felt a stiffening in my muscles and joints. I was lying flat on the ground, my rifle in my hand, shaking in fear as trees shake when storm winds blow. Every time a shell was fired, my heartbeat increased and my body shook and I realized the meaning of the saying: "Watching a battle is easy." I started cursing the hour I surrendered to my impetuousness and enlisted. My fear grew even more when I saw one of my friends lying on the ground, covered in his own blood. Had I been standing, my knees would not have held me and doubtless, I would have sunk to the abyss.

As I was lying on the ground, I fired randomly from my rifle, without aiming: I could only see the houses of the village. But after an hour in that situation, my strength returned to me and I regained my soldierly courage. I stood up and started shooting at the enemy and every time a soldier fell in front of me, I became stronger and more resolute. Soon, I started enjoying the sound of bullets as music delights the ear of the listener. I thought myself shooting in a marriage celebration, and not in some bloody conflict. At 2 pm, we were given orders to attack the city. The voices of the soldiers rose in victory: as we attacked, the earth shook under our feet and we were like the lion attacking its prey. In a few hours, the enemy contingent surrendered and we occupied the city with thrill and exultation.

I will tell this episode which is quite sad but which contains a lesson to him who does good to those who don't deserve it. The long and short of it is that while we were launching our aforementioned attack, one of my comrades saw a Spanish soldier who had fallen in a moat and was buried up to his neck in mud. It is likely that he was hiding there when one of the shells fell and pushed the mud and covered him. My friend the American soldier pitied that poor man, and so he started digging him out to save him from suffocation. When the Spaniard pulled his hand out he grabbed a bayonet next to him and stabbed the kindly American in his back and through his chest. When I saw that deed by the mean and ungrateful Spaniard, I took my *sinka* and struck him in the neck driving it through the rear of his head. He fell dead over the body of my afore-mentioned comrade. I was pleased with myself and found in that quick and just revenge great satisfaction and repeated the saying of the poet:

He who does good to those who do not deserve it
is like one who lights candles in the halls of the blind.

In the evening, we went around gathering the bodies of the dead along with the weapons and everything else that had been left behind. After dinner, we marched to San Juan Mountain [Battle of San Juan Hill, 1 July 1898] where we found the battle raging and the 72nd Company retreating before the advancing Spaniards. We shouted to them encouragingly so much so that they were reinvigorated and joined us in the attack on that aforementioned mountain. We climbed it like goats climbing oak trees and when we reached the fortifications we found that the staunch hero Theodore Roosevelt had gotten there first, accompanied by his hardened men, and had overrun those fortifications and driven away the enemy. His soldiers then scattered in different directions to prevent unexpected attacks and to protect us at night. I was assigned the 2 am shift and the spot in which we stood watch was between El Caney and San Juan Mountain.[12]

At 3 am, I went down with three friends to drink. It was very dark because of the thick trees in the valley. As we were drinking from a fountain and washing our faces and cracking jokes, gunshots were fired at us from the other side. Three of my friends fell down dead, covered in their own blood. I escaped as if by a miracle. I fled as fast as I could in the hope of safety and hid behind a tree which I used as a cover to protect me from enemy bullets. From my hiding place, I began firing back and soon I heard one screaming: "He killed me, he killed me, that gringo" (which is the way they call Americans). I continued firing until I felt the butt of a rifle slam my chest. I quickly grabbed it with all my strength and pushed it away. A bullet tore away one of my fingers and I felt bullets slamming into my back and thigh. I realized I would die soon and I started crawling on my belly until I fainted and could remember nothing.

When I woke up, I found myself lying on green grass under one of the trees and above me a young woman, more angelic than human, whose chest was adorned by a red cross. She looked at me with kindness and compassion, smiling a smile that made me forget my pain. It was a sincere and guileless smile. When she saw that I was reviving, she asked me how I was. I answered:

"I feel well as long as you are near me." And she started washing my blood-drenched wounds with her gentle hands which are sanctified by virtue and dedicated to acts of charity and relief of pain. I hoped that my wounds would continue to bleed so that she would spend more time cleaning them.

The company captain came up and said:

"Congratulations on your safety."

I asked: "How did you bring me here?"

"When we heard the sound of the bullets in the valley," he said, "we quickly sent a regiment of soldiers and they surrounded the valley until dawn and then descended and captured forty Spanish soldiers and found eight dead. We found you unconscious in the grass and thought you dead at first, but then we realized that you were alive and so, we brought you here. As for your friends, they are dead."

Three days later, we returned to Siboney and from there sailed to the city of Key West in Florida. From there, we boarded the Red Cross train which had been waiting there and it took us to an army compound in Atlanta, Georgia.

One day, while I was walking in the gardens admiring the beauty of nature and smelling the beautiful roses, I saw a young soldier, in the prime of his youth, tall, attractive, his stature reflecting his liberality and noble lineage. I stared at him and my heart yearned to speak to him. It is said: "There is a way for hearts to meet." He also looked at me, and so I went up to him and asked him about his origin. He said with a gentle smile on his lips, "I am Syrian." I swear: Jacob was not happier at finding Joseph than I was at that moment. That courageous man whom I had the honor of meeting was Khalil Bayk al-Aswad the Lebanese.[13] We sat down and started talking and thanking our good fortune (if there is anything like that) for bringing us together.

We spent two weeks in Atlanta after which I left with sixteen soldiers back to Springfield where the citizens had offered to pay for our medical expenses.

As we were sitting on the train, I did not realize that my cigar burnt through my military hat, making big holes in it. Anyone who looked at it would have thought it had been in the thick of battle. When the train reached the station in Richmond, Virginia, we went out to rest for half an hour. The citizens of Richmond had heard about our train journey and so a large crowd surrounded us in the station to see the "Heroes of Cuba" and to welcome them. They laid a table full of the best food and drink and so we sat down, grateful for their bounty and patriotism. Unexpectedly, a young woman of 16 years, as if of the *houri* from heaven, came up to me and said:

"I see that your hand is wounded. May I carve the meat for you?"

"I don't know how to thank you, my dear lady," I replied. "If you will feed me, I will be most grateful because my other hand is paralyzed with rheumatism." So, she sat near me feeding me just like a mother nursing her child.

I leave it to the reader to imagine how delicious that food was in my mouth and I wished I had the belly of the whale that had swallowed the Prophet Jonah and that this beautiful woman would fill it.

After we finished eating, I thanked her for her kindness and her consideration and went to the train. A man, who appeared to be rich, waved at me saying:

"Soldier, your hat has been in battle. I can see bullet holes in the sides."

"Yes," I said. "Bullet holes from the battle of San Juan."

He said: "How I wish to own it. Will you sell to me?"

"No," I said, "I have no wish to sell it. But if you really want it, I will give it you as a present."

He took it with thanks, wrote down my name and company number, and gave me twenty-five dollars. I returned to the train bare-headed, and after we started moving, I bargained with a soldier and bought his hat for five dollars. I then burnt holes in it with the bullets of my cigarettes so it would look exactly like the other hat which our friend took in Richmond.

When the train reached the station in the capital Washington, we were asked to go down and meet President McKinley who was coming to greet us. They set up chairs for us in the corridors of the beautiful Washington Station. Soon, the honorable president arrived, exuding grandeur and stateliness. He was surrounded by the country's ministers and dignitaries. He drew near and greeted us like a father to his children and not like a president to his subordinates. We said:

"God protect democracy and may the light of freedom and justice ever shine."

The president then shook hands with each of us, smiling and beaming with joy. At his order, cigarette packs and boxes of sweets were distributed to us as the crowds that filled the station and all the space outside called out in celebration: for we were the first they had seen of the wounded of the Spanish[–American] War. After the president and his entourage left, and as we were on our way out, an employee from the railway asked me about the holes in my hat. I answered:

"Don't you know that we are returning from war? Or do you think the soldier fights bare-headed?" He thought that rifle bullets had been shot through the hat and not the bullets of my cigarettes on the train. He said:

"Will you take fifteen riyals for it?"

"Twenty," I said.

He happily paid.

I returned to the train feeling certain I would buy another hat from one of my friends, but unfortunately, I had to remain bare-headed until we reached Springfield. When we arrived in New York City and left the carriage that transported us from the city, we found the people lining up the streets, like tightly built edifices, and as soon as they saw us, they welcomed us with shouts of celebration. Men shook our hands and women kissed us. The crowds were so thick we could not walk past them – we were to go to the train station that would take us to Springfield, and so a police force arrived and made room for us to pass through.

As I was climbing into the high train (*elevated train*) on my way to *Grand Central*, I heard a voice calling me by my name.

"Hello Jabr."

I turned and lo, it was my friend Khalil Ibrahim al-Shammas from Amyun al-Kurah [in North Lebanon, not far from Tripoli, Jibraʾil's birthplace]. I was overjoyed to see him and I told him that I will be going back to New York in the near future to see all the dear friends and compatriots there. When we reached the station and because there was still time before the train would depart, they led us into a special room in the station. Two policemen stood guard to keep people out, but a man entered without them preventing him. He came up to me and asked:

"Are you a Cuban?"

"No," I answered, "I am Syrian."

"Poor man," he said. "And what do you have to do with the war?"

I answered that I had enlisted in the army to fight the oppressors and to free the oppressed. I did everything for the love and honor of the victorious flag of America.

"Poor man, poor man," he repeated. Then he asked me: "Were you at the first battle in which the unfortunate sergeant Hamilton Fisher died?"

"Yes," I said, "and I was one of the four soldiers who carried his body to his last resting place."

No sooner had I finished my answer than he started crying and wiping the tears with his handkerchief. Truly, the sound of bullets and bombs did not have the effect on me as did the tears of this dignified man with such tender emotions. After he dried his tears and took control of himself, he took out from his wallet ten riyals and pushed them into my hand, as he did with every other soldier. He then left without saying a word. A policeman then entered and said:

"This rich and famous man is the father of Sergeant Hamilton Fisher who was killed in the first battle of the war."

When the time for departure came, we boarded the train and traveled to Springfield where we saw what no pen can describe. The citizens were crowding the station and its surroundings, carrying flags, and singing patriotic songs in praise of the "Heroes of Springfield." They had built special floats to carry us and so we left the train, amidst applause and victory cheers, climbed on, and started moving, with the police in front of us and the fire brigade behind us, followed by Civil War veterans in their official uniforms. In front of us all was a group of beautiful women dressed in white and carrying flags in their hands. Behind us came the carriage of the city mayor, government officials, major traders and others and the whole grand procession moved down the main street in the city until we reached the city hall. Whitman, the owner of the most important newspaper in town stood there, and delivered a speech that was most appropriate for the occasion:

"American citizens are by necessity called on to enlist to defend the flag of their country. As for this stranger, I mean Rose the Syrian soldier, he enlisted because of his immense love and concern for our country and our flag. We must all thank him heartily."

Everyone repeated words of praise, shouting "*Hurrah* to Rose, the Syrian soldier."

After that wonderful celebration, the families of the soldiers went up to greet their own. As for me, the stranger, the city mayor and the afore-mentioned newspaper owner took my hand and led me to a float and sat next to me until we reached the most famous hospital in the city. The mayor said before he left me:

"Valiant soldier, we will help with all that you need."

They led me into a room decorated with the best furniture, above which was the American flag, and said: "This is your room until you recover from your wounds."

Of the treatment and care I received at the hospital, the kindness of the nurses and doctors: I cannot praise them enough. The flowers that were sent to me by kindly people filled the spacious halls. Three days later, a distinguished lady/*shaykha*, advanced in age, came to see me, a woman of dignity and stature, accompanied by a very beautiful young woman. She was wearing black as a sign of mourning. The distinguished lady shook my hand and said: "I wish to introduce you to Mrs Blanche Whitman, sister of Ferrar Whitman who died in the battle of El Caney." She then asked me whether I had seen him at the time of his death and I answered that sadly I had, adding that before he breathed his last, he asked me to convey his love to his family. She broke down in tears. After she dried her tears, they started talking to me and continued asking ques-tions for an hour and a half. As they were about to leave, they gave me a gold watch and a chain. And they left.

It is worth mentioning something about the aforementioned Ferrar Whitman:

The day before we reached El Caney, I ran out of cigarettes just like everyone else. But I really needed to smoke and, not knowing what to do, I looked, and lo, the aforementioned Whitman was smoking. I went up to him and asked him for a cigarette. He said that he had searched in all his pockets and had found that very last cigarette. But a short while later, I saw him smoking again, and so I started watching him and found out that he would hide behind a tree and take out the tobacco box from his breast pocket, roll a cigarette, and then hide the box. So, I walked up and said to him:

"Your lie will not work on me. Give me some tobacco."

He answered: "Even if my father came all the way from Springfield I would not give him a cigarette."

Angrily I said: "I hope you die and I take your tobacco box."

As fate would have it, that poor man was killed the next day and as he was dying I went to him and he said in a faltering voice: "Rose, when you return to Springfield, convey my love to my family." He then died.

I stuck my hand inside his breast pocket and took out the tobacco box and lit a cigarette and turned to his dead body and said:

"May God have mercy on you for the relief you have given me. By God, I would not exchange this tobacco for its weight in gold."

After that, Mr Whitman came to my room and I told him that I wanted to go to New York to see my friends and compatriots but that I had no money and had no idea when the government was going to pay us our salaries. He consulted the doctor about the possibility of my travel who said: "It is okay only if he finds someone to change the bandage on his finger."

I answered: "There are doctors in New York who are my compatriots and they will look after me."

Mr Whitman bade me farewell and published in his newspaper, the most important in the city, as I have mentioned, that the Syrian soldier who had been wounded in the battles of Cuba wished to visit his friends in New York but had no money. Some hours after the announcement was made in the newspaper, the postman arrived with three letters addressed to me. When I opened the first two, I found money transfers for twenty-five riyals with the names of the senders. When I opened the third, I found fifty riyals without the name of the sender who wanted to show his generosity but remain anonymous. The next day, I received other letters, each with money in it. All in all, I collected (just) 460 dollars.

Two days later, I prepared myself for travel and took the train to New York City, home of the largest Syrian community in the diaspora. I was overjoyed to meet people I had known before and was lucky to meet many of the writers and distinguished members of the community. (19–39)

5. "The Greatness of America" by Bulus Effendi al-Khawli, 1905 (published in *al-Muqtataf,* 1906)

[*Azamat Amāyrka (al-Muqtataf,* November 1906)]

EDITOR'S NOTE

Al-Khawli traveled to the United States in the summer of 1905. He was a professor at the Syrian Protestant College [later the American University of Beirut], and he gave this talk in April 1906. That it appeared in al-Muqtataf is significant: the journal editor admired America, but was not unwilling to publish an article about the "Greatness of America" that also showed its dark side. Al-Khawli was familiar with the writings of Darwin and Marx and used their views about the survival of the fittest and the capitalist control of the means of production to criticize conditions in the United States. In his talk, he presented a measured analysis of the culture of the United States at the same time that he defended the values of the "East" – a defense that visitors and emigrants repeatedly presented to their readers.

Al-Khawli denounced duplicity and dishonesty in America, and defended his fellow Easterners, perhaps after hearing stereotypically "Orientalist" views about them from his hosts. He also discussed a topic that appeared in many other Arabic writings of that time: American greed and love of money. All authors who did not remain in the United States mentioned that fact, revealing the ambiguity they felt about the greed in the accumulation of wealth: on the one hand, there was poverty and the desire for amelioration and affluence; on the other, there was endless toil and labor. Al-Khawli praised hard work, as many other writers did, having discovered that it was not just a means of ensuring survival but also an ethic, a way of American life, a national goal.

The article ends abruptly. It is not clear why.

*   *   *

If you get the opportunity to write the history of a people, do not just focus on the past, but make space in your pages for explaining cause and effect and for showing how justice is the basis of government, and knowledge the bulwark of civilization. Show also that one nation rises and another falls according to the laws of nature, which operate in animates and inanimates.

When you arrive in New York for the first time, I do not blame you if you become confused and stand looking around at the various sides of American civilization. Your eyes will meet with constant movement – of people and trains, carriages and coaches of different kinds and shapes and names, all hurrying in great speed to which your eyes had not been accustomed before.

One goes to America with images in one's minds based on information gathered from past reading of books or from listening to speeches or from conversing with Americans, Syrians and others. But those images, much as they might be detailed and reliable, can never reflect reality because hearing is not like seeing, and because people rarely describe anything without inserting their own biases. If, for instance, one person believes that all Americans belong to a noble class as represented by the missionaries here [in Beirut] – the class of the learned and the virtuous, the trustworthy and the selfless – that person will soon change his mind after seeing immoralities and villainies the like of which he had not known before. And if he thought that America was the land of equality and justice: when he sees the prejudices of the government and the inconsistencies in laws, and when he reads about injustices so great of which he had never heard before, he will conclude: people are everywhere the same; we are all in the same boat. And if that person thought that America was the land of wealth and riches – the land that overflows with gold and silver where people find money pouring down on them wherever they go – it won't be long before he changes his mind and discovers that making money requires hard work and that many are the poor [in the United States] who spend days without food.

This is the problem: we hear so many things from people and believe them – until we experience them ourselves. Only then do we change our minds and find out the truth.

I reached New York in the middle of last August [1905]. The sky welcomed us with terrifying lightning, thunder, and rain the like of which I had not seen before, making me think that I was in a terrible December night and not in the middle of August. I said to myself: "I seek refuge with God from a country where its summer is winter." I then traveled west to St Louis and visited its great Exhibition and was stunned at the magnitude of wealth and knowledge. I returned via Chicago, Niagara Falls, and Philadelphia to New York. Throughout, I was astonished by what I saw but failed to detect what was behind what I was seeing – just like every foreigner looking at things he had not seen before.

I stayed in New York to teach at one of its famous universities. I listened to the lectures of its professors, read the books of its scholars, and followed the intellectual activity of the people as it was reported daily in newspapers and magazines and in game parlors and clubs. I apprised myself of events and analyzed matters and only then was I able to see what lay behind the externalities. I identified the philosophy of this state of affairs and I grew to despise this civilization because it crushed the weak person, not because he was unfit for survival but because he did not cheat in his dealings or oppress other people, as the wealthy do. I saw the struggle for survival in the sphere of business and realized that it was not the survival of the fittest but of the wiliest. So, I said to myself: "Sociologists should change the words 'survival of the fittest' to 'survival of the wiliest.'" I then reflected on my views of the East and wondered to myself: "When will the East awaken from its slumber and learn of the West's designs on it, and when will the Easterner open his eyes and see that Europe befriends him only to achieve its own objectives and not because of admiration? It rubs him with oil not to relax his muscles and strengthen them but to make it easier to swallow him. This is the age of trade and international rivalry and Westerners travel far and wide in the world to expand their commerce: they go to Asia and Africa on the pretext of enlightening the populations there and introducing modern civilization to them."

Cursed be what they do.

I saw the greatness of America and wondered: what has brought about its greatness? It is a country that is not famous for its history or for its traditions. The tourist does not visit it to admire its ancient ruins or to study its archeology, nor to enter its churches or stroll in its museums. It is a vast and spacious land: its soil is rich, its mineral resources and forests are vast, its rivers and lakes are enormous, its plains are immense, its mountains are high, and its [time] zones are varied. The constituents of civilization are amply available to the point where some have said that America is greater than its people.

But: is the secret in the land or in the people? And who are the people of America?

They are a mix of every nation and language: those who have left their homelands in search of religious and political freedom; the persecuted and the poor from the Old World who could not make a living; the seekers of fortune and worshippers of white and yellow [silver and gold] who were never deterred by obstacles or dangers; and the *zunuj* who were slaves but were later freed. The American character is made up of all these and has become a race strong in finance, trade and political institutions. This new nation, notwithstanding all the evils in it, has attained a very high level of progress so much so that it rivals the European countries.

So, what is the secret of its success?

The answer is that the Americans are a self-made nation built on the principles of fraternity, equality, and freedom. America left the chains of old and began to innovate: it freed its slaves who are now one ninth of the population, and it made them equal to all others in the eyes of the law. It recognized its deficiency in science and so it sought out the best researchers from Germany, England, and France; it so succeeded in organizing and improving its schools that even England, in recent years, has been sending delegations to learn about the educational system here and the courses of study. It opened its door to wage-earners and immigrants as a result of which its cities grew bigger and its industry, commerce, and agriculture flourished. Today, it is a populous nation of 80 million: its goal is unity, its motto is work, and its ally is wealth.

In America, you see wonders of nature and man-made wonders. You will see the power of the intellect, the might of the pen, the sharpness of the tongue, and the supreme authority of money. You will see how honorable work is, and you will find inscribed on the streets and the houses a rule not written in words – a rule saying that there is no shame in work, whatever it is; rather, shame, dire shame, is for man not to have work and to dream of living off the labor of others. In America, you will see everyone hard at work and not distracted from his goal. Even women vie with men in work and they have been widely successful.

Work is more important than pleasure. That is their golden rule: Americans chase after money and nothing will stop them, even if they sometimes have to resort to illegal means. And they make money to spend in whatever manner satisfies them; they do not save and thus do not live in frugality or abstinence. America is now in the age of money: all the nation pants after money. There are great industries: the meat industry, the ice industry, the petroleum industry, railway companies, the electrical trams, and life insurance companies. The companies are numberless and they monopolize and control all the sources of wealth.

The most effective means they use to publicize their goods and merchandise are advertisements; and how imaginative they are! This is one of the wonders of America.[14] Wherever one looks or walks, one's eyes will be drawn to colors or words or shapes, but most of the advertisements, ubiquitous as they are, are packs of lies: they accuse the Easterner of deceit and dishonesty, but had they been fair they would have said that the Easterner lies with his tongue because pressures force him to do so, but the Westerner lies with his deeds and finds financial justification for his deceit.

The most important place for placing advertisements is in the newspapers. They are the strangest that can be: they are quickly produced, widely distributed, cheap, impressively capable of collecting and presenting news, and read by all people. In New York alone, many newspapers are published and distributed numerous times daily, their size varying between ten to twelve large pages, and costing one cent (two *millims*). You find newspaper sellers calling out at every stop, station, and corner, and people buy the papers on their way to or from work. They read them on the trams or trains because they are pressed for time. But: "read and you will be happy; try [the objects that are advertised] and you will be disappointed" applies to many of the advertisements in the newspapers. Still, and notwithstanding jumbled reporting, exaggerated language, and extreme partisanship to political parties, these newspapers are proof of American glory and advancement. The freedom of the newspapers in their investigations makes them the vanguard of the ideas of the nation: they will not be silent about financial corruption or oppression by company owners but will attack them and expose their crooked ways in subverting the rights of the people. They point to errors that demand rectification. (885–8)

6. "From the Rooftops of New York City" by Ameen Rihani, 1907
(published in *al-Rihaniyyat*, vol. 1, 1968)

[*Fawqa sutūḥ New York* in *Al-Rīḥāniyyāt* (Beirut: Dar al-Rihani, 1968).]

EDITOR'S NOTE

Rihani arrived in the United States in 1888 and became one of the leading intellectuals among the mahjar *writers: in 1903 Muhammad Rashid Rida referred to him as, "that resident of America and one of the advocates of nationalism and an enemy to bigotry."[15] He was an active member in the Syrian community and wrote in Arabic and in English for numerous newspapers. He opposed the control of religion by the ecclesiastical Maronite institution, as a result of which he was excommunicated. Like Khawli, he excoriated the cruel American system of capitalism, and like other Arab writers in America, including Khalil Sakakini (see below), Rihani was a great believer in the Arab unity that Sheriff Hussein proclaimed at the beginning of the Arab Revolt in June 1916, ever hoping to see the model of the United States replicated in the East. He admired many aspects of America, but he bitterly criticized its unbridled capitalism; even in his first published article, which appeared on 10 May 1898 in al-Hoda in Philadelphia, with the ironic title "The Civilized American People," he expressed gratitude for the opportunities he had found, but denounced American political hypocrisy and militarism.*

Rihani traveled frequently between Lebanon and the United States, always remembering the beauty of nature in his homeland. After he returned to Lebanon for the last time, he started traveling around the Arab world, and wrote extensively about conditions there, having occasion to meet many rulers and potentates.

*   *   *

I once took the elevator in one of the high-rise buildings of New York and was whisked by the elevator boy in one minute to the top floor – the 25th. There, I climbed a spiral stairwell until I reached the dome of the huge building, a dome that nearly soared to the clouds during the day and to the stars at night.

This dome above the high-rise buildings of New York overlooks the miserable houses of the poor.

From here, like a bird, the viewer can see the great city of New York. But before seeing its busy markets, he should look from atop at its roofs filled with tangled telephone and telegraph wires, surrounded by smoke rising from chimneys and trains.

Standing far from the noise of work and business and the shouting of newspaper sellers and the clamor of trains and wagons, I breathed in clean air that is rarely found in houses and streets. I breathed in deeply and looked over the roofs below me with their chimneys from which smoke rises day and night. I imagined these chimneys as mouths of terrifying volcanoes warning of an imminent and terrifying eruption. The smoke was like the hands of the black miners raised to the sky, imploring God to spare them disaster. It is as if the smoke ris-ing from their fingers is the excess smoke of the darkness in which the miners live, digging in silent patience. Thousands of chimneys spew this gaseous soul into the face of the sky, protesting to the Creator those who advocate ceaseless work – unremitting motion with no rest or peace.

I gazed at the smoke intently and examined its shapes and qualities, its diffusion and concentration, its ascent and descent, its attack and retreat. I saw monstrous apparitions sometimes soaring and sometimes falling, then lurching at the air like tempests in the wind as if to pollute it with the lethal gas. They were like vaporous waves crashing and swelling and dissipating in the atmosphere – like a bull shaking its head and with its horns goring the sky, then returning defeated to disappear into the air; or like a snake, slithering, appearing and disappearing.

Close your eyes and come with me to the world of trade and toil.

Don't you see this bull at the stock exchange/*būrṣ* goring and killing the little ewes and then goring his maker and killing himself?

Don't you see that snake spewing its poison on society and exhausting its deadly power and then disintegrating like smoke?

Do you see those chimneys on the roofs?

Look behind the rising smoke and you will see misery and woe and tribulation. Behind those chimneys, or under them if you prefer, are thousands of human lives laboring with their pickaxes below the earth's surface for ten hours a day. Smoke is the soul of coal that is burning in thousands of stoves, hearths, and boilers. As coal burns, the souls of those men and children are incinerated, as they mine in deadly darkness with neither air nor light or water – except by artificial means. They extract the coal and carry it to trains, which carry it to cities and villages. It is their holy labor that burns right now in front of you and goes up in air. The fruit of their labor is great for the world, but it is deadly for them. It is like the smoke that is dispersing now before your very eyes.

We rely on coal now, but will not its use be discontinued in the future? For cooking and heating, many households are already replacing it with gas; some railway companies are using electricity instead of coal.

Someday, there may be no more coal and so the miners will be freed of a slavery the like of which did not exist even in the past – slavery that was ended by the edge of the sword and for which the blood of the free was spilled.

Not a month passes but a disaster befalls the coal mines of this country and elsewhere, killing hundreds and thousands of them. How many times did the mines collapse on the slaves while they were at work below, resigned and long-suffering, leaving hundreds of widows and thousands of orphans? Extracting coal is like a slow death: each miner dies as if by suicide. For suicide is not just by ingesting poison, or breathing gas, or firing a gun: the man who has to labor with his children under the surface of the earth and is denied fresh air and light and the beauty of the skies never dies a normal death.

A society which cannot progress except by the misery of others is flawed and cruel, a corrupt society that needs change and reformation.

We have progressed, as some claim, in civilization and civility, and we have freed the slaves and spread freedom – in the West – to every man, rich or poor. But the new slavery assumes new guises and wears new clothes: what good is it to say to the prisoner – you are free? What good is it for him to change his striped uniform for that of a free man if he remains chained in iron, imprisoned in his dark cell?

The chains have changed and the manacles are different and the slavers have been replaced by others. The causes are many but death is the same, for in the United States, there are so many forms and types of slavery: slavery in the mines, in the oil fields, in the textile factories and in all the world of labor. When will man be truly freed, and happiness and ease prevail among all?

Enough about mines and factories and smoke.

Let us turn to the world of trade, to the showground of clamor and motion and clatter. I heard the newspaper man on the street calling out: "Latest news! Important news!" So, I bought the evening paper and went back to my lodgings, my thoughts fogged and my spirit depressed. I sat near the heater and read: "Instability in the market as stocks plunge! The loss in one hour is fifty million dollars because of the sudden fall."[16]

Fifty million dollars lost and won in a short time, while thousands of miners labor with their pickaxes ten hours a day and risk their lives and the lives of their children in total darkness under the ground for one or two dollars.

What a world!

And what a civilization that comes at us from every corner with bizarre spectacles!

7. From "Syrians in America" by Yusuf Jirjis Zakham (published in *al-Muqtabas*, 1910)

[*Al-Sūriyyūn fī Amāyrka (al-Muqtabas 5, 1910)*]

EDITOR'S NOTE

Zakham was a regular correspondent from the United States for al-Muqtabas. This periodical was edited in Damascus (and later in Cairo) by Muhammad Kurd ᶜAli, a Syrian scholar and literary critic, who had started it in 1900. Like all others appearing at that time, it was eclectic: it included essays on important writers, chiefly Arabs, book reviews from both the Arab World and Europe, information about new inventions, and reports about government institutions. Kurd ᶜAli was very optimistic about the Arab World and wrote accounts about his travels in the "West" in which he praised what he saw and expressed his hope that the Arabs transform their lives and achieve what the West had achieved. There was a sense of imminent change in Syria in 1910 after the constitutional reforms in the Ottoman government, and so he wrote about the "Nahda" in Syria that was emanating from Beirut and other cities, notwithstanding the violence of 1860.

Hopeful as he was, Kurd ᶜAli was anxious about the pull of the United States. In an earlier issue that year, he had reviewed a 1909 book, The Syrian Immigrant, published in New York, which offered advice to the potential emigrant about what to do and know.[17] For him, the Nahda was being undermined by the departure of large numbers from Syria. Instead of leaving, he wrote, Syrians should stay in their homeland, improve their mastery of Arabic, challenge the dominance of Turkish, and reform the state schooling system. It is against this backdrop that Zakham wrote his essay, showing the great advantages of emigration. Like the author of the The Syrian Immigrant, he showed how the Ottoman authorities were publishing false reports, supposedly sent by emigrants, about the dire conditions in America – in an attempt to stem the tide of emigration.[18] Two years earlier, on 1 October 1908, al-Hoda published an article about Ottoman attempts to force emigrants to return with their wealth so they would make their countries prosper. Zakham, however, reminded his readers that the Young Turks liked neither the Arabs nor, in particular, the Syrians.

In this essay, Zakham was blunt but polite in his rebuttal of anti-emigration arguments, and he turned his fury on the Ottoman governors and administrators while giving expression to a unique criticism of social relations in the Arab World: the patriarchy that went beyond the subjugation of women to the emotional control of the youth, specifically of young men. It was an unprecedented criticism because it downplayed what Arabs always prided themselves on – family ties – and praised independence and self-reliance. Having lived in the United States, Zakham realized that one reason for the failure of Arabs to rise was exactly those family ties which, in his view, were outdated and counterproductive.

* * *

Most of the Syrians who are in America today were illiterate when they left the Syrian region; now they can read and write.[19] They left ignorant of decorum and social graces; in America, they have perfected them.

They left ignorant of national and foreign politics; in America, they have grown to understand its meaning, process, value, and goal.

They left nearly ignorant of general knowledge; in America, they have become knowledgeable.

They left ignorant of the rules of trade; in America, they have become businessmen.

They left ignorant of modern industry; in America, they have become active in many of the industries.

They left lazy and unmotivated; in America, they have become ambitious.

They left with narrow and selfish spirits; in America, they have developed generous souls.

They left in humiliation; in America, they have gained dignity.

They left having been blindly tied to the oppressors; in America, they have become enlightened, advocating personal freedom.

They left without newspapers of their own; in America, Arabic newspapers are the best in the Arab World.

They left poor; in America, they have become rich.

They left without any social status; in America, they have filled high positions.

They left with a weak will and drive; in America, they have gained vitality and passion.

These are some of the ways in which emigrants were in Syria and how they have changed in America. As for the sums of money they have sent to Syria, they exceed ten million dollars, or two million English *liras*.[20] Whoever has any doubts about those figures, let him check specifically the London Bank and the Ottoman Bank in Beirut.

Two years ago, I asked the manager of the First Omaha Nebraska Bank, Mr Neecy, who is still alive, about the amount of money that the Syrians in the state of Nebraska had sent to Syria through that bank. He answered that what they sent in one month amounted to 60,000 American dollars – that is 12,000 English sterling. So, if that amount was sent by the community of the state of Nebraska in one month, how much is the total sum that was and is sent by others in other states?

The impact of that huge sum is evident to the eyes in Lebanon and in other provinces of Syria. When I was in Syria, I used to see with my own eyes the sums of money that reached the people in Rashaya al-Wadi [in south Lebanon] and its nearby villages. The sums always ranged between 500 and 1000 *liras*: people had so much money and indulged in so much buying and selling that the interest rate rose ten-to-twenty *bara* [small Ottoman coin] from what it had been before the emigration to America when it had been two or three *piasters*.

The beautiful buildings that can be seen today in the counties and provinces, municipalities and districts that are associated with the Syrians of America were all built with their money. Without that money, most of the towns and villages would have remained dilapidated, nor would the population have been able to pay their taxes because the Syrian regions, especially in the last decade of the nineteenth century and the first of the twentieth, were in great need of money. In those dark years, employment became a thing of the past, while the governors, officials, and those in power and authority usurped what remained of the wealth of the nation, leaving her nothing except death by hunger and poverty, humiliation and defeat.

Some declaim that what Syria has gained in American money is not equal to one per cent of what it has lost in its youth and men who have been claimed by death. I say to them: It is obvious that he who is going to die will die whether he is in Syria or in America; death is here as it is there. But keep in mind that dying is less brutal in America than it is in Syria because there are many health facilities in America, but few in Syria. And, the Syrians in America are healthier than they were in Syria.

As for the view that the pursuit of money for which the Syrians left their fathers and mothers is not worth the sorrow and tears of a mother for the apple of her eye: it is a view that I consider to be one of those stupid and outdated views which have been the reason for the decline of the East and the Easterners.[21] For a son to stay with his mother and father and family is wonderful and touching. But doing so will never make a man of him – which is why you see that the men of the East who can rightly and deservedly be called men are few indeed. In fact, that is the reason why there is a dearth of men in the East.

The American [father] nurtures and teaches his son, and when he reaches maturity he tells him: Go out and fight the world and let the world fight back. But the Easterner neither instructs nor nurtures his son the way the American does: rather, he worries if his son leaves the house even for a few miles and he thinks that he is doing the right thing by protecting him, claiming to know what is best for his future. He thinks that sheltering his son is the most important thing. He does not realize, however, that it is on that fear or the lack thereof that the rise of nations or their fall depends. And so, even if America's Syrians learn just this trait in America, it will be enough because with that principle they can build a great nation.

As for those who claim that vast lands in Syria have been ruined because of the "emigration" of America's Syrians; and that had they stayed in their homeland planting and building, it would have rewarded them by pouring on them and on Syria rivers of wealth by far more than the wealth they have earned in America; and that those lands would have been booming with buildings: that is a totally false view. It is false because the time in which they left their homeland was one of wretchedness. The sky and the earth were desolate, and so were the four corners of the land. In those times, neither America's Syrians nor others could gain wealth, nor could they even lead a life that was unexposed to the tyranny of oppressors or to the depredations of governors. They were not even able to utter one word about reform and progress.

Did not the farmer leave his land, destroy his crops, and ignore his fields to escape tyranny? Did he not leave his house in ruins, not willingly but because he lost all hope in those dark days and was unable to endure more than he had endured – nor could any human or wild beast endure as much? O ye free men: why did you desert your homelands and friends and families and the nearest and dearest? Was it not because you could no longer bear what could not be borne?

We had expected that you would be fair in what you wrote about us in this foreign land of ours. We expected honesty, not duplicity, but you and your rulers chose to deride and shame us, casting aspersions on us – even those among you whom we thought were noble and true and on whom we had pinned great hopes. But destiny has decreed that even those who are protectors of justice and upholders of virtue should oppress us.

Time will tell, for each timespan has its decrees.

In summary: America's Syrians did not destroy; they built. The causes of the infamous ruin in Syria lie in its infamous government. If it is true that all or most of the blame should fall on America's Syrians, then why did you flee from that oppressive government even before America's Syrians did – and continued to do so after them? Why did you not stay in Syria to repair what others have ruined and to rebuild, rather than assist in more and more destruction?

The governor of Beirut and others spread rumors about America's Syrians – rumors we have not heard except from him and them. Perhaps their concern for the welfare of the country made them do so. But: Let us assume that there is poverty among the Syrians in America and that they do not have enough to eat: be assured that there are many caring Syrians who will help them, offer them food, and furnish them with necessities.

Let us assume that the Syrians will not care for their hungry brethren: be assured that the governments in these compassionate and merciful lands will look after them; and even if they do not, there are numerous [charitable] societies in every corner of the land that care for the poor and needy.

Even so: I have not heard, nor has anyone else heard, of a Syrian who has starved to death since the first arrival until today. And how can a Syrian starve when rarely is his wallet empty of money, whatever his condition or profession in this foreign land?

As for the claim that these rumors appear in the reports sent by the officials of the Ottoman government in America: well, we do not know how these officials gather such reports since they know next to nothing about the communities of America's Syrians – and the Syrians know nothing about them except that they are in America.

I write about the Syrians and none others from among the Ottoman [subjects] in America. If there are communities of Turks who have emigrated from Salonica and Smyrna and other places, and have not learned how to make a living in America; and if government officials looked after their Turkish emigrant brethren because they were Turks and ignored all the rest because they were not; and if they sent reports because they cared about them and their welfare: it does not mean that the Arab Syrians in America have become Turks and that what the governor of Beirut proclaimed, based on what the government officials in America reported, applies to them. (766–70)

NOTES

1. Husband of Nellie, the Grants' only daughter. The marriage had taken place two years earlier.
2. For earlier Orthodox priests in New York, see Jacobs, *Strangers in the West*, 100–5.
3. See various references to him in Bawardi, *Making of Arab Americans* (16, 29, 60, 90). For a full biography see http://lebanesestudies.news. chass.ncsu.edu/2016/02/18/archive-spotlight-basil-m-kerbawy-early-lebanese-american-historian-and-advocate, accessed 2 January 2016.
4. Tannous/Antoni Tadros was born in Tripoli, Lebanon, in 1860 and died in New York City in 1938. He emigrated in 1883, Linda K. Jacobs, *Strangers in the West* (New York: Kalimah Press, 2015), 437. He started "N. Tadros & Co. Importers & Wholesale Merchants

in Persian & Turkish Rugs of Standard Quality. 39 Broadway, New York City," Abdou, *al-Safar*, 195. The advertisement opened with the following announcement: "The conflict between the Shah of the Persians and Ni'meh Tadros and Associates: Tadros defeated the Shah and seized from the land of the Persians the best textiles known as Persian Carpets."

5. Contrast the 1896 image of the Syrian agents who deceived the new-comers in Marseille by Saʿadeh, *Dalil*, 14–16.

6. In 1895, *Kawkab America* warned about the tough conditions that peddlers faced in Pennsylvania because the police arrested who-ever was unlicensed (1 February). In 1908, Sakakini wrote that his brother Yusuf had been arrested for peddling without a license (27 January 1908). See Jacobs, *Strangers in the West*, 166–7. Licenses were used by various states to restrict poor immigrants from work. "Laws were particularly common in the early twentieth century and were largely aimed at professional immigrants (lawyers, doctors, pharma-cists, teachers, others) as a way to reduce competition for US-born professionals . . . Sometimes states also used these laws to restrict the rights of working-class immigrants," communication from Brendan Shanahan, UC Berkeley, 6 December 2015. I am grateful to Brendan for his help.

7. His narrative about fighting in Cuba was included in a novel by the Lebanese author Rashid al-Daʿif, *Tiblit al-bahr* (Beirut: Riad el-Rayyis Books, 2011)/Reclaiming Land from the Sea.

8. *Al-Hoda* (10 May 1898).

9. The author (or the printer) used both forms of "Malone" and "Maloney," obviously for the same person. I have kept them as they appear.

10. The words in italics were transliterated in Arabic.

11. Turkish word.

12. For a contemporary description of this battle, see Richard Harding Davis, "The Rough Riders Charge San Juan Hill, July 1, 1898, San-tiago, Cuba," *Eyewitness to America*, ed. David Colbert (New York, 1997), 307–9.

13. In 1898, Aswad took over the editorship of *Kawkab America*, Jacobs, *Strangers in the West*, 270. See also for further details, Akram Kahter, https://lebanesestudies.news.chass.ncsu.edu/2017/06/08/lebanese-american

14. Advertisements had already been appearing in Arabic journals for some time: *al-Jinan* included the first pictorial ones, in 1885, 672. See also *al-Muqtabas* 5 (1910): 42–6 on advertisements in the United States, "Advertisement is the basis of Commerce." In 1912, Prince

Muhammad ʿAli marveled at advertisements, as did Jurji Zaydan during his visit to France in that same year, *Rihlat Awrubba 1912*, ed. Qasim Wahab (Abu Dhabi: Dar al-Suwaydi, 2002), 33.

15. *Al-Manar* 7 (1903), 838. For information about Rihani, see http://www.ameenrihani.org

16. The "Panic of 1907" started in mid-October and resulted in 50 per cent loss on the New York Stock Exchange.

17. *Al-Manar* 7 (1903), 423–4.

18. For Ottoman concerns about emigration, see also Khater, *Inventing Home*, 54–5.

19. In *al-Safar*, Abdou maintained that of the 4,500 Syrians arriving annually in the United States in the early 1900, one third were illiterate, 284.

20. The *lira* was the currency used in the Ottoman Empire until 1923. It was later used in Lebanon, Syria, and Palestine.

21. The Lebanese/Syrian authors concurred on the "decline" of the East (see also Hilwa, *al-Muhajir al-Suri*, 11).

Return

1. From *Diary of Khalil al-Sakakini: Diary, Letters, Reflections* by Khalil Sakakini, 1907–1912 (published 2003)

[*Yawmiyyāt Khalīl al-Sakākīnī: Yawmiyyāt, rasā'il, ta'āmmulāt*, ed. Akram Musallam (Markaz Khalil Sakakani al-Thaqafi)]

The selections below are from Book One (of a total of eight volumes): "New York. Sultana. Jerusalem, 1907–1912."

EDITOR'S NOTE
Khalil Sakakini was born on 23 January 1878 in Jerusalem and finished his schooling at the (English) Church Missionary Society school in 1893.[1] After establishing a name for himself as a teacher and writer in the city, he decided to go to the United States for a year or two in the hope of making enough money to return and marry his sweetheart Sultana Abdo (letter of 9 October 1907). In that year, a number of Maronites left to go to the United States from Acre; by 1911, the newspaper Filastin *regularly advertised travel to the United States via Marseille on French ships.[2] Sakakini stayed for a year in New York and in Rumford Falls, Maine, but he was not able to find suitable employment and was clearly not a man made for business. Throughout, he kept a daily diary in which he described his longing for Sultana and for Jerusalem, his poverty and unemployment, and his reaction to the grinding pace of life around him. As he noted, those who went to America without a sense of history or purpose stayed there because society absorbed them; but those like him with a strong identity rooted in land and love could not remain and returned to their countries of origin. After learning of the new constitution of Sultan 'Abdul Hamid in 1908, he felt hopeful about reforms in the Empire and boarded ship, arriving in Palestine on 9 September 1908.[3]*
  In Jerusalem, he worked as a journalist and a teacher of Arabic for foreigners. He clashed with the Greek Orthodox clergy because he called for the

Arabization of the Orthodox patriarchate in Jerusalem – and so the Greek-dominated church refused to officiate at his wedding with Sultana.[4] Although he got married in 1912 in Jaffa, he was excommunicated and the clergy warned the laity against his views.[5] Earlier, in 1909, and with two other Muslim Jerusalemites, ʿAli Jarallah and Jamil Khalidi, he had established a school with a progressive curriculum focusing on music, education, and physical fitness.[6] Throughout his life, and like other Christian Palestinians, he felt himself very much part of the legacy of Arab history, and in regard to Arabic, he deeply appreciated the stylistic beauty and depth of the Qurʾan (see his use of Qurʾanic phrases on 11 and 13 July 1908). The governor, notorious Jamal Pasha, appointed him as a teacher of Arabic in al-Madrasa al-Islahiyya, but when Sakakini started spreading nationalist/Arabist ideas, he was sent away from Jerusalem and imprisoned in Damascus.

The Arab Revolt of 1916 gave him hope and he supported the leadership of King Faisal in Mecca who launched a war of liberation from the Ottomans. So committed was Sakakini to the nationalist cause that he wrote the poem in praise of the Arab Revolt which became its anthem.[7] In 1919, he went to Egypt and after his return to Jerusalem, he began running the Teachers' College. He moved between Cairo and Jerusalem, teaching and working in journalism, and in 1932 he went to the American University in Beirut to give a series of lectures on education. He retired in 1938 and ten years later, as the Israelis drove out the Palestinian population, he was forced to leave Qatamun in Jerusalem. He died on 13 August 1953 in Cairo.[8]

Sakakini started writing and publishing in 1896 and contributed to many newspapers in his lifetime, but his most important work is the eight-volume diary which was first published in the early 2000s. As Salim Tamari points out in the introduction, Sakakini is unique because he may be the very first Arab writer to have kept a daily diary in which he gave expression to his emotions, fears, physical pains (hemorrhoids), and the inner workings of his personality. His daily diary furnishes a unique and detailed insight into the experience of emigrants to the United States whose stories have remained largely untold. Through his eyes, it is possible to see the plight of workers in factories (in his case, a paper mill), the peddlers and their trials (although he himself never took up peddling; his brother did), the poverty in which many emigrants lived, and their prayers and tears. Interestingly, Sakakini only started praying in Rumford Falls, falling on his knees before the Virgin, after he began to realize the failure of his American dream. Sakakini shows the very close-knit community of the emigrants who came from the same towns or regions: in his case, it is notable how the vast majority of his friends, helpers, and water-pipe smokers were from Jerusalem and whose family names can still be recognized, whether in Palestine or in the United States – as in the case of the Sununu family. What is strange about his daily recollections is that he never reflected *on events taking place around him or in the rest of the country – except to mention Christmas or the 4th of July. In many respects, Sakakini continued to live in Jerusalem in America, clinging to those around him and dreaming of those who had been with him in Jerusalem, both the living and the dead. As he wrote on 19 January 1908, "I was sometimes in New York and sometimes in Jerusalem." Coming from regions of open spaces and lovely natural scenery, Sakakini found New York and Rumford Falls grim and like other visitors and emigrants, he yearned for the forests and the rivers and the mountains of his native Palestine.*

The first entry in the diary is on 4 October 1907. His first letter to Sultana after arriving in New York was on 16 November (he had sailed from Jaffa on 22 October), and by late December, Sakakini wrote to his closest Jerusalem friend, Dawud al-Saidawi, about his plans for work. He had settled on Atlantic Avenue, Brooklyn, with a roommate, but regularly "went down" to New York/ Manhattan.

* * *

NEW YORK

Wednesday 1 January 1908 [a letter][9]

Dear Dawud,

Read and laugh.

I used to weep at the condition I had reached, but today I laugh.

I mentioned to you earlier that after great effort, I found three students who will ensure me of an income of four riyals per week. That is if they all show up – which is rare because in every lesson, one of them is absent and so I lose one riyal. With four riyals, I eat, wash my clothes, pay my room rent, and socialize with some members of our community from Jerusalem. I wish things had continued that way, for the students have now stopped coming because of the Christmas holiday, and it has now been two weeks since I earned anything. I sent my clothes to the washerwoman fifteen days ago, but I could not pay for them so I left them with her. I don't have any more clothes except what I am wearing, and two days ago, I had to wash my socks and handkerchiefs myself.

All that is manageable, but yesterday, the last day in the year, I just had ten cents in my pocket. So, I went with Niqula al-Barghut to the market and bought bread for nine cents and we returned home where we ate it with some tea. At night, and while America was having wild parties to bid farewell to the old year and welcome the new, we sat at the table playing cards, totally oblivious to everything around us. Then we went to sleep.

I thought of borrowing some riyals from Rafla al-Homsi [his room-mate and a relative of Messrs Mallouk] and so I went hesitatingly to him but when I stood in front of him, my pride prevented me from mentioning the subject, and so I left not knowing what to do.[10] I wrote to my brother Yusuf in Philadelphia, but he too must be financially tight because he did not answer. So, I decided to start fasting, saying that the best thing was to stay in bed, night and day.

It was ten o'clock in the morning and I was still in bed. Then Hanna Farraj along with the other guys came and said: "Get up and let us wander the streets: today is a big day for Americans." I excused myself, and so they went on their own, leaving Niqula al-Barghut with me. After they had gone, I got out of bed, put on my clothes, took a cent from my pocket and asked him to buy us a loaf of bread, to silence our hunger. When he returned, I divided the loaf with him but he did not even taste it because he was crying. He left the food and walked out and so I called him back and started calming him down. He said: "I am not crying for myself but for you Khalil. You have nothing to eat."

For one like me who had lived in prosperity and never thought of consequences and never paid attention to the value of money: nothing will change him for the better except such harsh lessons. I would not have endured had I known of a way out, but there was none. I am here, and I know no one from whom I can borrow money except Rafla al-Homsi, but I have borrowed enough from him already. Yesterday I thought of volunteering in the army, but the commitment is for three years which cannot be broken. No one can find a job anywhere: the nephews of Mrs Rafla, Messrs Mallouk, lost more than 13,000 riyals last week. They had had eleven employees who were so busy they did not have time to scratch their heads – but now they have fired them all. If you visit their store today you won't find anyone except one of the two brothers poring over the ledgers, with worry and distress on his face. Every day, we hear of the bankruptcy of this or that firm and trader – May God have mercy on His people. I consider myself lucky for having found a few pupils.

Yesterday, my friend Farah Antoun said to me: "Had you consulted me before coming to this country, I would have advised you against it." He commissioned me to translate an English pamphlet for him about the life of Muhammad Abduh for a professor at Columbia University, which he might publish in next Saturday's issue.[11]

I go to his office every day and sit and chat about various subjects. Yesterday appeared in print the novel *Atala* by Chateaubriand, translated by *al-Jam͑iah* man.[12] So Antoun asked me to read it and write a review. I did, adding some comments, which he liked, and so he urged me to write them down so he can print them in the first issue of his newspaper. It appeared to me that he needed a good friend in his *ghurba*/being a foreigner – and so I will be such a friend because I cherish him.

As for my health: I am in good shape, thank God! My spirits are high and although my longing for home increases every day, I turn the difficulties I face into strengths which I add to my own strength – may God be my succor.

Talking about health: one night, I joined some guys who started playing rough, each slapping the other about. All were bigger and taller and heavier than me, and so they ignored me at first. But I soon joined them and lifted weights and did moves they could not do. I then started wrestling with them: I would let them grab me in whichever way they liked whereupon I would wiggle and twist their arms, just like green twigs. Their legs gave way and their bodies bent over, as if their bones were bamboo reeds. I then would let the strongest try and grip me wherever he wanted, in my leg or chest or arm, even my face. But he would not be able to take hold of me. I became so elated I felt I had strength to twist iron whereupon one said: "You could be a wrestler." I then remembered the words of Tennyson, the English poet: "My strength is as the strength of ten, because my heart is pure."[13] If you had seen me, Dawud, walking in the street, you would have thought me a cannon ball.

Generally, the Syrians here are morally degenerate. Whenever I attend any of their gatherings, I have center stage and none dares mention women in my presence.[14] How I wish they had a literary society in which I could give voice to my values which are way beyond them. What a sorry lot: what if Miss Mannana [Dawud's sister] were to show up among them? I do not exaggerate in saying you won't find even among American women anyone who can rival her in culture and poise.

What would happen if fate brought you to this land? Doubtless, and in a short time, you will become famous.

O Dawud, I can achieve nothing if I am not motivated. Motivate me and you will see wonders. When I saw Farah Antoun, reeling under the attacks on him in one of the newspapers, I said to him: "Either try and forget that such enemies exist in the world or stand up and challenge them." There was a man standing near me and blood rose in his face and his eyes shone brightly at what I said. Do you remember Dawud, what I told you one night in your house: "I love the wild and chaotic life? Truly, I love the wild life; otherwise, there is no point for my existence."

Let me now take up the pen and write to my Sultana. Perhaps it will be dawn before I finish writing to her. Farewell and till another time.

God Almighty, in His kindness and benevolence, keep you as my support and source of pride.

Saturday 11 January AD 1908

I bathed, had breakfast, and went directly to Farah Antoun in New York and gave him the article. He was pleased with it and said: "Had you brought it yesterday we would have printed it today." Then a boy entered with issues of today's *al-Jami*ᶜ*ah* newspaper. Farah Effendi handed me one and when I opened it, I saw in it my article on the novel *Atala*, prefaced by a few lines by him introducing me to readers and commenting on my literary knowledge. I took great pride in that and then went to the store of Messrs Mallouk in the hope of finding a letter, but there was nothing.

It was noon and so Khawaja Rafla [al-Homsi] invited me to lunch but I apologized, having had lunch earlier, and so he invited Niqula al-Barghut and we all went to an American restaurant.[15] Afterwards, we walked in the streets of New York and I left them to go to Columbia University to visit the professor of Arabic, Dr [Richard] Gottheil. We sat at a table and lit two cigars and started examining the first galley proof [of a manuscript Gottheil was editing] and checking it against the original. We spent two hours at work, in which we corrected the typographical mistakes and changed the spelling of some words to make them comprehensible.[16] The result of all this labor, which took five hours of my time, traveling to and fro, and editing: he stood up and thanked me profusely. I left not knowing what to do [at not having been paid] but then I said to myself: "Fine. Perhaps I will gain favor with him and if he needs an assistant some day, he will remember me and my labor."[17]

I returned to Washington Street. I was so hungry I could not restrain myself and entered a Syrian restaurant where I ate for one quarter riyal. I stopped by the washerwoman and picked up my clothes and as I was returning to the room, I saw Niqula al-Barghut, Ilyas Haydar, and Yusuf al-Salfiti. They gave me two greeting cards that had been sent from Jerusalem, one from Salim al-Salfiti and the other from Suleyman al-Diddeh in which they wished me Merry Christmas. In the letter by Yusuf al-Salfiti, there was a page from his brother Ilyas assuring me of the well-being of my brother Yaᶜqub and passing on his greetings, along with greetings from my family and from Jurji al-Khuri and the rest of the friends.

I wandered in my thoughts to Jerusalem, and a black cloud came over me. I was in a state of utter confusion for a few minutes and I wondered why my relatives and friends don't write to me.

We then returned to the room and the landlady came for the rent, which I paid. I was left with half a riyal but neither Yusuf nor Niqula had any money to pay their rent and they had relied on me to pay them back the few riyals I owed them, four to the first, and two to the second – riyals I had borrowed from Khalil Hababu [so I could pay them]. I decided to borrow some riyals the next day, either from Khalil Hababu or from Khawaja Rafla [al-Homsi].

Sunday 12 January W[estern] AD 1908[18]

Rainy day. So, I stayed in.

I read *Atala* for the second time and underlined a few passages to send to my Sultana. In the afternoon, Khalil Hababu and Iskandar Ghazal came to see me, so I borrowed a riyal from the former and I paid it back to Niqula al-Barghut so he could pay his room rent. We then visited Khawaja Hanna Hishmeh and found his wife sick.[19] I returned to the room and with Ilyas Haydar we bought some fish for dinner. As we were finishing, Iskandar Ghazal walked in and insisted that we join him for dinner and so we went and had dinner with him. When fruit was brought, they peeled an orange so that the peel came out in one piece, just like a string. So, each of us started swinging it three times above his head and throwing it behind him: when it fell, it sometimes made the shape of a letter which was the initial of the name of the one whom the thrower loved. It fell in different ways but not always clear. So, I took the rind and swung it above my head and threw it behind me. It formed the letter S very clearly. I clapped, and my face turned red. I said: "This letter is the letter I want." They looked at me trying to read my thoughts; doubtless, that was strange.

We sat in the sitting room and played some music on the piano after which I returned to my room, sat at my desk, and wrote a letter to my mother telling her about the day's events. I had a hole in my shoe: "Those above say I have shoes; those below think I am barefooted."

Monday 13 January W[estern] AD 1908

I dreamt that I had returned to Jerusalem. O God, when will my dreams come true!

I bathed and had bread and yogurt for breakfast. I wrote an article for Farah Antoun, completed the Saturday article, and then went down to *al-Jami ͨah* newspaper office in New York and gave it to him. But he saw in it a deviation from the plans he had for me and so he thanked me and apologized. From there I went to the store of Messrs Mallouk where I found a letter from Jerusalem. I looked at the address trying to guess who had sent it, but I could not. I opened it and found it to be from the

American [Colony] in Jerusalem. I started reading but as soon as I was halfway, I came across news that shattered my heart and shook the earth under my feet: the death of Afif, Dawud's brother.

I sank in a chair, turned my face to the wall and started crying as Khawaja Rafla tried to console me. I took hold of myself and walked back to my room, my tears streaming. I sat at my desk with the picture of Dawud before me and wept and groaned. Khawaja Rafla came and consoled me and so did Yusuf al-Salfiti and Ilyas Haydar. All were very sorry.

Who will not weep for you Afif, and who will not commiserate with you Dawud?

Continued. Thursday 16 January W[estern] AD 1908

Farah Effendi Antoun asked me to pay him a visit on the next day at 10 in the morning. I bumped into Khawaja Khalil Hababu at Khawaja Hanna Hishmeh's house and he accompanied me to Brooklyn but all the way I could not but think of Dawud and could not hold back my tears. Dawud, Dawud, you are my life, my joy, my happiness, may God not deprive me of you and may I redeem you from every mishap. Meanwhile, Khawaja Rafla continued talking to me about work, but if he offered me the world, I would have turned it down. First and foremost, the safety of Dawud . . . Neither love nor power nor wealth nor progress – nothing in the world equals the safety of a friend. May you be safe, Dawud. Was it not enough that life was bitter and that I worried about my brother Yusuf or that I worried about my family whom I had left without support? Nothing will stop me from thinking about you Dawud.

I paid Khawaja Yusuf al-Salfiti two riyals but I still owed him two. I sent a letter to my brother Yusuf and two copies of *Atala*, one to Sultana and one to my sister Milia; I included with the letter to Sultana the issue of *al-Jami^cah* which had my article on the novel.

Dawud, if you are weeping for Afif, I weep for him, and weep for your weeping, and weep for my distance from you.

Friday 17 January W[estern] AD 1908

I dreamt that I was in Jerusalem, but I don't remember anything except that I saw my father.

I went down to New York and directly to the newspaper office and found that Farah Antoun needed me to help him for a few days. Work had accumulated because of the New Year holiday, and so I sat at the desk and wrote thirty-one letters at one go so that my back felt stiff and my eyes popped from my head. Meanwhile, Farah Effendi Antoun was poring over his notes and papers, never leaving the office except for lunch and then returning to work again. This constant and exhausting work had enfeebled him and changed his color; he looked like he was in his sixties. I will write at length about him some day.

I then went to the store of Messrs Mallouk and found a letter from the professor of Arabic [at Columbia University] which included the second galley of his book. I said to myself: "He surely will pay me for making corrections or else he will give me another job for which he will reward me for my pains." So, I returned to Brooklyn and I gave a lesson to Dr Ness. I sensed that he was happy to see me. The lesson took more than an hour and he gave me a riyal; previously, I had received half a riyal more. I dined and returned to my room and we started talking about various Jerusalem topics.

Nothing matters to me about Jerusalem except your well-being Dawud. Tell me good news and I will never mention Jerusalem. Your well-being is more important than Jerusalem or anything else.

It seems I will have to [do manual] work in this country. If I find a job at a store for one or two hours, along with my day and night lessons, I will be able to sustain myself and my family and pay back my debts. And if my brother's business improves in Jerusalem, I will return a rich man. But if news about you Jerusalem is not good, then farewell O world. I can never work and succeed in the world unless I am happy, contented, safe, and at peace. The least piece of bad news from Jerusalem ties up my hands and kills my enthusiasm. My soul is for you, relatives and friends. May God return me to you. Your happiness is my happiness, your well-being is my well-being, and your calamities are my calamities. When I wish you happiness and joy, it is as if I wish those for myself.

Saturday 18 January W[estern] AD 1908

I dreamt I was in Jerusalem. I tried to get together with you [Sultana], but you refused. Then I dreamt that I was with Dawud. I walked in and out with him. I had other dreams but I don't remember anything.

I woke up at seven, bathed and went to the market where I had breakfast of bread and yogurt for seven cents. I then went directly to the newspaper office and found that the writer Philip Ghurayyib had arrived there a few minutes earlier. I sat at the desk and wrote thirty letters. Farah Effendi Antoun gave me the new issue of al-Jami'ah which I took after which I went to the store of Messrs Mallouk.

I was depressed.

I found a card from Khawaja Bandali al-Jawzi and another from Messrs Saba Abdou and his brothers, all extending wishes for the Eid [Christmas according to the Orthodox calendar]. I went to a restaurant where I ate honey and bread for six cents and then had a haircut. I received a card from Doctor [Najib] al-Jamal asking me to visit him the next day in the afternoon at three o'clock.

Afterwards, I went to Columbia University and on the way I started reading the newspaper and found that the piece I had written in the previous week was included, prefaced by the following words: "Khalil Effendi Sakakini, the distinguished new author who joined the community of emigrants two months ago, urges support for the demands, in eloquent and straight-forward language." I was delighted and when I entered the office of the professor of Arabic, Doctor Gottheil, he handed me a cigar and we sat comparing the second galley with the original. I made some comments about misspelled or unclear words, even in the original, always referring to some historical, linguistic, and grammatical books. And everything [of what I suggested] proved to be correct. We spent three hours, but we only finished half of the work, and when I rose to leave, and as if realizing his need for me, he said: "Please visit me next Tuesday in the afternoon to finish the rest." So, I promised him to come. He then took me to the library of the University of Columbia and showed me the Arabic book section and borrowed a book by Professor Margoliouth about Islam and gave it to me to read.[20]

I returned to Brooklyn and, with Khawaja Yusuf al-Salfiti, bought some fish on which we dined. We then returned to my room and brewed some tea. I was waiting today for a letter from my brother Yusuf but I received nothing. Perhaps what prevented him was something good. I wrote a letter to my maternal cousin, Ya'qub.

Sakakini leaves New York and goes to Rumford Falls via Boston .

BOSTON

Sunday 21/8 June AD 1908[21]

I went this morning to a nearby bath house which was free to the public. Then we had breakfast after which we went and bought tickets to Rumford Falls. They told us that there was no train that day and so I had to wait till the next day – which made me happy as I could visit Messrs Sununu and see Boston. Around noon, I went to the Messrs Sununus' house and they and their wives welcomed me warmly. They complained about the bad [economic] conditions and said that they were thinking of not staying too long this time because their wives missed home very much. We remembered Jerusalem with as much longing as a weaned baby yearns for nursing. In the afternoon, I went with Khawaja Mikha'il al-Sayigh and his wife and his cousin and Bandali Abdou to the public park where there is the reservoir from which Bostonians drink. We walked around it and I remembered Suleyman's Pools [in Jerusalem] – so many memories flooded my mind that I felt depressed.

Khawaja Mikhaʾil is happy in his marriage: he is in good health and quite exuberant so much so that when he laughs he cannot stop. He loves his wife and helps her: I saw him serving at the table just like women do to relieve his wife who was about to give birth. I understood, however, that there was some disagreement between him and Salih al-Sununu. Bandali, meanwhile, continues to chase after women all the time: no woman passes by him but he ogles her and devours her with his eyes. He now works in sales but is not successful and does not make more than four or five riyals per week. Khawaja Mikhaʾil's paternal cousin is completely American and owns a factory which employs a large number of girls.

Boston is a beautiful city: the buildings are no more than two or three storeys high but they are quite elegant, and there is less bustle here than in New York. Khawaja Mikhaʾil said to me that he was thinking of writing to my brother to come to Boston, manage the merchandise, and join Bandali in peddling. For dinner, I had upside-down *maqlouba* [a rice and yogurt dish served upside down] after which I smoked a water pipe.

We did not stop talking about Jerusalem.

Around 10:30, I left with Khawaja Bandali. I wished I could find work in Boston and so live among my compatriots. I sent a card to my brother Yusuf.

Monday 22/9 June AD 1908

I woke up early and did not bathe and left with Khawaja Bandali Abdou. I had a haircut and stopped by a shoe repair store where I replaced nails that had fallen from my shoes. We then went to the house of Messrs Sununu. Alexandra, the wife of Khawaja Salih, came down so I said goodbye at the door and left. We passed by the store of the uncle of Khawaja Mikhaʾil and said goodbye, and then went to the store of Khawaja Adolph, cousin of Khawaja Mikhaʾil, to say goodbye. From there, we continued to the store of Khawaja Adolf, paternal cousin of Khawaja Mikhaʾil, to bid him farewell. I was impressed at what I saw of his competent administration, his shrewdness at work and his manliness, and I said goodbye. We returned to the house where we had breakfast, said goodbye to everyone, and then went to the train station where I boarded the train.

We passed through forests and jungles, with rivers running on both sides: sometimes you could see them, sometimes not, hidden as they were by the trees. I enjoyed seeing nature after being deprived of it for eight months [?] amidst the large buildings of New York. We passed by a station called Hebron [Maine] and reached Portland where we sat for an hour waiting for the train. I bought two post cards there. When the train arrived, we boarded and continued through jungles and valleys and rivers until we reached Rumford Falls around four o'clock.

It is a city rich in natural scenery. It lies at the foot of a high mountain around which are other high mountains covered by thick forests; from a distance, the viewer might think them clouds clinging to the mountains. Among the trees perched houses and chimneys like bird nests. There were three waterfalls the sound of which could be heard from afar, and so I imagined I was approaching Ayn Karim or the promontory over Wadi Qalt [near Jerusalem].

At the station, Khawaja Ilyas Khoury, a young well-built man who exuded manliness, welcomed me warmly. We walked to the depot of Khawaja George Ilyas Barbara, a young, handsome, gentle man who owns a store. We spent the night talking about Farah Effendi. I noticed how much they cared for the newspaper, *al-Jami‘ah* – which I liked very much.

I slept at their place.

RUMFORD FALLS

Tuesday 23 and 10 June AD 1908

I did not bathe because there was no place to do so in the house. We had breakfast and I smoked a water pipe which I found at Khawaja George's and then sat down to write a letter to my brother Yusuf, and another to Niqula Effendi Haddad. I insisted that he publish an article by George Effendi which he had sent him the day before. I sent post cards to Mikha³il al-Sayigh, Salih Sununu, Miss Sincair, Sultana, and my sister.

The town is small and its people friendly and simple, most of whom work in the factories. Wherever you look, you see the city and hear its waterfalls: I had never seen anything like this, even in pictures. Had this town been in our country, there would be a coffee shop under every tree; even under the waterfalls, there would have been wooden bridges with coffee shops. People would have truly enjoyed themselves: no sooner would evening come than men would leave their stores and women their homes and all would relax near the banks of the waterfalls to smoke water pipes and have a good time.

Here, however, people don't care for the scenery. You cannot even find a coffee shop. They just build factories above which rise clouds of fumes which destroy beauty.

Khawaja George Ilyas met all the overseers in the factory where I was destined to work. They gave him every assurance [of their commitment] – for he is a man of authority and status among them.

In the afternoon, I went alone to the bridge and stood looking at the water crashing on the rocks. I lifted my eyes to the high mountains and continued walking near the riverbank. I thought of all my relatives and friends.

I learned that my job was manual and that I would be with workers of the lower class. I was overcome by sorrow that nearly crushed me. But then I remembered Peter the Great who had worked in factories.[22] So I took courage: Perhaps this time I will walk the road to success because I will start at the first rung of the ladder. I looked for a room to rent but found none. When I look at my shabby clothes and imagine what my work will be, I see myself as one of the menial workers.

Well, it cannot be helped. There is no strength or help except in God.

Wednesday 22 June and 11 June AD 1908

I did not bathe today nor did I change my clothes. I was disgusted with myself.

We had breakfast which was paid for by Khawaja George Ilyas and then I went down to his store. I waited for the mail but it did not come. That day, there was a big celebration of the Organization of Masons: many members came from nearby towns, all dressed in official gear as if they were military commanders. The Masons in town welcomed them and then all the people lined the streets as the Masons entered in disciplined columns, with their swords drawn, to music played by four bands. They marched in the streets of the town and went up the mountain.

I found a room in the house of one of the overseers in the factory. It was a new and attractive house, with furniture that was up-to-date. My bed was new, my mattress clean and unused, and in one of the corners there was a closet with clothes hangers, one especially for overcoats which are mounted on the hangers so they would not slide. The room was lit by electricity and there was a beautiful bathroom, everything in it well polished. It was a room the like of which I had not lived in before and so I was very happy; additionally, the house owner and his wife were quite friendly.

I brought my suitcase and arranged my clothes and books and in the afternoon, I wrote down everything that had happened to me since leaving New York. Then, with Khawaja Ilyas Khoury, I went to the room of

Khawaja George Ilyas and turned on the phonograph. Among the songs were songs from Baghdad and Isfahan which moved me deeply and gave me strength.[23] In the afternoon, I took my pipe and walked near the river bank and wandered into the valleys of fancy.

My room rent is one and a half riyal.

I bought a food coupon for the whole week for three and a half riyals so that my expenses for food and lodging were five riyals. So, if I earned ten riyals from my work, I could save five or four riyals. Whoever thought I would one day work in a factory after all the glory? But maybe I will no longer be accused of being proud and supercilious.

I went to bed at eleven. Where ever I go, you are all with me.

Thursday 25 and 12 June AD 1908

I rose at 4:30 after a good sleep and went into the bathroom to shower. The water was very cold. I changed my clothes, did my exercises and thereby wiped away the rust of laziness.[24] I felt overjoyed as if I were a new-born. I put on my clothes, left, and stopped by Khawaja George, who was already fully dressed. In the previous two days, I had convinced him of the value of exercise, and so he started exercising on the chairs, the way I had shown him. If I settle down in my work in this town, I will slowly convince him of my principles and ideas, foremost of which are love of nature and attention to health. Since most of the townspeople are French, I will, God willing, seize the opportunity to learn French, among other subjects.

I went into the French restaurant and had breakfast while he had breakfast in the house to which he had taken me numerous times for breakfast and lunch. Then we went to the factory, but the workers had not arrived yet, and so we stood in the shade and soon one of the overseers came, followed by the workers, including girls. I met the nephew of Khawaja Ilyas Khoury whose name is Ilyas Maria. When I saw the workers in their shabby outfits and realized I would be working with them, I was engulfed by dark clouds of despair, but I forced myself and tried to forget my anxieties. The overseer in whose house I lodged arrived and said to me: "Today I will give you work." After we finished, I returned to my room, feeling languid. Later, I went to the store of Khawaja George and after spending some time there, I walked back with Khawaja Ilyas Khoury to my room and we chatted until noon. I left and had lunch and at one o'clock, I returned to my room and went to sleep. After sleep, I sat sewing buttons on my trousers and jacket – perhaps one of the things I learned in this country.

Al-Jami*ah* arrived, along with two letters, one from Niqula Effendi al-Haddad apologizing for not printing the article by Khawaja George because it would be like advertisements for the novels of Khalil Gibran – who is not loyal to al-Jami*ah*. The other letter was from Khawaja Makrouchian.

Before sunset, we went to the falls and sat under the trees. We then went for dinner. There was a Syrian with us who worked at the factories. He drank until he got drunk and kissed the woman owner of the restaurant.

Friday 26 and 13 June AD 1908

I dreamt of Dawud and saw in his face red spots, signs of a disease we always feared for him. I said to him: "Thank God you are recovered. From now on, you have to look after your health." He shook his head and said: "Yes," but rather indifferently [sometime before 25 January, Sakakini had received a letter informing him of the death of Dawud].

I rose early, bathed, massaged my body and exercised. I left, had breakfast, and then returned to my room, but I was depressed and my body lethargic. I sat at my desk not knowing what to do. I would take a book, read a couple of lines, and then put it down. I started recalling the past hoping memories would cheer me up, but to no avail. Then I opened the drawer and started reading letters from her [Sultana] and asking myself: Why did she stop writing? Perhaps she got mad at me because I mentioned that Aftim had written and pleaded with her at a time he hoped to marry her; she received his letters but never answered him. He told me all about that and I kept the secret until we made our covenant of love – so I wrote to her and teased her.

I filled my pipe and started writing a letter to Miss Sincair telling her that I was planning to work in the factories. I then dropped the letter in the mailbox. The postman came but had nothing for me – and so I became more depressed. I returned to the room and slept for an hour, then sat at my desk and wrote various cards from this town which I mailed to Ya*c*qub my maternal cousin and to my teacher Nakhleh [Zurayq], Jurji Habib, Aftim Mushabbak, Jamil al-Khalidi, Shurki Hishmeh, Ashil Seikaly, and Khalil Ra*c*d.[25] The postman arrived with a letter from Jerusalem in the handwriting of my brother-in-law Abu Salim. It included a letter by my cousin Salim about Salim Istfan and his brother: they had bought a piece of land in Beereh and started building. Also, that my brother Ya*c*qub had gone to help them, which was reassuring.

I received a card from Miss Sincair. At six o'clock, Khawaja George Ilyas closed his store and we went and stretched on the grass under the trees. One of the overseers in the factory came up, and I went with him to town. On the road, I saw members of the Salvation Army:[26] they were praying, preaching, and collecting alms, so I gave them five cents. Then I continued with him to the library.

I returned with him to the room of Khawaja George who said: "A guy came today looking for work, and perhaps he found a job" – as if he meant that I might not find work.

Saturday 27/14 June AD 1908

I stayed late in bed until seven o'clock. I bathed, massaged my body and exercised: had I not persevered in my exercises, I would have been like an old rag. I thank God that exercise is a habit so engrained in me that I do it without thinking and I never ignore it even in my most miserable days. I left and had breakfast and waited for the postman in the hope of receiving a letter from anyone who might write. He came but he had nothing for me, so I thought, maybe I will get something in the afternoon. I returned to my room, shaved, had lunch, and then had an afternoon nap for an hour. I got up, sat at the desk and wrote a letter to my brother Yusuf and mailed it, adding to it the Jerusalem letter. The postman came but had nothing for me, so I became depressed: it was not enough that I was far from home, I was also forgotten. I returned to my room, filled my pipe, and sat at my desk, perplexed. I tried to write to Sultana but I did not know what to say to her: should I plead with her? I had already written her letters that would melt flinty stone. Should I admonish her? I feared alienating her even more. Should I describe to her my situation which had nothing propitious?

Around six o'clock, I went to Khawaja George's store. One of the Syrians working in the factories came up to me: his name was Zayn Sfeir, perhaps from the Sfeir family in Jerusalem. He said: "Come with me to a beautiful spot." I did, and we reached a pond near the waterfall from which they irrigate the higher grounds. We sat there and he told me that he got engaged then broke off the engagement – a long story which I could not follow because I was distracted. I could not believe I had reached such a condition: to work in factories and to mix with those who were goatherds in my country.

I returned to Khawaja George's store and it was full of salesmen and customers. Near his store was a dance club in which young men and women met. I started walking up and down near the store, sometimes listening to the music and feeling depressed or looking up at the black sky and declaiming against injustice. The overseer came up to me and said: "You will work on Monday."

Sunday 28/15 June AD 1908

I took a good bath, went out and had breakfast. Then we all went and sat near the waterfalls under the trees until noon. We returned to Khawaja Jurji's room where we started competing in weight lifting. In the afternoon, I returned to my room, slept, and after I woke up, I sat at my desk, placed Sultana's picture in front of me, and started writing to her. When Messrs Jurji and Ilyas walked in, I hid the letter in my pocket but I could not hide the picture. George took the picture and said: "She is an empress! What beauty!" I was delighted to hear him say "empress." I marveled and said to myself: You should have said Sultana. They asked me who she was and at first, I said, my pupil, and then my paternal cousin.

We went out for a walk near the waterfalls where we found some tree branches. We broke some and played sword games for an hour in the fresh air. Whenever possible, I always take advantage of where I am: if I am in a healthy spot, I seize the opportunity to look after my health, and if I am in the company of a strong and mighty man, with him, I will exhaust my energies, and if I find myself in a literary circle, as was the case in New York near Farah Effendi and Niqula Effendi, I will not hesitate to participate.

We spent the evening at Khawaja George's talking and telling stories about men in battle. I became quite excited and returned to my room and finished the letter to Sultana saying: "Tomorrow I go to the factory – Khalil who kept Jerusalem busy and used to lord it over young and old, and used to prepare himself for leadership in his community – tomorrow, like a miserable worker, he will go to the factory." I slept at eleven o'clock so I would wake up early for work.

28 June W[estern] AD 1908 (Sunday evening) [a letter]

My beloved Sultana

My situation with you is like what Ibn al-Farid wrote in his *Kafiyya* poem which opens with this verse:[27]

> Revel in your might; you deserve it,
> And lord it over me; your beauty sanctions it.

The one verse that describes my condition today in regard to you is this one:

A slave who never pleaded for release:
He will never relinquish you even if you relinquish him.

Yes, my dear, thus has your might made me your slave, weeping and groveling, and much as you ignore or reject me, I do not let go of you, never forget you or discontinue my letters. You are my sultana and you have power. Judge in whichever way you want:

Do what you like, for [your] beauty has given you power to do so.

Read this poem for it is my message to you.

Eighty-six days have passed and while I write to you, you do not answer. I was hoping you would be mentioned in my sister's letters, or that you would mention me even in the margin. For your words, or words about you, delight me, as Ibn al-Farid said, too. I received a letter from her [his sister] saying: "Vacation time is near and so I have really started to prepare for it; I will be alone" – which indicated to me that you had also been cut off from her. O Sultana, fear God, I did not make my vow of love to you before you made your vow of friendship to my sister. Not only did I love you, but so too did my mother and my sister. I wish I had announced my engagement before I left, so that people would know you are mine and I am yours; and so, when you visit my mother or walk with my sister, there would be nothing for you to worry about. And, let us assume I did not get engaged to you or make my vow of love: were you not a sister to me? Did I not walk with you in the sight of people? What are those illusions that frighten you? Did we not visit one another? If you have forgotten the vow of love and amity, have you forgotten that we are relatives and that we have a paternal cousin living with you who is like my sister? Do you think that if I returned I would not visit and greet you before everybody else? Would you be embarrassed to visit my family and greet me had I not been a dear one and a friend – like a relative or an in-law?

O Sultana, however much you deny me, you cannot deny our relationship. Between us there is more than love that makes us one family. I left you and was confident that we had many ties that bound me to you and you to me. So, if you don't want to write as a beloved, write to me as a friend, or a sister. If your heart were made of stone, O Sultana, it would have melted for me; if I had committed a grave offense towards you, it is time for you to forgive me. I invoke you by what is pure in the love between us, by our evening meetings and promenades, by the first letters I sent you and the first letters you sent me, by the moment of our good-bye, and by the heavens: take pity on me, and if there is an offense of which I am ignorant, I appeal to your kind and gentle heart that is better than the angels'. Listen to your heart, O Sultana, for it is my intercessor to you.

[The letter continues with a repetition of what Sakakini had written in his diary above about Boston and his friends there. He ends:] My dear: it is now eleven o'clock and I have much to say to you but I will leave it for another time. I need to sleep in order to wake tomorrow at five to bathe and have breakfast before starting work. Imagine my condition O Sultana, and send me a letter to console my broken heart. Otherwise I will kill myself, for death is better than this bitter and miserable life.

What shall I say in conclusion: I hold back my pen, my tongue, my heart lest an expression of my love angers you. May you ever remain true to your lover who dies and lives for your love.

Margin: If you still have copies of *al-Jamiᶜah* which contain my articles, cut the articles out and save them because I gave my copies to someone to read, but he lost them. And there are no more copies at the office.

Monday 29/16 June AD 1908

I rose at 4:30, bathed, and exercised. I then had breakfast and afterwards went with Khawaja George to the factory. The overseer sent me to work with Khawaja Ilyas Maria, the nephew of Khawaja Ilyas Khoury. So, I took off my jacket and vest, rolled up my sleeves and laid one hand on the cart and with the other I shook hands with Khawaja George who smiled at me like a brother.

My work all day was in hauling: the overseer would give us a list of the merchandise and we would push a cart from one place to another, sometimes underground, sometimes on the first floor, and sometimes on the second. As I carried the packages [of paper] on my chest into the cart, I would sometimes drift away in my mind, and sometimes I would break out laughing. Sometimes, I would tell myself that I should write to Jerusalem and describe my work, and sometimes I would decide not to, for fear of shame. I remembered one time when Shibly, the late Dawud, and I were in my room in the city [New York]: we had undressed and lain on our backs with our feet on the wall. I told them as I looked at my feet: these feet are only good for hauling. I then wrote a contract and signed it – Shibly still has it. Sometimes I say: I have Peter the Great as a model – he left his throne and went to Europe incognito and worked at factories to learn about manufacturing. I then would add: Peter the Great left his throne not out of need but to learn in order to improve his country. As for me, I descended to the factory because of need – and what have I gained?

I started imagining ethical possibilities: if I am asked what my work is, I will answer that I discipline my body and scrutinize workers' morals.

And I laugh.

In the evening, I returned exhausted after a long day, ten non-stop hours. I was hoping for some letters, but there were none. I dropped Sultana's letter in the mailbox. As we were sitting on Khawaja George's balcony, two women came to visit his neighbors and one entered his room whereupon he started kissing her. So, I left them and returned to my room.

Tuesday 30/17 June 1908

I rose at 4:30, bathed and did my usual exercises. I then had breakfast and filled my pipe and walked to the factory. Whoever saw me then had no doubt that I was one of the workers, for male and female workers were ahead and behind me. We crossed the bridge and I looked at them eager to see if any paid attention to the beautiful scenery, but they were looking only at the ground, marching like oxen in yoke. All the males in the village are factory workers, and so are the females. And all have very, very low moral values.

I reached the factory, took off my clothes, rolled up my sleeves and started pushing the cart. Work that day was very hard and it felt as if we were not carrying paper bundles but rocks. I sweated all the way down to my feet; my arms were tired, my palms were scraped, and my hands stiffened. On that day, my mate was an American worker: and so, whenever we reached the place where we were to pick up the packages, [one of the overseers] would point at him saying: twenty bundles, or twenty-five, and so I would lunge ahead of him to haul them. There was no difference between us and horses pulling carriages except that they pulled and we pushed. Yes, I worked like a drudge, but I worked with energy and dedication, even chivalry – meaning I did not let my friend get tired.

At noon, I walked to the restaurant and arrived at 12:30, and so I had to swallow my food quickly and left still chewing the last mouthful and returned to the factory and to the same work. There is no difference in the factories between the laborer and the dumb machines – he goes and comes without thought or will; he does everything mindlessly. No wonder that the souls and thoughts and emotions of the workers die: the workers labor for ten hours non-stop after which each does not get more than a riyal and a half per day. How cruel the capitalists and how horrible this city; factories kill craftsmanship because the workers have nothing to do with what is being manufactured. Machines do that. Workers are mere porters.

In the evening, I took a bath. I was overwhelmed with memories and nearly cried.

I bought a new pair of shoes.

Wednesday the first of July W[estern] and 18 June E[astern] AD 1908

I dreamt I was in Jerusalem: Dawud, Askuhi (the fiancée of Ashil Say-qali), the mother of George Halabi, widow of the late Ya'qub Halabi, the wife of Khawaja Yanko Diddeh, and I. I sat near Dawud and wrapped him in a gown and started staring at his face and inquiring about his health because I was worried about him. He stood up to leave and I walked with him to his house. I then returned and met Askuhi on the street, so I apologized to her for leaving them.

I rose at 5:15 and took a bath, had breakfast, and went to work. Work was very tough: a lot of orders and very heavy bundles, just like rocks. When we finished we sat in the shade for a spell of fresh air, and so I started a conversation with myself. Meanwhile, the workers started flirting with the women who looked out from the windows of the factory across from us. They exchanged indecent words and gestures that would make you sweat in shame. We were called back, not for hauling but for sweeping. Each carried a broom and started sweeping. It was too much for me. I nearly put on my clothes and left.

While I was leaning on the broomstick considering my condition, I imagined my mother in these dark halls appearing to me, like an angel. She talked to me and wept for me. Suddenly there was another order to which I and another worker were called. So, I dropped the broom and hurried. That afternoon I felt broken. It was extremely hot, and so I did not go to work but lay in bed and slept. After I woke up, I took a bath and went out for a haircut. The postman came but brought me nothing. I returned to my room and wrote four letters to Farah Effendi Antoun describing my condition and telling him that I was leaving work the next week, returning to New York, and from there to Jerusalem. I wrote the same to my brother Yusuf, to Mikha'il al-Sayigh, and to Ilyas Haydar. I then dropped them in the mailbox.

In the evening, I filled my pipe and walked near the waterfalls, my mind wandering. I had to return right away for I had no future in this country. And no man can have other than what is decreed for him.

I walked back to my room and from my drawer took out letters from my teacher Nakhleh and from Bandali al-Jawzi and read them. I decided to return. "What God has destined will be."

Thursday 2 July W[estern]/19 July E[astern] AD 1908

I saw my father in my sleep. We were sitting in our house and there were some visitors, including Jamil Hababu who started singing *mayjana, mayjana*. My father was delighted and started humming joyfully at every pause in the song. I would say to him: "Listen father, how beautiful this singing is."

Today is the 90th day since your last letter, O Sultana. May God forgive you!

I got up at 4:15, bathed, dressed, and left for breakfast. I then went to the house of Khawaja George and found them all asleep. I sat on the balcony smoking my pipe. The ground was wet with dew and I remembered how I used to wake up early, when I used to be Dawud's guest, and sit on the balcony of his house overlooking the sea [Dead Sea].

Energetically, I went to the factory and worked till noon. It was very hot and I went to lunch without my jacket and vest, nor did I put on my tie but carried them all on my shoulder. I rolled up my sleeves like the rest of the workers and after lunch, I returned full of energy.

I received two letters, one from my sister Milia, which made me nearly cry, especially a sentence saying: "Your absence has been too long for those whom you wanted us to look after. Nobody pays any attention to us now." I paused as I read it, my heart bursting and full of longing. Another letter was from Ilyas Tarazi. After work, I bathed and had dinner. I took a riyal and a half from Khawaja George and on meeting the landlord paid him last week's rent. He said: "I am thinking of finding you another job – one as a clerk." I told him that I earned that much and more, and besides, the workers had more rights. He said: "Most of them are illiterate and cannot read." I was delighted and decided to work for a week or two and if I did not get the job, I would have at least disciplined my body and stopped needing people.

We spent the evening at Khawaja George's house. We turned on the phonograph and listened to Baghdadi and Isfahani songs. Blood burst into my head and I felt strength that could twist iron. In all honesty, I had started to like the work because it strengthened my body and renewed my vigor. I decided to have pictures taken of me in workers' clothes and send some to Jerusalem. I planned also to have some pictures taken near the waterfalls and under the trees. They will be a good souvenir.

Friday 3 July W[estern]/20 July E[astern] AD 1908

I rose at five o'clock, bathed and left for breakfast. Afterwards, I sat on Khawaja George's balcony as the sun was rising from behind the mountains. I filled my pipe and started talking to myself. I said: I will work at the factory and make some money; and if in the meantime I find no other job, I would have disciplined my body and refined my spirit.

I went to the factory. Work was light that day. Most of the time, I sat on the paper bundles in the dark factory corridors – like the corners of the Church of the Holy Sepulchre. Thoughts whirled in my mind. I said: I will return to the homeland and work in the Orthodox school for ten liras; twice a week, I will go to the school in Bethlehem, and I will give private lessons. I will contract the monastery to pay me 100 liras in advance.

I said to Khawaja Ilyas Maria: "The overseer, Khawaja Hashi, promised to find me another job as a clerk very soon." But it seems that he had made the same promise to him, too, because he became irritated. He said: "Do not believe a word he says." Then we talked about his uncle Khawaja Ilyas and Messrs Barbara and he told me some of their stories, which made my heart cringe and made me want to go back home. He said: "Some of their Muslim countrymen had a store in front of his store, selling the same merchandise. He made a false accusation against them, and so they were imprisoned and ruined."

In the evening, I returned to my room, bathed, and had dinner. I received a letter from my brother Yusuf, saying how much he missed me. He wrote "This separation has been more difficult than that in Jerusalem." There was also a card from Dr Jamil rebuking me for not visiting him and not asking about him all this time. There was another letter from Ilyas Tarazi in which he wrote encouragingly and consolingly, ending with two lines: that nobody liked my articles in *al-Jami'ah*, and he urged me to fill the columns with some of my noble thoughts instead of such commonplaces. I was hurt by this comment

Tomorrow is America's Independence Day. Children started playing with fireworks, which blasted my brain. I could do no better than to stay in my room but I slept restlessly. At around one o'clock, Messrs Ilyas and George, along with the landlord, came to see me. The landlord promised to offer me a job as a clerk in two weeks. They wondered why I stayed away from women. They made disgusting accusations which made me want to get married.

Saturday 4 July W[estern]/21 July E[astern] AD 1908

I woke up late, bathed, and went for breakfast. We spent the morning in Khawaja George's house. Men, women, and children were on the streets, piping and lighting fireworks. You would see a beautiful woman with a gun shooting in the air, and an old man, with beard and moustaches, blowing into a horn, walking in the street as if he were a little boy. I had

seen the same things in England. The man can be a father, even a grand-
father, but he behaves like a child. And when they call on each other,
they use "boys"; in our country, that would be an unforgivable insult.

In the afternoon, I went to bed and after sleeping I sat to write to
Milia to encourage her and to tell her that if I do not find a good job
that will allow me to pay off my debts, I will return, rich in myself. Even
if I am burdened by debts and even if I wear the shabbiest clothes, nothing will change my self-esteem. It was a long letter in which I excluded
nothing. I finished and went to Messrs George and his brother and
Ilyas Khoury; we stood in front of the house. Near us were three
youths, like the branches of a banyan tree in elegant clothes and hats.
One of them joked with a policeman who passed by them whereupon
the policeman turned on him like a ferocious beast, in front of everyone, and grabbed him by the throat until I saw his eyes pop out of his
face. His head was twisted by the policeman's grip. Then the policeman let go of him and the humiliated youth straightened up and said
in a faltering voice: "I said nothing to him." The policeman turned
at him again and seized him by the throat as he had done earlier, and
threw him on the ground and started dragging him – the youth meanwhile doing nothing, and his friends standing motionless like statues.
That poor youth said to him: "Why are you dragging me? What have
I done?" The policeman pulled out his baton and bashed him on the
head. Blood flushed in my head and all my body shook. Even so, none
of the bystanders moved to stop that ferocious beast from the youth.
Had something like that happened in our country, we would have said
they are savages.

I was livid for the rest of the day and the night.

Sunday 5 July W[estern]/22 June E[astern] 1908

I woke up, shaved, bathed and went out for breakfast. I then returned to
my room and finished the letter to my sister. I went for lunch, slept, and
then wrote a letter to Ilyas Tarazi saying: I must return. I have knocked on
every door and appealed to every contact I know. Nothing is left for me
to do; this is the last straw. I will return with great hopes in my heart and
with high spirits; I will return to renew covenants of fealty and of friendship; I will return to make amends with those who have grown distant,
etc. I am happy with the outcome even though it is not what I wanted,
because it has given me experiences more valuable than riches. At the
end, I asked him to greet Dawud's family whereupon memories surged
and I could not control my tears. I took up Dawud's picture and paced up

and down in my room, crying and groaning quietly, lest the landlady hear me, until my eyes grew dim and my tears dried.

I got dressed and carried Dawud's picture in my pocket and went out to be alone near the waterfalls, to mix my tears with the running water. I found Khawaja George with his brother Ilyas Khoury and I sat with them on the green grass under the trees. We went to another place where the water crashes over the rocks and sat there on wooden planks. As they talked, images of Dawud, Sultana, and my other friends passed before my eyes. I even imagined Dawud and Sultana sitting next to me. After we left, I returned to my room, took a bottle and walked to the water source and filled it and returned. I sat at my desk and smoked while writing a letter to Dr Jamil, and another to Sultana.

Before going to sleep, I knelt before the pictures of Jesus and Mary and invoked their spirits and the spirit of Dawud to guide me in the course of my life and to help me live above the evils of this world.

Monday 6 July W[estern]/23 June E[astern] AD 1908

I dreamt that I had returned to Jerusalem. And Mrs Mary, wife of Khawaja Yanko Diddeh, and her sister Cleope and other ladies came to greet me.

I woke up at four o'clock but stayed in bed till five o'clock. I then rose, bathed, dressed, and left for breakfast and from there to the factory. The workers arrived, lazy and yawning, having spent the two previous days drinking and indulging their appetites. As for me, I had spent those days in my room, going to bed at the beginning of the night and sleeping in the afternoon, and bathing in the morning. And so, while they yawned and dragged themselves around, I was moving with great energy. I worked happily as if I were doing my exercises rather than working. Khawaja Ilyas Maria told me stories about women in this country which I found appalling. I thought of collecting information about the lives of women and girls, especially those working at factories, and writing an article.

After work, I returned to my room, bathed, got dressed, and went out for dinner. I then went with Khawaja Ibrahim to town and found a letter from Dr Ness at the post office. I returned to my room and took my jug to fill it from the fountain from which all the inhabitants of Rumford drink. On the way, I met Khawaja Ilyas Maria with another Syrian who worked with us in the factory and so they came to my room. The landlord joined us and we started chatting about various subjects until eleven o'clock. After they left, I went to my desk and wrote my diary.

Today I mailed four letters, to my sister, Sultana, Ilyas Tarazi and Dr Najib. Before going to sleep, I knelt at my bed and prayed.

Tuesday 7 July W[estern]/24 June E[astern] AD 1908

I dreamt that I was in Jerusalem with my maternal cousin, Ya°qub, and with Nayfeh and Mary.

I wish today were not a day of my life; I wish I had died before this day; I never felt as humiliated and broken. I went to the factory: it was not enough that we worked like beasts of burden, but in the afternoon, they told us to clean a large room full of stones, wood, and dust where machine oils had congealed. It was a sinkhole of filth. The overseer handed me a broom – I hesitated out of pride and self-esteem; I nearly walked out of the factory never to return. But then I remembered: I was there because of debt and that I will have nothing to spend on myself if I quit. And here, for the first time, my pride deserted me – it was like my soul leaving my body.

It was very hot, enough to melt iron and I was sweating all over, as if stepping out of water. I could not wipe my sweat with my hands because they were dirty. I swept and lifted the beams and the barrels and metal pipes, all covered with grime. My clothes were soiled and I looked like a coal seller or a lamplighter. I carried the pipes on my shoulder from one place to another, then took a shovel and lifted the trash into a barrel outside. The smell of the oils was nauseating and gave me a headache. To whom can I complain? To heaven, which has closed all doors in my face? Or to the people who have abandoned me and left me all alone? All my past and future happiness will not equal this day. Who will blame me if I return to my country?

I left in the evening, my body worn with fatigue and worry and humiliation and misery. I shaved and bathed and went to dinner, but had no appetite. The first thing I was served was meat which looked like it had been chewed and masticated; I could not eat it and nearly threw up. I asked instead for eggs. Since coming to this town, I have just eaten leather-like meat and potatoes. If I stay here for another month, I will die of starvation and misery. I got a letter from Khawaja Mikha°il al-Sayigh saying: "I advise you to stay in your job."

Wednesday 8 July W[estern]/25 June E[astern] AD 1908

I bathed, prayed, and had breakfast: fried eggs and a glass of milk. I then went to the factory as if to prison. My thoughts were tumultuous: sometimes I reflected on my dire condition and bad luck, and sometimes I remembered Dawud only to find myself crying, and sometimes I remembered Sultana, and sometimes I imagined that I was in Jerusalem. As soon as I reached Jaffa, I went directly to Bank Credit-Lyon and stood at the door, my head lowered, my eyes to the floor, calling on Dawud. I then went to the cemetery where ʿAfif was buried, stood there and wept and groaned. Then I went to Jerusalem and on reaching the foot of Mount Zion, I went up to Dawud's grave and knelt and called out on Dawud. I crawled on my knees until I reached his grave and wept and wallowed in the earth.

At noon, I went to lunch and found a letter from Ilyas Haydar telling me that I could have till Saturday to send the money, adding: "If you ask me for my life, I will give it to you." He continued: "Your brother Yusuf went out peddling with Niqula al-Barghut and each made eight riyals." I was happy because, first, they had partnered together, knowing that Yusuf could not work alone, and secondly, that they had been lucky and had made some money. I returned to the factory; our work that day was under another overseer.

Meanwhile, I did not stop studying the condition of the workers. I saw that the factories kill the nation: they kill craftsmanship and thinking, the mind and the body, for the workers do not see the sun all day. Factories kill dignity and extinguish independence, for the worker learns no craft and can never hope to be independent. That is the reason why the factory owners can bully the workers in whichever way they want. Etc. I decided to write down notes every day.

They paid me last week's wages based on nine riyals per week. I will not be able to pay back my debt – i.e. the twenty riyals – in a year, and so I started thinking of another way. In the evening, I returned totally exhausted and depressed. I wrote two letters, one to Ilyas Haydar telling him not to send the money; and another to my brother, urging him to save me.

Thursday 9 July W[estern]/26 June E[astern] AD 1908

I saw my brother Hanna in my sleep and I stopped him and we kissed each other. I also dreamt that my paternal cousin Salim had opened a small store in the *souk* of the new Orthodox monastery near the Church [of the Holy Sepulchre], so I went there and sat on a chair in front of the shop.

In low spirits, I bathed, had breakfast, and dragged myself to the factory. There were lots of orders and my back was nearly broken as I lifted the bundles and hauled them to the cart and then to the train wagon. I was hoping I would get letters with the morning post, but nothing came. I returned in the afternoon and we went to work at the factory where the girls worked. I entered one of the corridors and found a girl standing at the entrance. As a carriage drove past, I stood aside and nearly melted with pity for her. I thought of my sister and became angry, saying: Far be it that you, Milia, should enter such factories. And even if you visit, who would even dare to look at you or say anything [impolite] to you?

Farah Effendi in *al-Jami*ᶜ*ah* says that he has begun to love America. If you look superficially at this country, you will praise its modernization and think people are living in bounty. But if you look carefully, and if you enter the factories where honor is tarnished and virtue is disgraced and souls are sold cheaply, you cannot but say: May this modernization disintegrate and leave no stone standing. I became very, very emotional and wanted to leave work in the afternoon and go to my desk and write down all the ideas in my mind. I regained my pride and self-esteem: my spirit was lifted and my head raised. I started viewing the workers as insects and vermin: what is there in their hearts? Do they care for their dignity, which is a tattered cloth? Do they care about their honor, so sullied and fouled? I left the factory and walked slowly, proud and haughty. When an attractive woman passed me by, I averted my eyes in aloofness.

I took a good bath. Messrs Ilyas Khoury and George Ilyas came after peddling in nearby villages for two days. They made fifty riyals. Every day, I grow more eager to leave this miserable and sickening place.

Sakakini returns to New York on his way back to Palestine.

NEW YORK

27 July W[estern] AD 1908 [a letter]

My beloved Sultana,

I left Rumford Falls where I had stayed a month, which was more like a century, and arrived in Boston where I was greeted by Mikha'il al-Sayigh and your [paternal] cousin Bandali. Khawaja Mikha'il works for half a day but can only make three-quarters of a riyal and your cousin goes out to peddle but can barely make enough to cover his travel expenses. I don't think he will succeed even if he stays in this country all his life. I nearly encouraged him to go back home had I not feared to interfere in what is none of my business. He said to me that he would wait for a few months and if conditions improved, he would stay; otherwise, he would return.

The next day, I called on Messrs Sununu and with them went to visit Boston's institutions and beautiful historical sites. When we reached the public garden, we sat on a bench facing a small lake. Boats sailed up and down and so I wandered in my thoughts to Artas and I remembered you. Then we went for lunch, *malloukhiyya* and rice, after which I sat near a window smoking a water pipe. I was dazed as if out of my senses and wandered in the world of imagination and remembered you and Dawud whereupon I could not hold back my tears. In the evening, I bid Mikhaʾil and Bandali farewell; Mikhaʾil's wife was about to give birth. I rode the train for an hour, and then the boat, and reached New York.

Everyone I talk to advises me to leave this country for this country is not for the likes of me. But whenever I decide to leave, I think of you and remember my promise to struggle until I reach the highest rungs of glory and then return to you and bring you and Milia to visit America. Truly, my beloved, America is worth seeing, but it is not good as a home-land. It is a land of work, not of happiness. But how can I return to you a failure? The only hope I have is to return and try my luck again in our land. I hope conditions will be good, especially after the sultan granted a constitution for the land [3 July 1908], as you may have heard. Just give me one more year and then decide what you will. I am getting ready to travel and wish I could fly. Separation has devastated me, but I pray our meeting after this excruciating absence will herald the beginning of a new and happy life, God willing:

They say reunion is tomorrow near the bend of the road
But for the ardent lover, tomorrow is so far away.

I will return to you, my love, full of sorrows and fears. But they will all vanish when I see your smile. You are my cure and my happiness. Two days ago, I dreamt that I was in a meeting with your teacher Katie and Mr Amin Nasr. It was as if she knew of our relationship and so she said, probingly: "May God realize for you your hope." She then asked me to join her for tea on another day and promised to try all she could to remove the hurdles. What misery. Even in my dream I see hurdles.

May God forgive you Sultana: I never thought you would avoid me and thus leave me to anxieties and doubts. Tomorrow, I will explain every-thing; tomorrow, I will tell you about all that I encountered; tomorrow, I will cast my worries at your feet and my burdens in your arms; tomorrow, you will see with your own eyes my wretched state. I bid you farewell now. Until later: it is dark and I cannot see what I write. May you ever remain safe for him who loves you.

Tuesday 28 and 15 July AD 1908

I bathed and had breakfast. Yusuf went to peddle. I sat at my desk and wrote three letters, to Professor Bor, Dr Ness, and Khawaja Makrou-chian telling them of my return to New York. I went to the store of Messrs Mallouk in the hope of letters but found nothing. Then I went to the office of *al-Jamiʿah* and again found nothing. I picked up copies of *al-Hoda* and *Mir³at al-Gharb* newspapers and went to a Syrian coffee shop and asked for a water pipe and a cup of coffee and sat reading about the Turkish people's joyous celebrations and patriotic demonstrations: I wished I could have been in my country to join them.

I returned to the office but only found Miss Rose who told me something about Metropolitan Howadini [sic] which made me livid.[28] It was this: a young man, dear to his community, died and after the funeral, the metropolitan stood up and said: "I regret that the deceased did not care about spiritual matters; nothing will now save his soul from damnation." The brother of the deceased ground his teeth but remained patient until after the burial when he confronted the metropolitan, raging and fuming and hurling cruses at him.

Back in my room, I slept, bathed, dressed, and went to New York, straight to the store of Messrs Mallouk. Khawaja Ilyas hurried up to me saying: "You have received a telegram from Jerusalem advising us to give you sixty riyals for the return journey." I held the telegram and could not believe my eyes. It was from Khawaja Salim Mallouk, and the money from Yaᶜqub my maternal cousin. I turned reddish for joy and could not control myself, saying: "It is finished. It is finished." I then turned to Khawaja Ilyas and said: "Please keep this sum with you until I get some more money from my friends; this sum is not enough." I went to the *al-Jamiᶜah* office and told them the news and passed by Ilyas Haydar and told him, too. May the heavens bless you Yaᶜqub, successor of Dawud, and God have mercy on your soul, Dawud.

Yusuf returned from peddling having made one and a half riyal. I told him about the telegram and he was happy. Messrs Fuᵓad Salfiti and his brother and Khalil Dabdub spent the evening with us.[29]

Wednesday 29 and 16 July AD 1908

I bathed and had breakfast. I received a letter from my Armenian student Khawaja Makrouchian inviting me to dinner with him that evening or the next. I went to New York and found my brother Yusuf, Hanna Hishmeh, and Khalil Dabdub on the ferry. When we disembarked and I saw my brother carrying the *jizdan*, I nearly went blind with anger. The *jizdan* is just like the *kashkul* and those who carry it are no less than beggars going around from door to door.

I went directly to the store of Messrs Mallouk for letters, but found nothing. I continued to the office of *al-Jamiᶜah* where there was a bundle of mail for me from Rumford Falls. It included my pictures, a letter from Ilyas Khoury the Tripolitan [Tripoli in Lebanon], with redirected letters, two from Jerusalem and one from Ilyas Haydar. The former letters were from my sister Milia and from my mother but written by Ya°qub. There was also a letter to my paternal cousin Salim. I was piqued by what my mother said in the words of Ya°qub, my maternal cousin: "As for your coming here, that is what I desire most. But as you know, I have no means to help you. If you can manage on your own, do so and return. You will find us waiting for you." And if I could not on my own, what then? In her letter, my sister said that Sultana had sent her a letter but she could not understand its meaning; and that the grandmother of Dawud had died. In general, I felt depressed.

I went around the shipping agencies trying to find a passage via England, but I discovered that such a route would cost me more than my whole journey to Jerusalem. So, I decided to return via France on Saturday 8 August.

I wrote a letter to Messrs George and Ilyas in Rumford and enclosed six riyals. Then I returned to my room and wrote a letter to Miss Sincair. I tried to write to my maternal cousin and completed two letters but did not send them because I wrote them in anger. Then I wrote a letter to my mother. Messrs As°ad Hishmeh and Farid Salfiti spent the evening with us and Yusuf returned having made one and a quarter riyals only because he was not well. When we went to dinner, he came very late and when I asked him why he had been late, he became angry.

Thursday 30 and 17 July AD 1908

I bathed and had breakfast, then sat at my desk to write some letters. I received a letter from Dr Ness inviting me over on the following Tuesday. So, I went down to New York and passed by the store of Messrs Mallouk and found two letters, one from my mother telling me that my brother Ya°qub is now in Ramallah overseeing the construction of the Istfan family house and wishing for my return. The other was from Miss Sincair encouraging me to go back to my country and urging me to visit her in London. I continued to *al-Jami°ah* office and we sat talking about our country after which I went to a Syrian restaurant for lunch and a water pipe. I returned to my room, nearly melting from the heat and so I went to bed, but no sooner had I closed my eyes than Khawaja As°ad Hishmeh came and so I rose, got dressed, prepared coffee and we played cards. At 5:30, I went to my Armenian student, Khawaja Makrouchian, and we had dinner together. Then we went to a public park near his house and sat for a while. We returned to his room and I asked him to write a letter to Nikogos in Armenian. We then went looking for Wartnan, brother of Sikiyas the barber, but could not find him. Afterwards, we watched the moving pictures which included a report about the Salvation Army.[30]

I was very much moved and became tearful. He invited me to spend the evening with him the next day.

I returned to the room around 11:00 and asked Yusuf about his work. He did not have much to say.

Friday 31 and 18 July AD 1908

I dreamt I was in Jerusalem standing near the Khalil Gate. I saw the late Mrs Misterman on a donkey and so I said: How did they spread the rumor that she had died? I was told: She did not die but had a quarrel with her husband and her father sent for her.

I bathed and had breakfast. I received a letter from Professor Bor bidding me farewell and apologizing for not being able to see me because he was away. I sat at my desk and wrote three letters, to Messrs Sununu and Mikha'il al-Sayigh and Yusuf al-Salfiti bidding them farewell. I then went to the store of Messrs. Mallouk in New York inquiring about letters but found nothing. I then continued to the office of *al-Jami'ah* and took a clipping from *Mir'at al-Gharb* reporting the arrest of Augustine al-Qirri for fraud: he claimed to collect money for the charitable restoration of a leprosy hospital in Nablus which had recently burnt down. I added it to the English newspaper that had reported the whole story and sent them to my teacher Nakhleh.

I lunched and returned to my room. It was very, very hot and so I slept and then bathed and wrote a farewell card to Khawaja Yusuf Karaidian. Soon after, Khawaja As'ad Hishmeh came and so we played cards and then I had dinner, and went to my student only to find him busy moving to a new room. I went to an Armenian coffee shop where I met Khawaja Wartnan, brother of Sikiyas the barber. I found him very eager to return to the homeland. Back in my room, I found Yusuf and Niqula al-Barghut, the latter having shaved his moustaches. He looked like the Jews of Yemen. There were also As'ad Hishmeh and Ilyas Haydar and so we played cards.

Yusuf earned 3.30 riyals. I decided to have a new suit tailored for me, and if I run out of money, I will borrow twenty more riyals here.

Saturday the first of August W[estern] and 19 July E[astern] AD 1908

I dreamt I was with Dawud and lo, Yusuf Raheel ran towards us followed by my brother Ya'qub. When they drew near, my brother Ya'qub started beating him with a rod on his head. I lunged at Ya'qub and snatched the rod away from him and shouted at him. Then I saw myself standing in front of Dawud's house when his sister Mannana came, covered in black. When I saw her I wept. I then entered the house where his mother greeted me. She was skinny and pale, and so I threw myself at her feet and started crying. Then I dreamt that I saw ʿIsa Nakhleh Qurt and Mikhaʾil Mushabbak, their eyes red with rage. I asked them: What is the matter? ʿIsa said: My children were playing in front of the house near the Russian consulate when the consul came out and beat up their mother. Then I saw my maternal cousin Yaʿqub and Yaʿqub Khoury and told them the story. They found it strange.

I bathed and went down to New York and had breakfast. Ilyas Haydar said to me that he had quarreled with Miss Saʿdi al-Hajj and so decided not to go to work that day. I went to the store of Messrs Mallouk numerous times asking for letters, but found nothing. Then I went to the office of al-Jamiʿah where I also found nothing. I took a copy of al-Jamiʿah, both the periodical and the newspaper, and went to a Syrian coffee shop where I ordered a water pipe and coffee and sat down reading.

I was depressed all the time because I was worried about my brother's heavy drinking. I nearly gave up on reforming him and feared he would have a terrible future that would bring infamy on us. I went to the shipping companies but found no news. I returned to the room and slept.

Khawaja Asʿad Hishmeh came and we played cards. Then Khawaja Niʿma al-Hajj came with Ilyas Haydar and we sat for a while. I mentioned Dawud a hundred times in our conversation. We left and I went with Ilyas to dinner. He said: He had gone to Gibran ʿAwad and yelled at him, leaving nothing unsaid. We returned to the room and Asʿad Hishmeh, Simʿan Hishmeh, and Fuʾad Salfiti and his brother came and we played cards. Then Yusuf with Niqula al-Barghut returned from peddling, having gone out together, but they had made only two and a half riyals. I wrote a letter to Hanna Farraj and started another letter to Miss Sincair. We slept at 11:30.

Sunday 2 August W[estern] and 20 July E[astern] AD 1908

I bathed, and then we bought bread, yogurt and cantaloupe and had breakfast. Afterwards, I smoked a water pipe while writing a letter to Sultana. At noon, I went to bed until one o'clock, got dressed, and left for lunch. We then got on the tram – I, Ilyas Haydar and Niqula al-Barghut – heading to Coffee Island, but Yusuf and Simʿan Hishmeh lagged behind. On our way, we passed by the house of Khawaja Niʿmeh al-Hajj who insisted that we join him and prepared a water pipe and played the phonograph. We got on the tram again and went to Coffee Island: the tram was packed and we could find no space except on the outside steps. The wind was gentle and pleasant and when we got there, we walked to the seashore where men and women were bathing. You saw a man holding the hand of a girl and wading into the water, and once in a while, the two of them would come out and stretch on the sand and cover one another with sand in a manner that is disgraceful and shameful.

We then took the tram that runs on inclining lines going up and down until we reached Fairy Land and watched lions, tigers, and other creatures at play. Fairy Land is a large space full of wonders that startle and amaze, which no tongue can describe. Alone, I walked into the Arabic Dance Hall as Americans were entering in droves: men, women, and children. I liked nothing there except the man playing with a rifle. Then we went to a spacious dance hall and when the music started, hundreds, maybe thousands, started dancing. We continued to another coffee shop with a stage on which girls danced and, once in a while, a very strong man appeared and lifted weights at which even elephants would balk; he carried twelve men and women on his back. It was enough to watch the crowds on the streets: wherever you looked, you saw licentiousness, dissipation, and depravity.

We returned at 2 am I was very hungry and we stopped by a bakery and asked for bread. They said: "We don't sell at night."

2 August W[estern] AD 1908, Feast of St Elias [a letter]

My beloved,

This is the last letter I write to you from America. I have decided to leave on Saturday 8 August, and today is the end of the fourth month since I received a letter from you. Four months, O Sultana, which I spent in misery and despair, suffering and anguish. I could confront separation, overcome difficulties, resolve challenges, and deal with all hurdles had you not turned away from me, thereby chaining my hand and blinding my eyes, leaving me weak even to face the littlest problem. If I now return a failure, you are the cause, not time. As the poet said:

> "Away from us, Time seems to have wreaked havoc on you,"
>   she said.
> "By no means," I said; "it was you, not Time."

I hope to find you happy and contented after all the alienation you showed me. One smile from you, Sultana, at our meeting will give me back my happiness which I have just about forgotten this past year. One smile is enough to make me forget all my uncertainties and sorrows and instill life in me and renew hope in my heart. It will invigorate me and I will then show you my perseverance and dedication which, I hope, will win favor with you, God willing.

I thank God that I return with the banners of freedom fluttering over the land, with restrictions having been eased, and opportunities for work increased. I have many plans which I will share with you when we meet. But neither the freedom that has revived the land from its slumber, nor the plans I dream of, nor the many mediators will be worth anything if my eyes do not see your sweet smile, if we do not return to how we were: meeting in the evenings and celebrating the nights and going out into the open to greet the sun and breathe the pure air and pick flowers and listen to the singing of the birds and climb the mountain-tops. Add to that a visit to the grave of Dawud, where we speak to his good soul. I do not, Sultana, mean to fill your life with empty dreams, but if you accept me, I will make it a life of happiness for which all young women will envy you, God willing. May you, Sultana, not be one who cares for money but for glory and honor: otherwise, all education and good breeding and family origin will have been wasted. Of course, we need money to live a happy life: the least income I can make is fifteen liras/month. Such a sum in the hands of one who is capable and wise will ensure peace and happiness. It is enough that we share the same values and principles. A month might pass before we meet, so reexamine your promises and reflect on our beautiful past and imagine a future in which we attain joy and befriend the stars. Consult your gentle heart and turn to your honorable principles – and may God guide you to the good.

If you wish to be faithful, this heart is of that mettle, and if you wish for honor, this chest is its abode. God forbid that I will deceive you, Sultana, or tell you of what is not in me. Here is my past life laid out before you and if you see one black spot, reject me categorically. If I knew that you cared for money, and not honor, the opportunity for me in this land was not open and I will tell you my news that will vindicate my failure and deprivation. And if I am unable to make you visit America, Sultana, believe me, there is nothing here worth seeing. I never thought of you but said: May you never live in this miserable and sordid place; our country, with all its defects, is more beautiful and dignified.

Believe me: since arriving in this land, I have liked nothing, and nothing has given me joy. I cannot believe that I go back to you! So, get ready. I only ask of you to be happy and satisfied, God willing. I will end now because some Jerusalemites have arrived. Farewell and until we meet: you who give joy to the one who loves you.

Khalil

Monday 3 August and 21 July AD 1908

I bathed, had breakfast, and went down to New York, directly to the Messrs. Mallouk store hoping for a letter from anyone. But there was nothing. I then went to the office of *al-Jami‘ah* and found only a card from Farah Effendi Antoun with the picture of Niagara Falls. Then I went to one of the shipping companies and learned that there was no way of returning directly to Jaffa except via France. I then stopped by Hanna Hishmeh and asked him to come with me to order a suit, but he was busy, and so I went to Ilyas Haydar, who too was busy.

I returned to my room depressed and dismayed, had lunch, and went to sleep. I then bathed and sat at my desk to write a letter to Sultana which I dropped in the mail in New York, along with a letter to Hanna Farraj, and I inquired again about letters but found nothing. I dined and returned to my room. Khawaja As‘ad Hishmeh came over and we played cards. Then Ilyas Haydar came and we started singing our church hymns which aroused in me my religious feelings: I so missed praying in our old churches. Yususf and Niqula al-Barghut came and we all went to the house of Khawaja Iskandar Ghazal so I could bid them farewell.

Yusuf did not stop smoking, one cigarette after another, which I did not like at all. As we stood to leave I said: "If you feel that your eyesight is becoming weak, it is because of your excessive smoking." He got furious and said: "Even if I am to die, I will not quit smoking." I said: "I did not mean that you should quit; just be moderate." "Rather," he answered, "I will smoke even more until I die." I did not answer him although I felt very sad. We returned to the room and I slept but was deeply worried. I received a letter from Messrs Sununu.

Tuesday 4 August and 22 July AD 1908

I bathed and had breakfast. Yusuf did not go peddling because he had a fever, so he took a laxative and stayed at home. I went down to New York with Khawaja Farid Salfiti and reached the store of Messrs Mallouk in the hope of a letter from ‘Isa al-‘Isa, but there was nothing.[31] And so I decided to borrow twenty liras over and above the sixty so I can return. We then bought two suits, one for twelve and a half riyals and the other for 5.95. We took the underground and reached the public park on 84th Street and visited the museum [Metropolitan Museum of Art] but we did not have time to see everything.[32] Actually, there was nothing significant there in comparison to the London and Paris museums. It was very hot and I came down with a headache and so I returned to the room, had lunch, and went to Dr Ness. He took me to New York where we entered the big building called the "Metropolitan," the tallest in New

York, indeed, in all the world, and built of superb marble. We had *Ice Cream* and sat in the park nearby where we read a little in the original. We took a car that passed through 5th Avenue where he showed me the houses of the American rich – Rockefeller and Vanderbilt – and the big hotels. I had expected the houses of the rich to be very opulent but they were just like other buildings without the luxury that their wealth could afford. No wonder: although they may be some of the richest on the face of the earth, they still retain the spirit of common workers.

I promised Dr Ness to collect funny episodes and send them to him. We then discussed an album of Jerusalem photos and he said: "Send me at first a dozen and if we sell them and find a market for the book I will write you to send me more." We then took the *Subway* and reached New York and entered a building where church ministers meet. We read a little and then as we were leaving, he paid me five riyals and bade me farewell. He asked me to mention him to Khalil Doughan and the American [Colony] and Mr and Mrs Hensman. I returned to my room, prepared a water pipe and bathed. Khawaja Salfiti promised me to take my brother to live with him: he would be like a brother to him to guide him. I was thus comforted. I sent a letter to Professor Bor. They spent the evening with us.

Wednesday 5 August W[estern]/23 July E[astern] AD 1908

I bathed, had breakfast, and went down to New York. Yusuf went peddling. I stopped by the store of Messrs Mallouk but found nothing. I got depressed and my spirit grew cold. It had been a long time since I sent my letter to ʿIsa al-ʿIsa: forty-nine days and no answer. There must be an important reason why he did not write back sooner. I cannot believe that the delay is out of indifference. But what do I do now? The sixty riyals are barely enough for the two suits, the ticket, and some necessaries and I cannot wait until I get the money. I went to al-Jamiʿah office and took that day's paper. I read in the English papers that one of the officers of Yildiz [palace in Istanbul] had attacked his majesty the sultan [ʿAbdul Hamid II] and struck him with a dagger; had it not been for the steel armor plate he was wearing, it would have pierced his heart.[33]

I took twenty riyals from Khawaja Ilyas Mallouk and went with Hanna Hishmeh and bought a blue suit and then went to the Syrian restaurant where we had lunch, for which I paid. It was very hot and I was sweating all over and could not continue wandering and so returned to my room, slept, bathed, and went down to New York to buy some necessaries. It started raining and so I returned to Brooklyn, had dinner, and then went to bid farewell to Eugenie Khairallah, our friend in Jerusalem.

She was surprised that I was returning so quickly and said: "You must have a sweetheart from whom you cannot be long separated." She then asked me to choose a name for her daughter. I nearly gave her the name Sultana. We reminisced about Jerusalem and our days there. I then bade her farewell and returned to my room.

Yusuf did not sell anything that day. I wrote a letter to Dr Ness asking him to lend me twenty riyals and to send them with my brother Yusuf. Khawaja Hanna Hishmeh said to me that he would send two English pounds sterling with me to Shukri Hishmeh and that if I needed them on the road, I could use them and re-pay them later to Shukri when I reached Jerusalem.

Thursday 6 August W[estern] and 24 July E[astern] AD 1908

I bathed and had breakfast. I received two letters: one from Dr Ness asking me to go over to him at eleven o'clock so he could give me the twenty riyals I had asked him for; and another from Khawaja Yusuf Karaidian. I stayed in my room until eleven o'clock and wrote a letter to Miss Sincair, then went to Dr Ness who gave me the twenty riyals. But he asked me to sign a receipt that I would repay the loan after six months. I had not expected that of him.

On my way back, I met Khawaja Yusuf Karaidian and so we went and had lunch together. After we finished, I headed to New York but it rained so heavily I got completely drenched. I went to the store of Messrs Mallouk and found two letters: one from Miss Sincair asking me to visit her in London, and the other form Ilyas Tarazi saying that they had heard I was in dire need and apologizing for not being able to help me with any money. I took from Khawaja Ilyas Mallouk forty riyals, the remainder of the sixty, and then continued to the office of *al-Jamiʿah* and found a letter from Khawaja ʿIsa al-Tabbeh with other letters to *al-Jamiʿah*, saying that they heard I had been unsuccessful and was planning to return; and that Antoun Halabi was very sick. I became deeply concerned.

I bade farewell to Khawaja Karaidian in the hope of dining with him in the evening with my brother Yusuf. Then I went to the store of Khawaja Hanna Hishmeh where I found Khalil Shabab who was also planning on returning. We went together and got tickets to Jaffa for thirty-five riyals. When I paid the money, I saw a cloud of despair rise before my eyes. I got to Brooklyn and Yusuf came, having sold for five riyals. I told him I got my travel ticket. He was dumbfounded and so I started railing at the world. He tried to calm me down. Then, my brother, Ilyas Haydar, Hanna Hishmeh, and I went to the house of Khawaja Karaidian and had dinner.

We did not stop talking about Jerusalem.

Friday 7 August W[estern] and 25 July E[astern] AD 1908

I bathed and had breakfast. Before leaving the room, I received two letters: one from Professor Bor, my very good friend, which included a present of a check for ten riyals. He was so kind in the letter I nearly cried.
The other letter was from Khawaja Yusuf Salfiti bidding me farewell. I
went with my brother and bought a suitcase along with other necessaries
and then I bade farewell to Messrs Dabdub and everyone I met on the
street. Most of them promised to visit me in the evening in my room. We
then had lunch, Yusuf, Ilyas Haydar, Hanna Hishmeh and I, for which
we paid. In the afternoon at two o'clock, I went to the store of Khawaja
Hanna Hishmeh to get the phone call from Hanna Farraj, as we had
agreed. When it was two o'clock, the phone rang and we exchanged
parting words. He asked me to write to him about the situation that had
caused him to leave for America. I then returned to Brooklyn and went
to the store of Messrs Mallouk and bade them farewell.

I returned with a broken heart and worn-out emotions. I looked at
the scenery there for the last time, my tears pouring down. In my room, I
wrote to Professor Bor to thank him for his letter and gift, and I wrote a
card to my mother, and another to ʿIsa al-ʿIsa informing all of them that
I was leaving the next day.

I wrote ten commandments for my brother Yusuf.

*The above letter was the last of Sakakini's writings in America. He arrived in
Jerusalem on 19 September 1908, and later got married to Sultana.*

**2. From *The American Journey* Farewell by Prince Muhammad ʿAli
Pasha, 1912 (published 1913)**

[*Al-Rihla al-Amrīkiyya* (Cairo, 1913)]

EDITOR'S NOTE
*The prince's words recall the Greeting to Paris/Tahiyyat Bariz that Muhammad
Kurd ʿAli had addressed to Paris in which he had opened with "Peace be upon
you" – the same words that Muhammad ʿAli used, signaling perhaps the beginning of the shift from Europe/France to the United States. The prince wrote his
farewell on board the ship sailing away from New York.*

*   *   *

While thinking of my country and longing for it, I looked behind me
and thought of America. But then I would think again of my country.

And so my soul continued to waver between two emotions: affectionately recalling my country and homeland and remembering America and its people and all its refugees from among my brethren, sons of the East. I reminisced about my traveling days, as I observed customs, compared mores, visited historical sites, wondered at innovations, and delighted in landscapes and breathtaking vistas. But then I said to myself that every moment that is now taking me away from America is drawing me closer to my country: my country is ahead of me and America is behind me.

It was therefore time to address America with my last farewell:

Peace be with you, New World, and peace to you America, and to your children, hardworking and persevering, aspiring towards lofty goals and high ambitions;

Peace be with you for handing your children the keys to the treasures of your earth which enabled them to reap vast bounties from its surface and from under it. Nearly all of them are now possessors of thousands upon thousands of gold and silver;

Peace on you for smiling at your new white children, but frowning and turning your back on your old red sons. This is the punishment of every people who do not unearth the bounty of the land: God will send them a people who know the value of that bounty and they will enjoy it, while the original people will be denied;

Peace be with you and your children who have recognized the value of knowledge, and in its pursuit, have expended riches to build your prosperous schools and great universities;

Peace be with you for taking in all who have left their homelands and for opening your arms to them, even though it is the white population from among your ruling sons that have most benefited from their labor;

Peace be with you and your children who have excelled in all ways of profit-making and advertisement;

Peace be with you for the energy of your children in trade: they have reached all ends of the earth;

Peace be on you for endowing your sons and daughters with the blessing of freedom, even though it is sweeping and without check;

Peace be on your majestic palaces which nearly touch the sky;

Peace be on you for all the wonders with which God has endowed you to show the might of His creation: of mountains and rivers, springs and trees and streams, such beautiful scenery before which the mind is awed;

Peace be on you for unlocking to your children the realms of imagination, and opening up the doors of temerity that they can turn a seed into a dome, and make us imagine the silent rocks as flying eagles, and turn inert stones into raging lions.

Peace be on you as long as you remain a place of refuge for immigrants whose countries can no longer accommodate them, and whose homelands have rejected them: in you, all mankind have assembled.

Peace be on you for welcoming whoever visits you and bidding farewell to whoever departs.

I bid you a last farewell and leave with you a trust which I hope will be returned to its people. The trust is the following: you my brethren of the Syrian East, I now leave you but amity will always tie me to you, even across distances.

I leave you in God's care: I pray that He will protect you and grant you success in all that you seek, and guide you to prosperity in all your endeavors, and keep goodwill among you as you aspire to do good, and to nurture in your souls what I read on your faces and what I heard from your mouths about the great love you have for your homelands, and faithfulness for your government.

I hope you will safely return to your homelands after you realize your goals so you can work with the same dedication there that I saw in you in your *house of immigration;*[34]

I hope you will labor to improve conditions in your countries and discredit with your great achievements all those who deny the Easterner his ability to undertake mighty projects.

Salaam.

NOTES

1. For a detailed biography, see Ya'qub al-'Awdat, *Min a'lam al-fikr wa-l-adab fi Filastin* (Al-Quds al-Sharif, 1978), 273–84.
2. Kamal H. Karpat, "The Ottoman Emigration to America, 1860–1914," *International Journal of Middle East Studies*, 17 (1985): 180 in 175–209; "The travels of Shukrallah Khoury," *al-Machriq* 18 (1907), 822. As of 1907, the number of Syrians in Brooklyn, according to Abdou, was 10,000, *al-Safar*, 155.
3. See the reference to Sakakini in Michelle U. Campos, *Ottoman Brothers: Muslims, Christians, and Jews in Early Twentieth-Century Palestine* (Stanford: Stanford University Press, 2011), 20–1, 84–5.
4. See references to Sakakini and his role in confronting the Greek hierarchy in Bedross Der Matossian, "The Young Turk Revolution: Its Impact on Religious Politics of Jerusalem (1908–1920)," *Jerusalem Quarterly* 40 (2009): 18–33.
5. Nadim Bawalsa, "Sakakini Defrocked," *Jerusalem Quarterly* 42 (2010): 10–13.

6. See Khalidi, *Palestinian Identity*, 50 and 228, n. 71. See the entry in the diary on 11 July 1908 where he discussed the Orthodox-Latin situation in Jerusalem.

7. See Fadwa Ahmad Mahmoud Nsayrat, *al-Masihiyyun al-ʿArab wa fikrat al-qawmiyya al-ʿArabiyya fi Bilad al-Sham (1840–1918)* (Beirut: Markaz Dirasat al-Wihda al-ʿArabiyya, 2009), 399–400 for the poem. See also the references to his house and legacy in Ghada Karmi, *In Search of Fatima* (London: Verso, 2002), 90, 112, 126.

8. For references to his life, see Wasif Jawhariyya, *Al-Quds al-ʿUthmaniyya fi al-mudhakirat al-Jawhariyya*, ed. Salim Tamari and ʿIsam Nassar (Beirut: Muʾassasat al-Dirasat al-Filastiniyya, 2003), 1: 93, 123–6.

9. See Salim Tamari, "A Miserable Year in Brooklyn: Khalil Sakakini in America, 1907–1908," *Journal of Palestine Studies* 17 (2003): 19. See also Michael W. Suleiman, "Impressions of New York City by Early Arab Immigrants," in *A Community of Many Worlds*, eds Benson and Kayal, 33 in 28–45.

10. The Mallouk were a Christian family from Jerusalem, living in the Muslim quarter of Bab al-ʿAmud. The same applies to the Sununu and Khamis families: see Tamari and Nassar, eds, *al-Quds al-ʿUthmaniyya*, 2: 267. In 1919, Ward dedicated his book, *Kitab al-jundi al-Suri*, to the "famous merchant in New York . . . Salim Effendi Mallouk."

11. Muhammad ʿAbduh was an Egyptian Islamic reformer, 1849–1905. Farah Antoun was the editor of this newspaper which he had started on 1 July 1906. He edited two others, *al-Jamiʿah al-yawmiyya* (first issued 2 January 1907) and *al-Jamiʿah al-usbuʿiyya* (first issued 22 February 1907). See Husayn ʿAbdallah al-Manasra, *Farah Antoun, ruwaʾiyyan wa masrahiyyan* (PhD dissertation, University of Jordan, 1984), 34.

12. The novella had originally been published in 1801. It had been translated by Antoun and appeared in 1908 in 48 pages. It is strange how Sakakini refers to Antoun, as the man of the daily newspaper *al-Jamiʿah*.

13. From *Sir Galahad* (1842).

14. Sakakini saw himself as a very moral and upright man, emotional to the point of frequently crying, censorious, devoid of religious bigotry, perhaps even atheistic, critical but also admiring of Americans. He never indulged himself with women because of his commitment to Sultana – to the point where some around him mistook his chastity for homosexuality.

15. Sakakini used the Turkish title, *khawaja*, repeatedly, even though he was writing a private diary. He wanted to retain a sense of the social status that prevailed in Palestine.

16. The book was published in Paris in 1908 by Paul Geuthner, *The History of the Egyptian Cadis, As Completed by Abu Omar Muhammad ibn Yusuf ibn Ya'qub al-Kindi*. At the end of his introduction, Gottheil thanked Sakakini for his help (xx). He also thanked Khalil Bishara – but his name did not appear in Sakakini's letters.

17. Did Sakakini ever know about Gottheil's Zionist views – how the professor ardently supported the idea of Jews settling Palestine, in accordance with Theodore Herzl's plans? Sakakani must have described his Jerusalem community to Gottheil, with its history, music, and social activities: yet the latter never seemed to associate Sakakini with the people whose expulsion he was advocating in his *Zionism* (Philadelphia, 1914, but completed 1912). The only reference Gottheil made in the book to the Arabs of Palestine was to them as "tillers of the soil" (169). The book on which Gottheil was working appeared in 1908 and was praised in *al-Muqtabas* as a sign of how Westerners were taking interest in Arab history, 3 (1908), 143.

18. In Palestine, the Orthodox community used the Julian Eastern calendar, as Wasif Jawhariyya also shows in his memoirs, *Al-Quds al-'Uthmaniyya*, 2 vols. Later, Sakakini will use both calendars to date his letters.

19. See the reference to "John Hishmeh & Co. Importers of Religious & Fancy Goods, on 35 Broadway, New York City," Abdou, *al-Safar*, 212. Hishmeh is described as coming from "West Jerusalem"/*Urushalim al-Gharbiyya*. As the advertisement explained, Hishmeh had artifacts designed for him in Jerusalem, Haifa, and Jaffa.

20. A distinguished British orientalist and Laudian Professor of Arabic at Oxford from 1889 to 1937.

21. The first date is according to the Gregorian calendar, the second to the Julian.

22. In 1697, Peter the Great went incognito to Western Europe on a "Grand Embassy" during which time he acquired first-hand knowledge of European innovations, from shipbuilding to urban planning.

23. *Al-Hoda* often advertised records of Isfahani music.

24. After his return to Palestine, Sakakini included exercise and athletics in his school curriculum, Jawhariyya, *Al-Quds al-'Uthmaniyya fi al-mudhakkirat al-Jawhariyya*, 1: 128.

25. Zurayq (1861–1921) was born in Beirut and moved to Jerusalem in 1899 where he worked at the British-sponsored Church Missionary Society bookstore. In 1893, he became principal of the high school on Mount Zion where Sakakini studied. He remained in that position until his death. He was known for his immense love of the Arabic language and his high admiration for the Qur'an. See the article in Ya'qub al Awdat, *Min a'lam al-fikr wa-l-adab fi Filastin*, 234–6. Ra'd

was the "first" Palestinian photographer: Badra al-Hajj, "Khalil Raad – Jerusalem Photographer," *Institute for Palestine Studies*, 12 (2001): 34–8 and Robert Fisk, "Khalil Raad's Palestinian Pictures Chart the History – and the Tragedy," *Independent* 7 April 2013. I am grateful to Ms Samira Kawar for the information.

26. Sakakini admired the work of the Salvation Army: see also his entry on 11 July 1908.

27. The greatest poet in the history of Arabic Sufism, AD 1181–1234.

28. Bishop Raphael Hawawini, Syrian Greek Orthodox, Brooklyn, New York: Abdou, *al-Safar*, 327. He was editor of *al-Kalima*, an Orthodox periodical published in New York.

29. An advertisement in Abdou's *al-Safar* mentions "S. G. Dabdub and Bros." as importers of beads, wooden crosses, and holy merchandise from Bethlehem, 206.

30. Did Sakakini see also "Aladdin's Lamp," a silent film, which had been released the year before? For a study of the earliest silent films, see Abdelmajid Hajji, *The Arab in American Silent Cinema: A study of a Film Genre* (PhD dissertation, University of Kansas, 1993).

31. ʿIsa al-ʿIsa founded the *Filastin* newspaper and supported the Arab Orthodox cause against the Greek hegemony over the Church. After returning to Palestine, in 1908–10, Sakakini contributed to the newspaper in support of the Arab cause. See R. Michael Bracy, *Printing Class: ʿIsa al-ʿIsa, Filastin, and the Textual Construction of National Identity, 1911–1913* (Lanham: University Press of America, 2011).

32. The museum was still small, having been established in 1872.

33. It is not clear what newspapers he was reading: the assassination attempt had occurred in July 1905.

34. Muhammad ʿAli uses the phrase *"dar hijra"* which connotes a place of refuge from persecution.

Bibliography

Abdel-Malek, Kamal, *America in an Arab Mirror: Images of America in Arabic Travel Literature: An Anthology, 1895–1995* (New York: St. Martin's Press, 2005).

Abu Ghazaleh, Adnan, *American Missions in Syria* (Brattleboro, VT: Center for Arab and Islamic Studies, 1982).

Anbinder, Tyler, *City of Dreams: The 400-Year Epic History of Immigrant New York* (Boston and New York: Houghton Mifflin Harcourt, 2016).

Ayalon, Ami, "The Arab Discovery of America in the Nineteenth Century," *Middle Eastern Studies* 20 (1984): pp. 5–17.

Bawardi, Hani, *The Making of Arab Americans: From Syrian Nationalism to U.S. Citizenship* (Austin: University of Texas Press, 2014).

Behar, Moshe and Zvi Ben-Dor Benite, *Modern Middle Eastern Jewish Thought: Writings on Identity, Politics and Culture, 1893–1958* (Lebanon, NH: Brandeis University Press, 2013).

Beshara, Adel (ed.), *The Origins of Syrian Nationhood: Histories, Pioneers and Identity* (London and New York: Routledge, 2011).

Boosahda, Elizabeth, *Arab-American Faces and Voices: The Origins of an Immigrant Community* (Austin: University of Texas Press, 2003).

Bracy, R. Michael, *Printing Class: ʿIsa al-ʿIsa, Filastin, and the Textual Construction of National Identity, 1911–1913* (Lanham: University Press of America, 2011).

Campos, Michelle U., *Ottoman Brothers: Muslims, Christians, and Jews in Early Twentieth-Century Palestine* (Stanford: Stanford University Press, 2011).

Cioeta, Donald J., "Ottoman Censorship in Lebanon and Syria, 1876–1908," *International Journal of Middle East Studies* 10 (1979): pp 167–86.

Conklin, Nancy Faires and Nora Faires. "'Colored' and Catholic: the Lebanese in Birmingham, Alabama," in Eric J. Hooglund (ed.), *Crossing the Waters: Arabic-Speaking Immigrants in the United States before 1940* (Washington, DC: Smithsonian Institution Press, 1987), pp. 69–84.

Dahir, Masᶜud, *Al-Nahda al-ᶜArabiyya wa-l-Nahda al-Yabaniyya* (Kuwait: ᶜAlam al-Maᶜrifa, 2006).

Elias, Leila Salloum, "The Impact of the Sinking of the *Titanic* on the New York Syrian Community of 1912: The Syrians Respond," *Arab Studies Quarterly* 27 (2005): pp. 75–87.

Elshakry, Marwa, *Reading Darwin in Arabic, 1860–1950* (Chicago: University of Chicago Press, 2013).

El-Enany, Rashid, *Arab Representations of the Occident: East–West Encounters in Arabic Fiction* (London and New York: Routledge, 2006).

Fadda-Conrey, Carol, *Contemporary Arab-American Literature: Transnational Reconfigurations of Citizenship and Belonging* (New York: New York University Press, 2014).

Farah, Mounir A, *The United States Identity from its Origin to 1876 in Syria*, PhD dissertation, New York University, 1986.

Friedlander, Jonathan, "Rare Sights: Images of Early Arab Immigration to New York City," in Kathleen Benson and Philip M. Kayal (eds.), *A Community of Many Worlds: Arab Americans in New York City* (New York: Syracuse University Press, 2002), pp. 46–53.

Gharayibah, ᶜAbd al-Karim, *Al-ᶜArab wa-l-Wilalayat al-Muttaḥidah min al-qidam ila al-khamis min Tishrin al-thani 2008* (Amman: Dar Ward, 2009).

Gonzalez-Quijano, Yves, "Reading Muḥammad al-Muwayliḥī's Description of Paris: A Modern Egyptian Glimpse of the West at the Beginning of the 20th Century," *Middle Eastern Literatures* 13 (2010): pp. 183–90.

Gualtieri, Sarah M. A., *Between Arab and White: Race and Ethnicity in the Early Syrian American Diaspora* (Berkeley: University of California Press, 2009).

Haiek, Joseph (ed.), *Arab-American Almanac*, fifth edition (Glendale, CA: News Circle Publishing House, 2003).

Hajji, Abdelmajid, *The Arab in American Silent Cinema: A Study of a Film Genre* (PhD dissertation, University of Kansas, 1993).

Hakim, Carol, *The Origins of the Lebanese National Idea, 1840–1920* (Berkeley: University of California Press, 2013).

Hanssen, Jens, *Fin de Siècle Beirut: The Making of an Ottoman Provincial Capital* (Oxford: Clarendon Press, 2005).

Hilmi, ᶜAbbas, ᶜAhdi: mudhakirat ᶜAbbas Hilmi al-Thani, Khedawi Misr al-akhir 1892–1914, trans. Jalal Yahya (Beirut: Dar al-Shuruq, 1993).

Hilwa, Jamil Butrus, *Al-Muhajir al-Suri wa ma yajib an yaᶜrifuhu wa yaᶜmal bih* (New York: al-Hoda Publisher, 1909).

Hitti, Philip, *The Syrians in America* (New York: George H. Doran Company, 1924).

Hooglund, Eric J. (ed.), *Crossing the Waters: Arabic-Speaking Immigrants in the United States Before 1940* (Washington, DC: Smithsonian Institution Press, 1987).

Houghton, Louise Seymour, "Syrians in the United States," *The Survey*, Survey Associates, Charity Organization of New York, vol. 26, 1911.

Hourani, Albert, *Al-Fikr al- ᶜArabi fi ᶜAsr al-Nahda, 1798–1939*, trans. Karim ᶜAzqoul, third edition (Beirut: Dar al-Nahar li-l-Nashr, 1977).

Jacobs, Linda K, *Strangers in the West: The Syrian Colony of New York City* (New York: Kalimah Press, 2015).

Jawhariyya, Wasif, *Al-Quds al-ᶜUthmaniyya fi al-mudhakirat al-Jawhariyya*, eds. Salim Tamari and ᶜIsam Nassar (Beirut: Muᵓassasat al-Dirasat al-Filastiniyya, 2003).

Jingled, Naomi, "One of America's First Syrian Immigrants Helped Conquer the West – With Camels," *PRI's The World*, 15 May 2017.

Johnson, Rebecca C., "Importing the Novel: The Arabic Novel In and As Translation," *Novel: A Forum on Fiction* 48 (2015), pp. 243–60.

Karmi, Ghada, *In Search of Fatima* (London: Verso, 2002).

Karpat, Kamal H., "The Ottoman Emigration to America, 1860–1914," *International Journal of Middle East Studies* 17 (1985), pp. 175–209.

Khalaf, Samir, *Protestant Missionaries in the Levant: Ungodly Puritans, 1820–1860* (New York: Routledge, 2012).

Khalidi, Rashid, *Palestinian Identity: The Construction of Modern National Consciousness* (New York, 1997).

al-Khalidi, Salah ᶜAbd al-Fattah (ed.), *Amayrka min al-dakhil bi-minẓar Sayyid Qutb* (Jidda, Saudi Arabia, 1986).

Khater, Akram Fouad, *Inventing Home: Emigration, Gender, and the Middle Class in Lebanon 1870–1920* (Berkeley: University of California Press, 2001).

Khater, Akram Fouad, https://lebanesestudies.news.chass.ncsu.edu/2016/11/30/arbeely-family-pioneers-to-america-and-founders-of-the-first-arabic-language-newspaper

Khater, Akram Fouad, https://lebanesestudies.news.chass.ncsu.edu/2017/06/08/lebanese-american

Khayat, Nicole, "Historiography and Translation during the Arabic Nahda: European History in Arabic", PhD dissertation, University of Haifa, 2016.

Laroui, Abdallah, *The Crisis of the Arab Intellectual: Traditionalism or Historicism?*, trans. Diarmid Cammell (Berkeley: University of California Press, 1976).

Lee, Erika, At America's Gates: Chinese Immigration during the Exclusion Era, 1882–1943 (Chapel Hill: University of North Carolina Press, 2003).

Lindner, Christine Beth, Negotiating the Field: American Protestant Missionaries in Ottoman Syria, 1823 to 1860, PhD dissertation, Edinburgh University, 2009.

Lynch, William Francis, Narrative of the United States Expedition to the River Jordan and the Dead Sea, Philadelphia, 1858.

Mahafza, ᶜAli, Al-Itijahat al-fikriyya ᶜind al-ᶜArab fi ᶜasr al-Nahda, 1798–1914 (Beirut: al-Ahliyya li-l Nashr wa-l Tawziᶜ, 1978).

Mahfuz, Issam, Hiwar maᵓa ruwwad al-Nahda al-ᵓArabiyya (Beirut: Riyad al-Rayyis, 2000).

Makdisi, Ussama, Artillery of Heaven: American Missionaries and the Failed Conversion of the Middle East (Ithaca: Cornell University Press, 2008).

al-Maqdisi, Anis, al-Awamil al-faᶜala fi-l adab al-Arabi al-hadith (Cairo: Al-Muktataf Press [sic], 1939).

Marston, Elsa, The Lebanese in America (Minneapolis: Lerner, 1987).

Matar, Ibrahim, Haᵓulaᵓ khadamu al-Sharq al-Awsaṭ (Beirut: Matbaᶜat al-Mashᶜal, 1969).

McCabe, James, The Illustrated History of the Centennial Exhibition (Philadelphia: National Publishing Company, 1876).

Mruwwat, Ahmad, Al-Nasira, ᶜalam wa shakhsiyat, 1800–1948 (Akka: Muᵓassasat al-Aswar, 2009).

Naff, Alixa, "Lebanese Immigration into the United States: 1880 to the Present," In Albert Hourani and Nadim Shehadi (eds.), The Lebanese in the World (London: I. B. Tauris, 1992).

Naff, Alixa, "The Early Arab Immigrant Experience," in Ernest McCarus (ed.), The Development of Arab American Identity (Ann Arbor: University of Michigan Press, 1994), pp. 23–35.

Naff, Alixa, "New York: The Mother Colony," in Kathleen Benson and Philip M. Kayal (eds.), A Community of Many Worlds: Arab Americans in New York City (New York: Syracuse University Press, 2002), pp. 3–10.

Naimy, Mikhail, Sabᶜoun (Beirut: Dar Sadir, 1960).

Najjar, Michael Malek, Arab American Drama, Film and Performance: A Critical Study, 1908 to the Present (Jefferson, NC: McFarland & Company, Inc., 2015).

Nash, Geoffrey, The Arab Writers in English: Arab Themes in a Metropolitan Language, 1908–1958 (Portland, OR: Sussex Academic Press, 1998).

Nolan, James L., Jr., What They Saw in America: Alexis de Tocqueville, Max Weber, G. K. Chesterton, and Sayyid Qutb (New York: Cambridge University Press, 2016).

Norris, Jacob, "Return Migration and the Rise of Palestinian Nouveaux Riches, 1870–1925," *Journal of Palestine Studies* 46 (2017), pp. 60–75.

Nsayrat, Fadwa Ahmad Mahmoud, *Al-Masihiyyun al-ᶜArab wa fikrat al-qawmiyya al-ᶜArabiyya fi Bilad al-Sham (1840–1918)* (Beirut: Markaz Dirasat al-Wihda al-ᶜArabiyya, 2009).

Orfalea, Gregory, *Before the Flames: A Quest for the History of Arab Americans* (Austin: University of Texas Press, 1988).

Orfalea, Gregory, *Journey to the Sun* (New York: Scribner, 2014).

Pastor, Camila, *The Mexican Mahjar* (Austin: University of Texas Press, 2017).

Patel, Abdulrazzak, *The Arab Nahḍa: The Making of the Intellectual and Humanist Movement* (Edinburgh: Edinburgh University Press, 2013).

Perkins, Kenneth J., *Saudi Aramco World*, November/December 1976, pp. 8–13.

Philipp, Thomas, "Participation and Critique: Arab Intellectuals Respond to the 'Ottoman Revolution,'" in *Arabic Thought Beyond the Liberal Age*, ed. Jens Hanssen and Max Weiss (Cambridge: Cambridge University Press, 2016), 243–65.

Reid, Donald M., *The Odyssey of Faraḥ Anṭūn: A Syrian Christian's Quest for Secularism* (Minneapolis and Chicago: Bibliotheca Islamica, Inc., 1975).

Rihani, Ameen, *Rasaʾil Ameen Rihani*, ed. Albert Rihani (Beirut: Dar Rihani, 1959).

Rihani, Ameen, *Letters to Uncle Sam* (Washington: Platform International, 2001).

Saydah, Jurj, *Adabuna wa udabaʾuna fi al-mahajir al-Amrikiyya* (Beirut: Dar al-ᶜIlm li-l Malayin, 3rd ed., 1964).

Sharabi, Hisham, *al-Muthaqfun al-ᶜArab wa-l-Gharb, ᶜAsr al-Nahda 1875–1914*, second edition (Beirut: Dar al-Nahar li-l-Nashr, 1978).

Sheehi, Stephen, "Arabic Literary-Scientific Journals: Precedence for Globalization and the Creation of Modernity," *Comparative Studies of South Asia, Africa and the Middle East* 25 (2005), pp. 438–48.

Shwayri, Yusuf, *Al-Rihla al-ᶜArabiyya al-ḥaditha min Awrubba ila al-Wilayat al-Muttahida* (Beirut: al-Muʾassasa al-ᶜArabiyah li-l-Dirasat wa-al-Nashr, 1998).

Tibawi, A. L., *American Interests in Syria, 1800–1901: A study of Education, Literary and Religious Work* (Oxford: Clarendon Press, 1966).

Trollope, Frances, *Domestic Manners of the Americans*, ed. Elsie B. Michie (Oxford: Oxford University Press, 2014).

Wadiᶜ Suleyman, Mikhaʾil, "Tajribat al-muhajirin al-ᶜArab," *al-ᶜArab fi Amayrka* (Beirut: Markaz Dirasat al-Wihdah al-ᶜArabiyya, 2003), 15–46.

Walther, Karine V., *Sacred Interests: The United States and the Islamic World, 1821–1921* (Chapel Hill: University of North Carolina Press, 2015).

Wells, Robert V., *The Population of the British Colonies in America before 1776: A Survey of Census Data* (Princeton: Princeton University Press, 1975).

Werner, Louis, "Little Syria, NY," *Saudi Aramco World*, Nov./Dec. 2012, pp 2–9.

Wild, Stefan, "Negib Azoury and his Book, 'Le Reveil de la Nation Arabe'," in Marwan R. Buheiry (ed.), *Intellectual Life in the Arab East, 1890–1939* (Beirut: American University of Beirut, 1981), pp. 92–104.

Yarid, Nazek Saba, *Al-Rahhalun al-Arab wa hadarat al-gharb fi-l-Nahda al-ʿArabiyya al-haditha* (Beirut: Mu'assasat Nawfal, 1979).

Zallum, ʿAbd al-Hayy Yahya, *Amayrka bi-ʿuyun ʿArabiyya!* (Amman: Dar Ward, 2007).

Zaydan, Jurji, *Rihla ila Awrubba 1912*, ed. Qasim Wahab (Abu Dhabi: Dar al-Suwaydi li-l Nashr wa-l Tawziʿ, 2002).

Zeine, Zeine, *Nushuʾ al-qawmiyya al-Arabiyya* (Beirut: Dar al-Nahar, 1968).

Index

EU representative:
Easy Access System Europe
Mustamäe tee 50, 10621 Tallinn, Estonia
Gpsr.requests@easproject.com